Chas G Halpine

THE

POETICAL WORKS

OF

CHARLES G. HALPINE

(MILES O'REILLY).

CONSISTING OF

ODES, POEMS, SONNETS, EPICS, AND LYRICAL EFFUSIONS
WHICH HAVE NOT HERETOFORE BEEN
COLLECTED TOGETHER.

WITH

A BIOGRAPHICAL SKETCH AND EXPLANATORY NOTES.

EDITED BY

ROBERT B. ROOSEVELT.

NEW YORK:

HARPER & BROTHERS, PUBLISHERS,

FRANKLIN SQUARE.

1869.

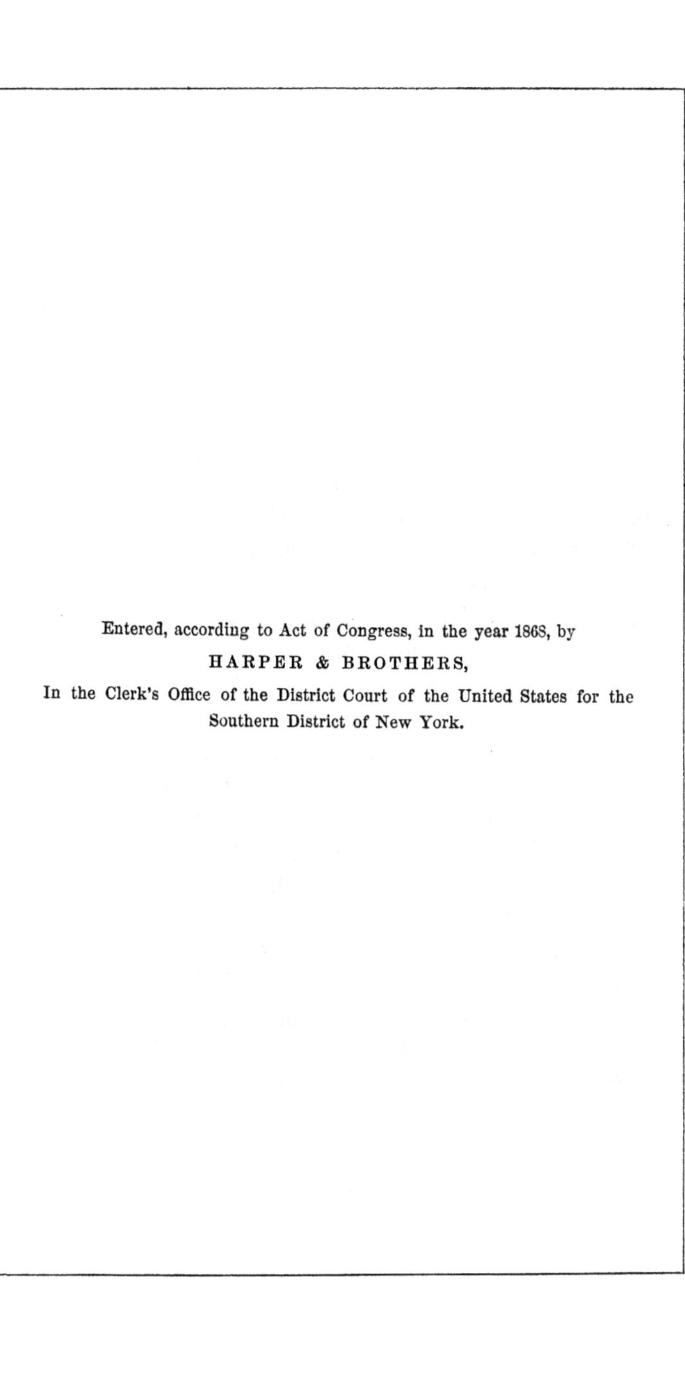

PREFACE.

This is not intended to be a complete collection of the poetical works of Charles G. Halpine. Some of these are already before the public in "Miles O'Reilly His Book" and "Baked Meats of the Funeral," from which it is not desirable to copy them, as much of their significance, in many instances, depends upon their connection with the prose matter with which they are interwoven. It would be impossible, if it were desirable, to make any extended extracts from those two books without explanations that would render this compilation cumbersome. Some of his earlier productions have been taken from the volume entitled "Lyrics by the Letter H," which he published in the year 1854, and which is out of print, but the great body of the following effusions are now for the first time collected. They are followed by notes describing the circumstances under which some of them were written, and giving personal reminiscences of the author that will grow in interest daily.

The habits, mode of thought, manner of work, and many individual peculiarities, although of no importance when they concern an unknown person, are of interest to the public when they affect a great man, one of the bright lights of his day and generation; and that Charles G. Halpine was a great man, a brilliant genius, and an uncommon intellect, his contemporaries have conceded, and posterity will confirm by more deliberate decision. The success of one laborer in the literary vineyard encourages others, and the life under consideration is a wonderful example of the effect of hard work when united with great gifts; for it is a remarkable fact that this talented writer invariably denied that he possessed any peculiar genius, and attributed his success simply to hard work and indomitable energy. His career is well worth studying to all those who are wearily toiling along the same hard path, and even the sketch of it which can be given in the narrow limits of this volume teaches a valuable lesson.

That this collection will not be as full as it should be is accounted for by the suddenness of the decease of the author, by the confusion in which his papers were necessarily left, and by the haste with which circumstances have compelled this compilation to be made. For the same and other reasons, no attempt has been made at classification, and it may be that omitted poems will have to be added at the last moment. General Halpine had never been in the habit of collecting or preserving his works; his pen was so busy, his brain so fertile, his time so fully occupied, that such an attempt would have been a severe tax upon him; and although he had before his death commenced getting together his poetical efforts, the collection, so far as it had proceeded, being incomplete and unfinished, was of little assistance. Although his memory was wonderful, yet his writings were so voluminous that he actually could not remember them all. For any deficiencies, therefore, this explanation must be the excuse of

THE EDITOR.

BIOGRAPHICAL SKETCH.

Charles G. Halpine was born near the town of Oldcastle, in the county of Meath, Ireland, in the year 1829. His father, the Rev. Nicholas J. Halpine, was an Episcopal clergyman of the Established Church, and a man of extraordinary abilities. A remarkable aptitude for literature, and especially that peculiar branch of it connected with the life of a journalist, existed in the family. The father was editor of the Dublin *Evening Mail*, and an uncle, Wm. Henry Halpine, was proprietor and editor of the Cheltenham *Mail.* Charles G. Halpine was the favorite son of his father, and early gave evidences of those abilities which brought him such distinguished honor in later years. At as early an age as the rules of the college allowed he was admitted to Trinity, from which he subsequently graduated with distinction, having won the affection of his fellow-students and the respect of his instructors. Subsequently he commenced the study of medicine, and obtained a superficial but not thorough knowledge of that science, when he surrendered it for the more congenial pursuit of journalism. He contributed to the Irish, and subsequently to the English press, spending several years in London; but feeling that his talents were kept down by the want of a proper opportunity, he determined upon emigration to the United States.

He came alone to this country, although he had been married some years previous to his departure from England; but so soon as he was fairly established, he sent for his young wife, who joined him immediately. He established himself in Boston, where for some years he was connected with the Boston *Post*, and subsequently became leading editor of a paper called the *Carpet Bag*, which had but a short existence in spite of the talent of its conductors, who were Mr. Shillaber (known under the soubriquet of Mrs. Partington), Dr. Shepley, and Chas. G. Halpine. After its failure he removed to New York, where he became associate editor of the *Times*, with Henry J. Raymond, and shortly afterward acquired an interest in the New York *Leader*, with John Clancy. To this latter paper he devoted his best efforts; he not only furnished the political matter, but gave sketches and stories, which were so well appreciated that the circulation of the *Leader* rapidly increased from a few hundred to eleven thousand, and it became a power in the land. At that period he commenced to exhibit his talent for fictitious inventions; and, under a wager that he would produce a sensation at a time when literary matters were excessively dull, he wrote a long account of the resuscitation of Hicks, the pirate, who was executed on Bedloe's Island a short time before. By this production, which was most adroitly done and complete in all minutiæ of detail, for which his medical knowledge furnished a good basis, he attained his object, and not only set the city wild with excitement, but originated a blind suspicion which was not allayed for many years.

He did not, however, restrict his pen to any single

journal, but contributed to almost all of importance that were published in the metropolis—a story for one, an editorial for another, a poem for a third, on any subject and in various styles adapted to each publication. In fact, his very first article for the American press appeared in the *Tribune;* and it was shortly after his arrival, when he was strongly alive to the wrongs of his native country, and naturally sympathetic with the down-trodden of every land, that he wrote for that journal a famous poem, the authorship of which has long been falsely attributed to Mr. Greeley, containing the lines,

"Tear down the flaunting lie,
Half mast the starry flag,
Insult no sunny sky
With hate's polluted rag."

This remarkable versatility has led to the charge against him that he possessed no literary conscience. But this accusation was most false. His temper, it is true, was mercurial, and his views would occasionally vary, but he never prostituted his powers to sustain a lie or to do an injustice. He had no control of many of the papers for which he contributed, and was required to furnish matter that accorded with the views and purposes of each, and so far he had to modify his own sentiments; but nothing that he ever wrote was in a bad cause or for an unworthy object, and his course of action was invariably the best that he could follow under the circumstances; but when he was his own master, and in such publications as he controlled, his conduct was guided by the highest sense of duty, often at great pecuniary loss to himself, and invariably to the disgust of those who would have warped him to their meaner views. When the war against the Union broke out he laid down the pen and took up the sword. Giving up all his connection with the press, surrendering the liberal income which his literary gifts secured to him, he accepted the moderate pay of a lieutenant in the Sixty-ninth Regiment, commanded by Colonel Corcoran. He rapidly mastered the details of military service, and his peculiar talents led to his promotion to the staff of General Hunter, with whom he served throughout the greater part of the war. His duties as adjutant general, both with General David Hunter, and subsequently with Major General Halleck when he was general in chief, were very arduous. Not only did he have the preparation of all the official correspondence, but he had to perform much literary work for the papers in moulding the public mind to military necessities. At that period the North was in uncertain humor, and the government had to feel its way carefully, and watch, and, so far as in its power lay, guide, public opinion. In his capacity as adjutant general he prepared for General Hunter's signature the first order ever issued directing the enrollment of a negro regiment, for which he was honored by the rebels by being included in the outlawry which was declared against that intrepid soldier, and which directed the immediate execution of both general and adjutant, if they were captured.

Both the commanding officers with whom General Halpine had served recognized his eminent merits, and strongly urged upon the government that his rank should be advanced, but the Secretary of War utterly ignored their applications, and left this patriot to the last a simple major. The reason for this action the party most affected by it could never clearly understand, but he supposed it was due to some informality; that the application was addressed to the President instead of to the Secretary of War, or for some other such trivial error, if error it could be called; for his final interview with the great organizer of the war dispelled many of his prejudices, and caused a thorough revulsion of sentiment toward one whom he regarded as his enemy for political reasons. His eyesight, which was always weak, having failed from exposure and excessive labor, he had twice sent in his resignation, accompanied with the certificate of the surgeon that farther service would probably result in total blindness. These resignations were not accepted, although a furlough was granted him on the latter—a furlough which, before it was half expired, he surrendered, that he might accompany General Hunter in his perilous expedition down the Shenandoah Valley. When that expedition returned, after enduring incredible hardships, he again applied to be permitted to resign, and obtained an honorable and complimentary acceptance of his resignation at once. The last of his doubts were removed when, in spite of his earnest support of M'Clellan as the presidential candidate of the Democrats against Abraham Lincoln, he was breveted lieutenant colonel, colonel, and brigadier general.

Few men sacrificed more for the cause; few men made less by it. If he had been a son of the soil he could have done no more, and was baptized in fire and blood as an American. Forever afterward he regarded himself as a citizen by birthright and inheritance instead of by adoption, for he had helped to save what came to others in the natural way and by accident. He had "paid a great price," and was entitled to all the rights of one "born free." His last connection with the army was under General Dix in the city of New York, where he had the congenial duty of arresting and punishing bounty swindlers. The frequenters of Lafayette Hall had deep cause to lament his fearlessness, unwearying resolution, and irrepressible energy. He worked night and day to bring the rascals to their deserts, and his skill in ferreting out fraud and in hunting down corrupt politicians which he had obtained in other walks of life was of vast service to him.

It was while he was on the staff of General Dix that the articles from his pen in the daily papers, exposing the corruptions of the municipal government, attracted the attention of the Citizens' Association, which had then just inaugurated its reform movements in that city. As soon as he was released from the army, application was made to him to assume the conduct of The Citizen newspaper, which had been started by the Association. He accepted the position, and finally purchased the entire journal and conducted it until the time of his death. He used it not only as a vehicle for reform in municipal affairs, but as an organ in party politics. With its aid and his own exertions he built up under the name of the Democratic Union an organization opposed to political corruption, and strengthened it by his personal popularity till it became more powerful within the sphere of its action than Tammany Hall itself. But, even when giving the larger part of his attention to THE CITIZEN, he still found time to contribute many articles to other papers. One of his earliest connections with the press was as French translator for the *Herald*, and from that period to the close of his career he had relations of the most intimate character with that journal and its editor, who from the first appreciated his remarkable and striking genius.

Such is a brief outline of his career as a journalist. His success as a politician was equally brilliant. In London he had connected himself with the "Young Ireland party." In this country his first essay in politics was as the private secretary of Stephen A. Douglas, and by virtue of that position he became identified with the leading political events of that exciting period. In consequence of his position toward Douglas, he naturally became the embassador between him and Buchanan in the negotiations for a settlement of their difficulties. The cunning sage of Wheatland, however, deceived him and his employer, and never did he forgive the baseness of that treachery toward the beloved leader of the Freesoil faction. It rankled in his heart, and he could not help expressing it when a thoughtless Republican Senate were offering incense on the grave of a double-dyed traitor—a traitor to his friends and his country.

For many years he was a member, and of course a most actively influential one, of the Tammany Hall General Committee. He was soon engaged in a reform movement, and his object of attack was no other than Fernando Wood, so notorious as the organizer and leader of corruption in the city of New York, and who, by his skillful combinations, maintained a bad eminence in that city. The struggle was fierce and bitter, but courage and honesty conquered duplicity and venality, and Halpine lived to rout his opponent and break his power. His admission to the army removed him in a great measure from the political arena; but no sooner was he free from military duties and trammels than he returned to an employment that gave especial scope to his talents. His fertility of resource was wonderful, his combinations beautiful and effective, and his grasp of the entire subject most masterly. At the period of his return to civil life, Tammany Hall had again fallen into the slough of iniquity, and, true to his nature, he commenced a battle against an organization that had once been his political home. The first brilliant success of this new combination was his own election to the Registership, a very lucrative office, against an adverse majority on other candidates of nearly fifty thousand. This was quickly followed by other triumphs, and at the time of his decease he was elaborating schemes and perfecting plans which would have rendered inevitable the defeat of his adversaries in the then approaching election.

But Charles G. Halpine was more than a journalist, more than a politician; he was a poet and an author whose writings were entitled to no mere fleeting popularity. So occupied was he, however, that he had neglected putting the great body of these productions in permanent form. He was so hidden under the impersonality of newspaper literature that he was hardly known to the public at large until the year 1862, when he assumed the *nom de plume* of Miles O'Reilly. His assumption of this soubriquet was merely accidental, and the rank of "private in the Forty-seventh New

York," instead of a similar place in the Sixty-ninth, to which he had belonged, came from the fact that the Forty-seventh was the only Irish regiment at Hilton Head at the date of his military lyrical effusions, and it was essential to his purpose to assume the character of an ignorant but well-meaning Irishman. His series of amusing poems referring to matters at Beaufort—or pretending to be connected therewith—were an immense success, and made his soubriquet a household word throughout the land—far more so than his own true appellation. But it is not generally known that they were written with a praiseworthy object, and for the good of the service. They were followed by his imaginary banquets and other fancy sketches, the force and purpose of which can only be fully appreciated by politicians versed in the mysteries of New York politics.

These entertaining and amusing poetic effusions, although so effective, were the least finished of his metrical efforts. Many of his amatory sonnets were exquisite as works of art, and in their delicacy and force of sentiment. He never ignored the passion which rules the world, but never made it gross or prominent. His admiration for woman was too pure and refined to make such a degradation of her possible to his thoughts or pen. Many of the finest of these are almost lost to the world, and are only preserved in albums and scrapbooks, his life being too full to allow him time to attend to the collection of his productions. Even more beautiful than his love-songs were his poems in memory of the dead who fell in the War for the Union. These were the natural outpourings of his heart; as no soldier crippled, sick, or out of work, ever applied to him in vain for assistance, so his regard for the dead was simple reverence. The poem on the dedication of Gettysburg is thrilling, and only surpassed in vigor by the grand lines of his latest work in commemoration of the Irish Legion—a work which gives evidences of greater capacity than he had then developed, and was the promise of even a higher career for the future, had his life not been brought to its sudden termination. The circumstances under which most of his productions were presented had possibly made him occasionally careless, and it was only for a worthy occasion that he exerted his full powers.

He had a slight knowledge of law, having been admitted to the bar, and having for some time held the position of assistant district attorney; but his knowledge was not thorough, and was rarely, except in this instance, put to any practical use. His mastery of a subject or a profession was, by the aid of his powerful memory, easy and rapid; but, unless he had sounded it to the bottom, he laid it aside entirely.

As for the circumstances of his death, although most deplorable, they are perfectly simple of explanation. He had always suffered at times from insomnia, or want of ability to sleep. It had been his habit to write without cessation for many hours, often for several days and nights in succession, without rest, until his brain was in so nervously excited a condition that sleep was absolutely banished. Then a nervine or sudorific was absolutely necessary to produce a normal condition of his system. At times he took opiates, but of late he had used ether or chloroform. His medical studies gave him some knowledge of the power of these dangerous drugs, he had seen them applied to Mrs. Halpine when suffering from violent hysterical attacks, and he used them upon himself to produce lethargy and sleep, or even to dull pain.

For some two weeks before his death he had been in perfect health, in excellent spirits, and in capital working condition. Early in the last week of his life he had written his poem commemorative of the Irish Legion, and on his final Saturday he was at the office of THE CITIZEN until about two o'clock, in gayer humor and more genial mood than usual, although he was invariably a charming companion. Later he was attacked with violent pain in the head, and he had recourse to chloroform. The apothecary, by a well-intentioned but unfortunate error, gave him a diluted article which had no effect, and which he detected as deficient in strength. Then he sent for more, and under the delusion that it also was weak or adulterated, while it was actually of full strength, inhaled too much of it and became insensible. Thus, by a mere accident, a most important life was taken away from the public at its period of greatest usefulness. He died ere more than half his natural term of activity had run, at the age of thirty-nine, at a period when his faculties were in their most perfect development.

Such is a brief outline of the life and death of a man who had few equals among his contemporaries. The details are meagre, the statements bald, but they are such as our limits will alone permit. The description of the character of him who has gone from among us is far more difficult; friendship and affection may guide

2

the pen, but will scarcely prove equal to the task; they will fail not from claiming too much, but by doing too little for one who had great talents, many virtues, and few faults. With the public he was a favorite, among his intimates he was beloved. He had a thousand qualities to win esteem, not one to cause dislike or even coldness. His imperfections, and they were but as the spots on the sun, brought suffering to himself alone. He possessed the largest generosity, the strongest affection, the most faithful friendship, the most unsullied honor, and not a single meanness. He was candid, straightforward, honorable, and upright; contact with the world had not dimmed the purity of his soul. He was kind, thoughtful, gentle, considerate to those under him, frank and honest with his comrades.

Charles G. Halpine from his earliest youth possessed a power of fascination, was surrounded with an atmosphere of electrical sympathy which it was impossible for man or woman to resist. He won his way to every heart without an effort. Kind to others, he never forgot a kindness to himself; open and frank, he recognized honesty and openness in others. He had a wonderful gift for creating friendship, and never in the course of his laborious life did he fall into difficulty but some one was near who gladly reached him a helping hand. If wronged, he was easily appeased. He was generous to an adversary, was merciful to those who were down; and never, in all his many contests and bitter political feuds, did "he strike below the belt," take an unfair advantage, or pursue a victory into revengefulness. He died almost without an enemy, and the press united as with one voice in expressions of affection to his memory.

It was innate with him, a part of himself that he could not escape from, to oppose fraud, venality, and corruption. Whether he was contending for reform in city politics, or ferreting out bounty swindles, or guarding against the corruptions of the quartermaster's departments, he was only obeying a law of his existence. He was once offered a fortune by a quartermaster at Hilton Head, when he was adjutant general, and he had but to shut his eyes and come home rich. The government had utterly ignored his services, and he was retained against his will in the army, and prevented from earning a suitable income by his independent exertions. It was a sore temptation, or would have been to most men, but he simply ordered the tempter under arrest, and presented charges at Washington. So he could at any time have made terms with his political opponents in this city, and secured any office he wanted; and yet he never swerved from his course, nor even hesitated as to his action.

He was generous to a fault. Appeals for charity were almost irresistible, although he might have little evidence that the object was worthy. In this, as in many other matters, he was a representative—a high-toned and noble one—of his race. Lively, kind-hearted, grateful, extravagant, versatile, inconsequent, mercurial, easily guided by his friends, he was a thorough Irish gentleman. Endowed with a wonderful memory, facile as wax to acquire an impression, like adamant to retain it, and possessed of a superior classical education, he had the groundwork for his genius to go upon.

The style of his writings has been praised, but in reality he cared nothing for style. He worked for a purpose. He used his pen to carve out a certain result, and wonderful was the skill with which he proceeded. This perception was intuitive, and the most effective plans seemed to present themselves of their own volition. He made no pretense to finish and adorn his style, and rarely read his productions except to correct the proof. But he was wonderfully fertile in argument and exhaustless in variety of mode of presenting a point. The most remarkable evidence of his ability to effect a purpose, even when that purpose was an entire revulsion of public sentiment, is furnished by his song "Sambo's Right to be Kilt." That was written to accustom the Irish—who had so great a prejudice against a negro that they did not like him even to be killed in the company of white soldiers—to the idea of negro regiments. Its effect was as astonishing as its arguments were unanswerable. Regiments of blacks were directly and indirectly a necessity of Northern success, and their possibility was mainly due to the wondrously skillful pen of General Halpine.

We have endeavored to give a slight insight into the character of the deceased from the point of view of one who knew him intimately, who understood him thoroughly, and with whom he was in perfect sympathy; but the pen is feeble that attempts this last act of friendship. No power can bring the bright glance into the eye that is dull forever; the smile to the lip that is silent and closed; the glow to the cheek that is cold as marble. No words can describe the fascination of his presence, nothing explain the force of his persuasive eloquence, more powerful in conversation than in declamation. The death of no single individual in the community would have reached so far, touched so many hearts, and affected so many interests. His activity had ramified into a thousand directions, and allied him with hundreds of public matters, until his death became a national calamity.

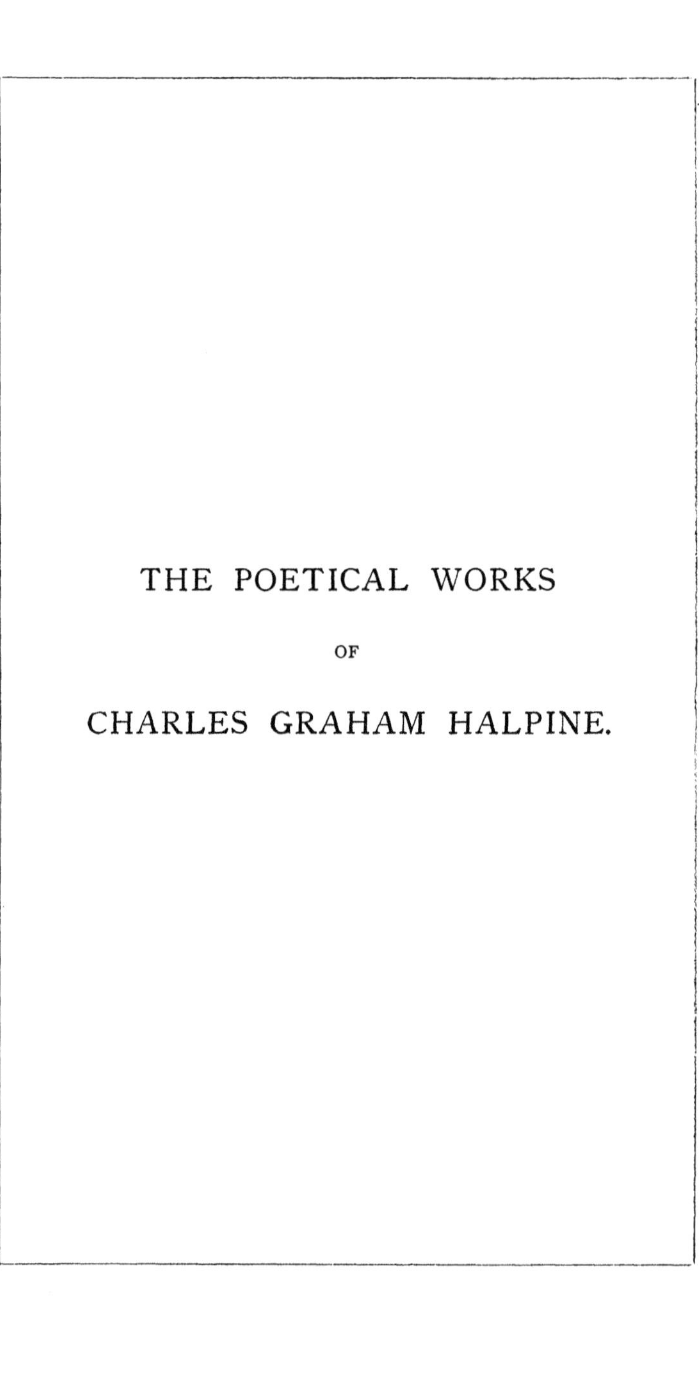

THE POETICAL WORKS

OF

CHARLES GRAHAM HALPINE.

POETICAL WORKS, ETC.

A VESPER HYMN.[1]

THE evening bells of Sabbath fill
  The dusky silence of the night,
And through our gathering gloom distill
  Sweet sparkles of immortal light;
  Such hours of peace as these requite
The labors of the weary week;
  When thus, with souls refreshed and bright,
Forgiveness of our sins we seek!

Oh! help us, Jesus, to conform
  Our spirits, thoughts, and lives to thine!
Beyond this earthly strife and storm,
  Oh! make Thy star of Love to shine!
  When we are sinking in the brine
Of doubt and care—oh come, that we,
  As Peter did, may safe resign
Our sinking helplessness to thee!

Thy Godhood—whence all glory flows—
  Thou didst not scruple to abase,
To rescue from undying woes
  The sons of a rebellious race!
  Who can, unmoved, unweeping, trace
Thy meek obedience to His will,
  Whose sole appointed means of grace
Thou didst, even to the Cross, fulfill!

Our wayward footsteps wander wide,
  Pursuing Joy's delusive rays;
And, in our hours of health and pride,
  Too oft from Thee our spirit strays;
  But soon descend the darker days,
When youth and strength their lustre hide,
  And, journeying through a pathless maze,
We turn to our neglected Guide!

Lead back, oh Lord! thy wandering sheep—
Oh, guide us gently to thy fold!
Instruct us all Thy laws to keep,
And unto Thine our lives to mould!
For we are weak, and faith grows cold—
Nor ever sleep the Tempter's powers;
Thou art our only stay and hold—
Through Thee alone can heaven be ours!

A darker shade, a denser gloom
Descends on all the folded flowers,
While, silent as the voiceless tomb,
Above them roll the midnight hours:
To-morrow's dawn, and their perfume
Again will fill their glowing bowers—
Lord, after death so bid us bloom,
Where no frost chills, no tempest lowers!

ON RAISING A MONUMENT TO THE IRISH LEGION.[2]

To raise a column o'er the dead,
To strew with flowers the graves of those
Who long ago, in storms of lead,
And where the bolts of battle sped,
Beside us faced our Southern foes;
To honor these—the unshriven, unhearsed—
To-day we sad survivors come,
With colors draped, and arms reversed,
And all our souls in gloom immersed,
With silent fife and muffled drum.

In mournful guise our banners wave,
Black clouds above the "sun-burst" lower;
We mourn the true, the young, the brave,
Who for this land that shelter gave,
Drew swords in peril's deadliest hour—
For Irish soldiers, fighting here
As when Lord Clare was bid advance,
And Cumberland beheld with fear
The old green banner swinging clear
To shield the broken lines of France.

We mourn them; not because they died
In battle, for our destined race,
In every field of warlike pride,
From Limerick's wall to India's tide,
Have borne our flag to foremost place;

As if each sought the soldier's trade,
While some dim hope within him glows,
Before he dies, in line arrayed,
To see the old green flag displayed
For final fight with Ireland's foes.

For such a race the soldier's death
Seems not a cruel death to die,
Around their names a laurel wreath,
A wild cheer as the parting breath,
On which their spirits mount the sky:
Oh, had their hope been only won—
On Irish soil their final fight,
And had they seen, ere sinking down,
Our Emerald torn from England's crown,
Each dead face would have flashed with light!

But vain are words to check the tide
Of widowed grief and orphaned woe:
Again we see them by our side,
As full of youth, and strength, and pride
They first went forth to meet the foe!
Their kindling eyes, their steps élate,
Their grief at parting hid in mirth;
Against our foes no spark of hate—
No wish but to preserve the state
That welcomes all the oppressed of earth.

Not a new Ireland to invoke—
To guard the flag was all they sought;
Not to make others feel the yoke
Of Poland, fell the shot and stroke
Of those who in the Legion fought:
Upon our great flag's azure field
To hold unharmed each starry gem—
This cause on many a bloody field,
Thinned out by death, they would not yield—
It was the world's last hope to them.

O ye, the small surviving band,
Oh Irish race wherever spread,
With wailing voice and wringing hand,
And the wild *kaoine* of the old dear land,
Think of her Legion's countless dead!
Struck out of life by ball or blade,
Or torn in fragments by the shell,
With briefest prayer by brother made,
And rudely in their blankets laid,
Now sleep the brave who fought so well.

Their widows—tell not them of pride,
No laurel checks the orphan's tear;
They only feel the world is wide,
And dark, and hard—nor help nor guide—
No husband's arm, no father near;
But at their woe our fields were won,
And pious pity for their loss
In streams of generous aid should run
To help them say "Thy will be done,"
As bent in grief they kiss the Cross.

Then for the soldiers and their chief
Let all combine a shaft to raise—
The double type of pride and grief,
With many a sculpture and relief
To tell their tale to after days;
And here will shine—our proudest boast
While one of Irish blood survives—
"Sacred to that unfaltering host
Of soldiers from a distant coast,
Who for the Union gave their lives:

"Welcomed they were with generous hand;
And to that welcome nobly true,
When War's dread tocsin filled the land,
With sinewy arm and swinging brand,
These exiles to the rescue flew;
Their fealty to the flag they gave,
And for the Union, daring death,
Foremost among the foremost brave,
They welcomed victory and the grave
In the same sigh of parting breath."

Thus be their modest history penned,
But not with this our love must cease;
Let prayers from pious hearts ascend,
And o'er their ashes let us blend
All feuds and factions into peace:
Oh men of Ireland! here unite
Around the graves of these we love,
And from their homes of endless light
The Legion's dead will bless the sight,
And rain down anthems from above!

Here to this shrine by reverence led,
Let Love her sacred lessons teach;
Shoulder to shoulder rise the dead,
From many a trench with battle red,
And thus I hear their ghostly speech:

"Oh for the old earth, and our sake,
 Renounce all feuds, engendering fear,
And Ireland from her trance shall wake,
Striving once more her chains to break
 When all her sons are brothers here.

I see our Meagher's plume of green
 Approving nod to hear the words,
And Corcoran's wraith applauds the scene,
And bold Mat. Murphy smiles, I ween—
 All three with hands on ghostly swords—
Oh for their sake, whose names of light
 Flash out like beacons from dark shores—
Men of the old race! in your might,
All factions quelled, again unite—
 With you the Green Flag sinks or soars!

AFTER THE BATH.[3]

A PICTURE IN WATER COLORS.

Her skin is moist, and cold, and pink,
 But warm and red the lips I press,
And all her beauty seems to shrink
 Compacter in her clinging dress;
While o'er her shoulders to the hip,
 O'er swelling bust and far adown,
In trailing gold the tresses drip
 Which form at night her braided crown.

No more her eyes in languor swim,
 But kindle with coquettish strife,
And every pulse in every limb
 Seems throbbing into radiant life;
Her cheek hath caught a ruddier stain,
 And her small feet in sand that sink
Are marble-white, with many a vein
 Down to the almond-nails of pink.

Her teeth are white as the flashing surf,
 Her eyes are blue as the bay in calm,
And her breath to the new-mown clover turf
 Is a rival in its fragrant balm;
Oh happy sea that has held her form,
 Oh happy sands by her white feet pressed—
With her beauty the whole bright scene is warm,
 Her beauty of gesture, and face, and breast!

Proudly she stands in her scarlet dress,
  And my eyes give a quiver and then grow dim
As I gaze on her infinite loveliness
  Of delicate color and rounded limb;
And the bright blue bay with its flitting sails,
  And the silver sands, and the rocks of brown,
And the woods that are dark on the distant hills,
  And the broad green meadows that slope adown,

All seem but a frame for my lady bright—
  A frame not worthy her matchless grace—
Her lips of red, and her eyes of light,
  And the wonderful charm of her winsome face;
Oh, here let me lie and die at her feet,
  Let my soul in its sighs for her pass away—
For my life hath its climax, and death were sweet
  With her eyes gazing down on me here to-day!

My senses swoon into blissful trance
  As her small, cool fingers touch my palm,
And through all of my veins the currents dance
  As I feel on my cheek her breath of balm;
All the springs of my life are in her control,
  For though faces more perfect I know full well—
In rich, womanly beauty of body and soul
  There are none to compare with my seaside belle.

The brown rocks glow as she bounds along,
  And the black weeds thrill in the silver spray,
And the birds in the blue sing a gladder song
  As my lady walks by the shining bay;
The waves that have shrined her glowing form
  Have been humanized by the saintly touch,
And will spare for her sake in the next great storm
  Some proud ship from their clutch.

THE MAN OF THREESCORE.[4]

A PHILOSOPHIC RANT.

Never grieve that youth flies!
  So the wise
  Mortal cries.
All the pleasure of life
In this one maxim lies.

Our youth is most dear;
 But does not the lover
 A pleasing pain suffer,
And is not his smile ever steeped in a tear?
 Never grieve, etc.

To love is to see
 New charms every hour;
 But is there a bower
Where sweet roses bloom that a thorn will not be?
 Never grieve, etc.

Our spring time departs—
 Let us laugh and not rage;
 For the laughter of age
Brings the sunshine of youth once again to our hearts.
 Never grieve, etc.

Sixty summers have fled—
 Poor, idle, and gay,
 I am wasting away—
But you can not find thirty gray hairs in my head.
 Never grieve, etc.

With a girl to adore,
 My godson, at twenty,
 Is satisfied plenty—
My grandmother lives, and I'm glad at threescore.
 Never grieve, etc.

Some people assever,
 As I have been told,
 That the world's growing old;
But, to my eyes, the world is more merry than ever.
 Never grieve, etc.

Old Momus, whose birth
 May be traced back for ages,
 Still laughs on our pages,
And reigns o'er us all as the monarch of mirth.
 Never grieve, etc.

Would not grief be destroyed
 Could we rest us content
 That our pleasures are spent,
And that, though we have lost them, they have been enjoyed?
 Never grieve, etc.

If my limbs grow so weak
  That I can not walk fast,
  Then I hope at the last
That the end of my term will be reached the less quick.
          Never grieve, etc.

And whene'er Death is pleased
  To forbid our delay,
  Let us hasten away
As an epicure runs from a fast to a feast!
          Never grieve that youth flies!
            So the wise
            Mortal cries;
          All the pleasure of life
            In this one maxim lies.

FAREWELL TO CLUB COMPANIONS.

Adieu to the glory of bachelor parties,
  The looseness of latch-keys, the cards, and the cup;
Old Hymen has caught me—so farewell, my hearties!
  The game, as we say in the vulgate, is up.
No more shall my voice, when 'tis mellowed by sherry,
  Troll out the wild glee of the "Grape and the Boar;"
Henceforward, without me, be social and merry,
  My voice shall be heard in your circle no more.

Yet sometimes, when Joy her white curtain is flinging
  Between your rapt eyes and the shadows of care—
When gaming, and dancing, and drinking, and singing
  Usurp the bronze of the giant Despair—
Let memory paint me as once, in your middle,
  I brimmed a full glass to the toast of "The Fair;"
When, with trumpet and gong, the cornopean and fiddle,
  We made the dull folk of our neighborhood stare.

Oh, of Hymen beware! Like a lion he's waiting
  To pounce on the careless who saunter along;
He sends a young Cupid, who, laughing and prating,
  Decoys us away with a smile and a song;
He leads up a path that is bordered with roses,
  A garden with every thing beautiful rife;
At the end of the vista a Venus reposes—
  We clasp her—and Hymen has noosed us for life!

Henceforward the fair one, whose mystical beauty
  Entranced every fibre and thrilled every bone,
Is ours by the law, and our business and duty
  Becomes to love her, and to love her alone;
But, you see, to the heart so abhorrent is bondage,
  It hates because right what 'twould love were it wrong;
And the path, all so green in our youth and our fond age
  Grows thorny, and tedious, and dreary, and long.

I'm married, alas! and, of course, I am happy—
  The married, you know, they must "all happy be;"
But I think of the nights when we "bowsed at the nappy,"
  And drop a few tears in my third cup of tea;
No more shall the polka's bewildering gyrations
  Inspire the warm lips till they whisper of love;
I must sit down sedately and shun such temptations,
  With my thoughts—or my eyes, at least—fastened above!

And don't, if you call—this for my sake, remember!—
  Don't whisper a word of the nights we have had;
Declare I was always as cold as December,
  A youth much religious, and gentle, and sad;
A man who detested all noise and confusion,
  Who cried that a polka was flagrant and vain,
And would never permit even the slightest infusion
  Of brandy or wine the pure element stain.

Above all, not a word of the girl of the ballet
  You found in my rooms when you called rather late;
Never venture a hint about Laura or Sally—
  Be silent, in mercy, and "mum" about Kate!
But tell her I loved still to linger and dandle
  The whole evening long o'er religion and tea;
Describe me a pattern young man, and a model
  Of all that a husband should properly be!

LINES

ON READING IN A LETTER FROM PARIS THAT "LOUIS NAPOLEON SPENDS HIS EVENINGS EITHER PLAYING BACKGAMMON WITH THE EMPRESS, OR EXAMINING THE PRIVATE REPORTS OF THE CHIEF OF POLICE."

Spirit of him who drove afar
  Rebellion's hydra-headed brood,
And quenched the torch of civil war
  In tides of foreign blood!

Thou, in whose ears the dying groans
  Of old Tradition ever sounded,
Thou, at whose step the reeling thrones
  Of Europe fell confounded!

Spirit of him whose mind did forge
  At once the weapon and the chain—
The prince of princes, and the scourge
  Of all who were too weak to reign;
Behold this jackal of renown,
  Who from your name its glory snatches.
This mannikin beneath your crown—
  This "king of shreds and patches!"

France weeps beneath the idiot sway
  Of shaveling priests and jeweled fools;
The Cross of Honor is the pay
  For Tyranny's most abject tools;
The land that couched the freest lance
  Now fears the informer's sightless arrow;
The eagle of imperial France
  Has dwindled to a sparrow!

And he who staggered to a throne
  Through broken oaths and civic broil,
Who sought his perjury to atone
  By drenching red the Roman soil;
This dwarf, tricked out with seven-league boots,
  This king of thimble-rigging science—
This rat, who gnaws the hoarded fruits
  Designed to foster lions.

This perjurer, robber, murderer, all—
  Religion's curse and manhood's jibe,
Whose only battle is a ball,
  Whose only victory is a bribe—
This rushlight that would be a star
  (Oh, Jupiter! Immortal Ammon!)
Foregoes the glorious game of war
  For one of mild backgammon.

His bulletins police reports,
  His aid-de-camp the mousing spy,
Falsehood the passport to his courts,
  His life one long-continued lie;
And this was all the First did win
  By Titan toil and daily battles,
And such "the pea that now within
  The giant's helmet rattles!"

QUAKERDOM.

THE FORMAL CALL.

Through her forced, abnormal quiet,
Flashed the soul of frolic riot,
And a most malicious laughter lighted up her downcast eyes;
All in vain I tried each topic,
Ranged from polar climes to tropic—
Every commonplace I started met with yes-or-no replies.

For her mother—stiff and stately,
As if starched and ironed lately—
Sat erect, with rigid elbows bedded thus in curving palms;
There she sat on guard before us,
And in words precise, decorous,
And most calm, reviewed the weather, and recited several psalms.

How without abruptly ending
This my visit, and offending
Wealthy neighbors, was the problem which employed my mental care;
When the butler, bowing lowly,
Uttered clearly, stiffly, slowly,
"Madam, please, the gardener wants you"—Heaven, I thought, has heard my prayer.

"Pardon me!" she grandly uttered;
Bowing low, I gladly muttered,
"Surely, madam!" and, relieved, I turned to scan the daughter's face:
Ha! what pent-up mirth outflashes
From beneath those penciled lashes!
How the drill of Quaker custom yields to Nature's brilliant grace.

Brightly springs the prisoned fountain
From the side of Delphi's mountain
When the stone that weighed upon its buoyant life is thrust aside;
So the long-enforced stagnation
Of the maiden's conversation
Now imparted five-fold brilliance to its ever-varying tide.

Widely ranging, quickly changing,
Witty, winning, from beginning
Unto end I listened, merely flinging in a casual word;
Eloquent, and yet how simple!
Hand and eye, and eddying dimple,
Tongue and lip together made a music seen as well as heard.

When the noonday woods are ringing,
All the birds of summer singing,
Suddenly there falls a silence, and we know a serpent nigh:
So upon the door a rattle
Stopped our animated tattle,
And the stately mother found us prim enough to suit her eye.

MY TOAST.[5]

"THE FIRST, LAST, AND ONLY GIRL I EVER LOVED."

Her hair is like a field of wheat
By autumn tinged with glistening yellows;
Her clear blonde face is always sweet,
Her little waist is round and neat,
And plump her bust, and small her feet—
Come, boys! "To Lucie Ellice!"

Her gentle hands of tapering white—
The rings that touch them make me jealous!
Her ripe red lips are with smiles bedight,
Her large blue eyes have a swimming light,
And her fair soft skin with health is bright—
We drink to Lucie Ellice!

Elastic as the delicate vine
That sways in June from the vineyard trellis;
Her step is dainty, her touch is fine,
And her breath is sweet as the perfumed wine
Which the votarist kisses before the shrine—
Even such is Lucie Ellice!

And then her voice! You mayhap have heard,
As dawn in the East to crimson mellows
(While the dews on the roses are yet unblurred,
And the gossamer web on the grass unstirred),
The song of the lark as aloft it whirred—
'Twas the voice of Lucie Ellice!

And her soul—'tis a spirit of subtle flame,
That kindles and softens, illumes and mellows;
'Tis an essence pervading and thrilling her frame,
And 'tis from it her wonderful gentleness came—
Her grace, and her beauty, and all that I name,
When we drink to Lucie Ellice!

But Fortune is cruel, and Love is blind—
  Cruel and blinded the fables tell us;
For with hearts revolting are hands resigned,
And the flowers are sundered that should have twined,
And darkly we drift on the path assigned,
    As I drift from Lucie Ellice!

Oh, give me a ruff that once touched her throat,
  And I ask no gems from a royal palace;
Give me a ribbon that once did float
Where the swelling lines her form denote,
Then send me to die in some land remote,
    My last thought—"Lucie Ellice!"

But why should I offer so pure a toast
  To the grosser ears of my feasting fellows?
To have seen her but twice is all my boast;
So back to our euchre, and call the host,
And that lad shall be king who can drink the most
    To the health of my Lucie Ellice!

BELLE OF THE BALL.

Oh, Lady of Kinsa!
  Dear girl of my heart,
With your teeth of cut pearl
  Where the crimson lips part;
And a breast o'er whose white hills
  With beauty aglow
The blue veinlets wander
  Like streams through the snow.
How proud is her glance,
  Yet how kindly to all,
As they halt in the dance
  For my Belle of the Ball.

My Lady of Kinsa!
  How royal her grace,
Yet how bright and how gentle,
  And winsome her face;
And her eyes, large and blue,
  Are as soft as a fawn's,
And her smile is as genial
  As midsummer dawns;

And her wealth of brown hair—
  See its hues rise and fall,
Golden, chestnut, and fair—
  In my Belle of the Ball.

My Lady of Kinsa!
  In silver and green,
By the sceptre of beauty
  A true Irish queen;
As she raises her train,
  For the dancers are fleet,
See how small in their white
  Satin buskins her feet;
Oh! to be but caressed
  By the white arms that fall
To the partner now blessed
  By my Belle of the Ball!

My Lady of Kinsa!
  The clover that dips
To the scythe has no perfume
  To equal your lips;
And your little pink ears
  Crown an ivory neck
Which the jewels of empire
  Might worthily deck;
And your voice is as bland
  As the murmur of streams,
And the touch of your hand
  Is the thrill of my dreams;
And I glow in each pulse
  As I bow to the thrall
Of my beauty of Kinsa—
  My Belle of the Ball.

TO SHERIDAN.

FROM ONE WHO LOVES HIM VERY DEARLY.

Phil Sherry was of knightly build,
  A soldier of renown,
His sabre flashed on many a field,
  His flag o'er many a town;
And when the limbs to weakness grow
  Now filled with youthful flame,
Our children's children yet shall glow
  To bold Phil Sherry's name.

With stormy oath and bugle-blast,
  And eyes of kindling fire,
When the skies of war were overcast,
  And hope might well expire,
Our Phil with gleaming hand and heel
  Led on his fiery flock,
And the victor foe would turn and reel
  Beneath his desperate shock.

Who has not heard, with tears and smiles,
  Of the hot and headlong ride,
When, after twenty galloping miles,
  He checked the rebel tide?
And how, when Lee was brought at length
  To final bay or flight,
'Twas Phil that hurled our final strength,
  And won our final fight?

Oh, gallant leader of the brave,
  Whose fame for aye endures,
Soil not the crest that victory gave
  By work that is not yours.
Leap in the saddle once again,
  Let your wild plumes outflow,
Nor help to crush the beaten men
  Who sank beneath your blow.

To baser hands, to meaner souls,
  Resign the odious task—
'Tis love this passionate cry controls,
  'Tis for your fame I ask.
I want you still an image high,
  Niched in my heart—its king;
Oh, once more let your pennons fly,
  Let "boots and saddles" ring!"

You were not framed—the soul God placed
  Within your fiery clay—
That rarest gift of heaven to waste
  In the wranglings of to-day;
The base intrigues, the ready lies,
  The cold and coward hates—
The barb that in the darkness flies,
  The pitfall at the gates·

These form the politician's trade—
  Too base for you to know;
To fight deceit you were not made—
  You need a manlier foe;

And I tell you, Phil, I'd rather seek
  For friends in the foes we fought,
Than trust any "loyal" Southern sneak
  Whom success to our side has brought.

TO RAYMOND ON HIS TRAVELS.[3]

Oh, your boat is at the pier,
  And your passage has been paid,
But before you go, my dearest dear,
  Accept this serenade!
For with friendliness we burn,
  And rejoicing come the rhymes
To toast the health and safe return
  Of him who rules the Times!
    To toast the health and safe return
      Of him who rules the Times.

If we all could get away
  From this town of cares and frets,
To wander round the Elysées,
  And kiss the gay grisettes,
Such skedaddling there would be
  As was never known before—
Ten thousand steamers out at sea,
  And not a man on shore!
    Ten thousand steamers out at sea,
      And not a man on shore!

But oh! delusive dream,
  For us no chance remains;
Mere drudges of the desk we seem,
  With dull and throbbing brains;
But, though we must stay at home
  To earn the painful dimes,
Let us all rejoice that he can roam—
  Our brother of the Times!
    Let us all rejoice that he can roam—
      Our brother of the Times!

Oh, safely may he sail,
  And safely sail he back;
His virtue like a proof-of-mail,
  To ward off each attack;

No beauty of the Boulevard,
Or nymph of other climes,
To win even half a thought's regard
From him who rules the Times!
To win even half a thought's regard
From him who rules the Times!

Were I Marble of the World,
Or young Bennett debonair,
Do you think I'd see his sails unfurled,
And not his voyage share?
By this wine-cup in my hand,
By my hope of famous rhymes,
My foot should quit Manhattan strand
With him who rules the Times!
My foot should quit Manhattan strand
With him who rules the Times!

THE TWO VOICES.

FIRST VOICE.

Of all light troubles to heart or head,
The lightest of troubles are from the dead.

SECOND VOICE.

False teacher, no! All griefs I crave,
Save the grief that whispers me from the grave.

FIRST VOICE.

The grave is silent, and death is dumb;
No hint of reproach from the dead may come.

SECOND VOICE.

The living accuse us of folly or crime,
But the white ghosts whisper us all the time.

FIRST VOICE.

The living can witness with threatening eyes,
But never a witness from death may rise.

SECOND VOICE.

Cruel and coldly your thoughts keep track,
But I'd give my life could the dead come back.

FIRST VOICE.

A source of division, of care, and dread—
Why seek to recall the now happy dead?

SECOND VOICE.

To breathe a few farewell words in the ear,
"In heaven try forgive any wrongs done here."

FIRST VOICE.

Regrets for the dead can but torture the heart—
Whether living or dead, you were forced to part.

SECOND VOICE.

Living, though seas might between us roll,
We would still have communion of soul with soul.

FIRST VOICE.

And your life would wither, your head turn gray,
With the sorrows that Destiny cast in your way.

SECOND VOICE.

Oh, sainted and loved! could I call back thine,
How gladly the burden of life I'd resign!

FIRST VOICE.

The living may change, but the dead abide
In the passion that crowned them as they died.

SECOND VOICE.

Had the years estranged us and changed the heart,
It were gentle; but death tore us roughly apart.

FIRST VOICE.

But a living change were a little woe;
The love that died loving must ever glow.

SECOND VOICE.

Oh, friend! that was thought in a kindlier vein—
All my joys in the grave of the dead remain.

FIRST VOICE.

The soul is immortal—the body dies;
The dead smile down pity with holy eyes.

SECOND VOICE.

I try to believe it—to see the dead stand
As my guardian angel in God's bright land.

FIRST VOICE.

So think! And, thinking it, henceforth move
That the dead beholding you may approve.

SECOND VOICE.

I shall try, my friend; but a cold, dumb pain
Swims up from the soul to the clouded brain;
And I'd give—had I power—all beneath the sky
For the dead to revive, and myself to die!

A BREEZY DISSERTATION.

Two breezes in the forest met
  A little way from town,
The one was blowing up to it,
  The other blowing down;
They whispered kindly through the trees,
  Through foliage, branch, and fork—
And that one was a country breeze,
  And this was from New York.

They tossed the crimson leaves about,
  And whirling danced around,
They laughed to see the forest rout
  Fall eddying to the ground;
To shaking nests and stripping boughs,
  And such like sports they fell,
Till, tired at last, one said, "Suppose
  What each has seen we tell."

The country breeze—the sweeter far—
  Full pleasantly replied,
"I've driven upon my cloudy car
  O'er landscapes far and wide.
I've seen the harvest gathered home
  By ruddy men and maids,
I've cooled me in the cascade's foam,
  And slept in quiet glades.

"But most of all I loved to force
  My way through those old woods,
Upon whose murmurs, warm and hoarse,
  No human voice intrudes;
'Tis pleasant, too, to breast the top
  Of yonder snow-clad hills,
Then down into the valleys drop,
  And chase the flying rills.

"O'er lakes that slumbered in the sun
  Like mirrors broad and bright,
My path has been a pleasant one
  Of perfume and of light.

And now I seek the city—there
   I hear are glorious things—
Come, tell to me, my sister fair,
   Where you have spread your wings."

So loudly then the other sighed,
   She made the branches sway;
The squirrel, perching overhead,
   Affrighted, leaps away:
"Oh, sister! bless'd hath been your lot;
   Far different mine hath been;
Now hear my tale, and you will not
   Desert the forest green.

"Condemned by fate, I wandered round
   Yon pile of smoky brick,
And men and mud were all I found,
   And both have made me sick;
The towering chimneys volumed forth
   A choking cloud above,
And, looked I south, east, west, or north,
   I saw not aught to love.

"I fanned the cheek of brilliant girls,
   And kissed away—their paint;
I danced through many a dandy's curls,
   And caught their soiling taint;
From wretched rooms and filthy streets
   One reeking vapor rose,
And, mingling with these city sweets,
   The sound of shrieks and blows.

"At every corner hideous men
   With curses rent the air—
Creatures whom neither tongue nor pen
   To paint in full would dare;
I heard the wife's expiring shriek
   As the wretch drove home his knife,
And saw some scenes I dare not speak
   In yonder city's life."

The country breeze would hear no more—
   Away the sisters fled;
The wood shook down o'er each a crown
   Of foliage, brown and red:
And now round some primeval lake,
   O'er hills and pastures bare,
Their freshening flight those breezes take—
   Would I were with them there!

A CALIFORNIAN DITTY.

When lovely Araminter Jones—
  She always was a gadder—
Did marry, then I took my bones
  To the Seeraw Neevadder.

My pick it seemed to have a charm,
  So quickly did I pocket
Enough to buy a jolly farm,
  To build a house and stock it.

The gold became my child apace,
  And I did rock its cradle,
And for to clean its yaller face
  I used both pan and ladle.

And day by day the bright sun rolled
  Above a larger treasure,
And day by day, in gathering gold,
  I took a wilder pleasure.

The miners called me stingy Sam
  Because I played no euchre,
But yet I was not then, nor am
  The slave of filthy lucre.

There's no man that can see the heart,
  The bosom has no winder,
Else had they seen, from gold apart,
  The love of Araminter.

I vowed revenge against that prig—
  Her husband, he—Joe Slammers;
He is a cove as wears a wig,
  Is lame, and squints, and stammers.

I swore that Mrs. S. some day
  Should envy me prodigious;
I'd live beside her, and display
  What might have been her riches.

I'd lend her husband money, and
  I then would prosecute him:
Were he in that auriferous land,
  'Twould be no sin to shoot him.

For this it was I drove my stakes
  Away on Feather River—
Lord! but I had the ager shakes,
  And suffered from my liver!

At length, with forty thousand clear,
  I shipped among the sailors;
One April day I landed here,
  And went into a tailor's.

I told him that I wanted all
  My clothes of brightest colors,
The largest patterns—nothing small—
  They cost two hundred dollars.

With brooches and with golden chains,
  And rings upon my fingers,
I looked, as do upon the plains,
  Them gaudy birds—flamingers.

I started off, as luck did hap,
  To see my Araminter—
I seed her in a widder's cap,
  A-sittin' at the winder!

She told me that her husband, Joe,
  The very morn of marriage,
Had tripped and broke his precious neck
  A-gittin' in the carriage.

And how, although she bid me go
  When the night was dark and clammy,
She always loved me more than Joe,
  And then she called me "Sammy!"

DELMONICO'S DREAM.[7]

HIS APOLOGY AND EXPLANATION TO ROYAL PHELPS AND THE SPORTSMEN'S CLUB FOR SHERIDAN'S TROUT OUT OF SEASON.

Alas! my sin hath found me out,
  For, while away, unhappy man!
My caterer served unseasoned trout
    To bold Phil Sheridan!
And Roosevelt frowns, and Brady smiles,
  And young "Jim Bennett," too, was there,
And Russell Young, and Private Miles,
    With Raymond in the chair.

Since then, on all the winds about
  The arch of heaven my crime is blown—
"'Tis he that cooked the unseasoned trout—
    'Tis he, and he alone!"
That murdered fish pursues my sight,
  Flapping its tail, and cries "False host!"
And, starting in cold sweats at night,
    I see the troutly ghost.

Then other sights awake my fears,
  For soon the Sportsmen's Club are out,
With gaffs, breech-loaders, rods, and spears,
    In vengeance for the trout!
For pardon, mercy, vain to wish,
  For still they cry—that vengeful train—
"Remember, Del, this piteous fish
    Was out of season slain!"

"In silver brook, in lilied pool,
  Beneath brown boulders jutting out,
Where trees and tumbling rills were cool,
    Dwelt happily our trout;
A speckled beauty for his bride,
  In orange silk and silver lawn,
With not one care beneath the tide
    Except to love and spawn!

"But as on Denmark's royal prop,
  Taking his orchard-sleep at noon,
False Claudius crept, and down did drop
    The leprous hebenoon—
So on our trout's unguarded hour
  (Who deemed our game-laws were not vain)
Thy poacher crept, and sought the bower
    Where dwelt this happy twain.

"How gleam their silver sides below,
  How calm the kiss of throbbing gills,
As o'er the bank, with caution slow,
    Thy peering poacher wheels!
One splash! the bride remains—but oh!
  She sees the gaff her lord impale,
And now in weeds of troutly woe
    She wags her futile tail.

"From March through all the breezy spring,
  When violets first are leaping out,
'Twas thine, with flies upon the wing,
    To tempt and slay our trout.

But—in November! oh, 'tis worse
Than all the crimes at which men flout;
And cursed be he with Cromwell's curse
Who kills unseasoned trout!

"The glorious summer days were thine,
Their crimson dawns and skies of blue,
With supple rod, and curling line,
And flies of varied hue—
Yea! till September browned the corn,
Rounding the golden pumpkins out,
'Twas thine—without reproach or scorn—
To chase the speckled trout.

"But thou hast done a deed of woe
That sets a blister on thy fame,
If custom hath not brazed it so
That it be dead to shame;
A deed that blurs the modest grace,
Plucks off the rose, bids virtue doubt;
For it was here, Del, in this place,
You served unseasoned trout!"

—

From dreams like this I panting start—
Oh, will the morning never come?
And through the long, still night my heart
Beats like a Southern drum!
Spare me! 'tis at my caterer's door
The fault should lie, and not at mine,
And on unseasoned trout no more
Shall breakfast guest of mine!

For I a sportsman am, as true
As Barrett, Beebe, or Seth Green,
And Walton's pleasure oft pursue
Where Islip's ponds are seen.
Besides—and let each Cockney swell,
Who loves not sport, accept this reason—
That bad for health, in taste and smell,
Are trout when out of season!

By order of Major Gen. DELMONICO,
Commanding Caterer of New York.

MILES O'REILLY,
Asst. Bottle Opener and Chief of Staff.

MY BROKEN MEERSCHAUM.

Old pipe, now battered, bruised, and brown,
With silver spliced and linked together,
With hopes high up and spirits down,
I've puffed thee in all kinds of weather;
And still upon thy glowing lid,
'Mid carving quaint and curious tracing,
Beneath the dust of years half hid,
The giver's name mine eye is tracing.

When thou wert given we were as one,
Who now are two, and widely sundered—
Our feud the worst beneath the sun,
Where each believed the other blundered.
No public squall of anger burst
The moorings of our choice relation—
'Tis the dumb quarrel that is worst,
Where pride forbids an explanation.

Old pipe! had then thy smoky bowl
A tongue that could to life have started—
Knowing the secrets of my soul,
In many a midnight hour imparted—
Thy speech, perchance, had then reknit
The ties of friendship rudely sundered,
And healed the feud of little wit,
In which each thinks the other blundered.

A DOLLAR IN HIS POUCH.

'Tis pleasant, when our friends are rich,
To meet them day by day,
Or good or ill, no matter which,
Provided they can pay;
But is there one—you answer not—
Who would or could avouch
Esteem for one who hadn't got
A dollar in his pouch?

'Tis pleasant with our friends to dine,
To see them well arrayed,
To bumper them in costly wine
For which themselves have paid;

To smoke with them, to drive about,
  Share cup, caress, and couch—
But could we know a man without
  A dollar in his pouch?

The bride will love the pleading swain
  Who holds at his command
A handsome house, a goodly train
  Of equipage and land;
But should his fortune cease to smile,
  Even love away will slouch—
Why can't the creature show a pile
  Of dollars in his pouch?

On sea, on shore, they seem to say
  He is rich, and can't be dull;
The gold within his porte-monnaie,
  They think, can fill his skull.
Let mammon reign, let genius rot,
  Let wit, love, valor crouch—
Poor devil, if he has not got
  A dollar in his pouch.

If Christ again should visit earth,
  A man of toil and care,
Howe'er divine, whate'er his worth,
  How, think you, would he fare?
Hence with this vagrant! thrust him out!
  Some swindler, I dare vouch—
Think you God's Son would come without
  A dollar in his pouch?

AN ACROSTIC BIRTHDAY OFFERING.[8]

Here on her happy day of birth,
  Encircled by the loves and laughter,
No other thoughts but peace and mirth
  Resounding from the gilded rafter,
It is no easy task to trace
  Each trait of figure, voice, and gesture—
The Eastern beauty of the face,
The large dark eyes, the regal grace,
  And all the rich, good taste of vesture.

A woman with all graces crowned,
  Grand in her style, yet keenly tender,
  Needing a care we rarely render
Even where our love is most profound—
She pines for Italy's classic ground.

Beneath her dark Circassian lashes
  Each impulse in her eyes is shown;
No feeling moves her but outflashes,
  Needing no words or spoken tone,
Even as we gaze, to make it known;
The flashing glance and changing cheek,
These show her varying thoughts, and eloquently speak!

JAMES GORDON BENNETT, Jr.[9]

Och, Jim avic! you've done the thrick,
  Our chord of manhood sthriking;
An' now you stand before the land
  Our young and laureled Viking.
An' it isn't bekase you won the race,
  An' bate all them others hollow,
But, staunch and thrue to your hardy crew,
  You didn't say "go," but "follow!"
No men would you ask to face a task
  That you dodged from your wealthy station,
An' this was the part that has touched the heart
    Of this great Yankee nation.

THE KNIGHT'S ADDRESS.[10]

ON CROWNING THE LADY OF HIS CHOICE AS QUEEN OF LOVE AND BEAUTY, AT THE GRAND TOURNAMENT IN ST. CHARLES COUNTY, MARYLAND.

The old chivalric days are gone
When beauty was by prowess won;
But still—though lost the feudal cause,
Its knightly faith and courteous laws—
We here yet strive to keep aglow
  The old chivalric tone of feeling,
Thus crowning beauty's radiant brow,
  At beauty's feet thus humbly kneeling.

Oh, lady! in the good old time
Your fame had lived in minstrel rhyme;

And gallant knights, in gilded steel
From tossing plume to weaponed heel,
With lance in rest and whirling sword,
  To win your smile had dared all chances—
Repaid even by your slightest word,
  Or by one flash of your bright glances.

But, ah! the feudal cause is lost,
And palms must now with gold be crossed;
And trade, and toil, and Yankee greed
To knightly faith and love succeed;
But beauty still retains her power,
  And knightly faith yet warmly lingers
Where History—in this darkest hour—
  Writes the "Lost Cause" with nervous fingers.

I crown thee, lady, as my queen,
The loveliest earth has ever seen;
My sole regret that on your brow
The chaplet which I offer now
Is not the crown of royal light,
  Which beauty such as yours should wear,
And that, for your dear sake, your knight
  Has had no olden risks to dare.

HONOR THE BRAVE.

Honor the brave who battle still
  For Irish right in English lands;
No rule except their quenchless will,
  No power save in their naked hands;
Who waged by day and waged by night,
  In groups of three or bands of ten,
Our savage, undespairing fight
  Against two hundred thousand men.

No pomp of war their eyes to blind,
  No blair of music as they go,
With just such weapons as they find,
  In desperate onset on the foe.
They seize the pike, the torch, the scythe—
  Unequal contest—but what then?
With steadfast eyes and spirits blithe
  They face two hundred thousand men.

The jails are yawning through the land,
The scaffold's fatal click is heard,
But still moves on the scanty band,
By jail and scaffold undeterred.
A moment's pause to wail the last
Who fell in freedom's fight, and then,
With teeth firm set, and breathing fast,
They face two hundred thousand men.

Obscure, unmarked, with none to praise
Their fealty to a trampled land;
Yet never knights in Arthur's days
For desperate cause made firmer stand.
They wage no public war, 'tis true;
They strike and fly, and strike—what then?
'Tis only thus these faithful few
Can front two hundred thousand men.

You call them ignorant, rash, and wild;
But who can tell how patriots feel
With centuries of torment piled
Above the land to which they kneel?
And who has made them what we find—
Like tigers lurking in their den,
And breaking forth with fury blind
To beard two hundred thousand men?

Who made their lives so hard to bear
They care not how their lives are lost?
Their land a symbol of despair—
A wreck on ruin's ocean tossed.
We, happier here, may carp and sneer,
And judge them harshly—but what then?
No gloves for those who have as foes
To face two hundred thousand men.

Honor the brave! Let England rave
Against them as a savage band:
We know their foes, we know their woes,
And hail them as a hero band.
With iron will they battle still,
In groups of three or files of ten,
Nor care we by what savage skill
They fight two hundred thousand men.

TO FORSYTHE FROM O'REILLY.

SUGGESTED BY THE RECENT DEPLORABLE FREQUENCY OF MATRIMONIAL CASUALTIES TO YOUNG OFFICERS OF OUR ACQUAINTANCE.

They fall, my friend! the young, the proud,
  The gay, the festive cusses fall—
An orange wreath instead of shroud,
  A ring in lieu of Minié ball;
The men who faced a battle's roar
  Now yield to ruffled chemisettes,
And lion hearts bow down before
  Some twilled, frilled pair of pantalettes.

And we, who with them marched and slept,
  Sharing advance, retreat, attack—
When revel on "salt horse" we kept,
  Coffee, hard bread, and apple-jack—
Shall we not heave one pitying breath
  For these our comrades as they go,
Not happy to a sudden death,
  But doomed to lingering lives of woe?

"'Twas their own fault," the cynic cries;
  "For if a moth will seek the flame,
And scorch his wing until he dies,
  Is it moth, or lamp, or both we blame?"
Ah! true, my friend; but think how long
  These hapless moths through War's dark night
(When rains were chill, and winds were strong)
  Had pushed their cold and lonely flight.

So when, at last, they saw the gleam,
  And felt the warmth of woman's eyes,
Who blames them if they dreamed the dream
  Which every moth in dreaming dies?
They were the youngest, tenderest kids,
  And saw no snake beneath the flowers,
Nor knew that under Beauty's lids
  Dwelt bolts of more than Whitworth powers.

And now, my friend, with moaning sore,
  They yield the latch-key, and resign
The sacred corkscrew which of yore
  In every pocket used to shine;

And henceforth, it is known to each
  Of this once gay and festive band,
It matters not what rank they reach,
  Their wives are in supreme command.

For them the idle badge of power,
  The strap with bar, or leaf, or bird—
But on the wives to whom they cower
  Far higher brevets are conferred;
The throated frill, the scented glove,
  The crimson lip, the throbbing breast—
These high commissions, signed by love,
  What slave of Hymen dares contest?

Ah! no; unhappy, it was theirs
  To ride unhurt through fields of strife;
But now—like rabbits caught in snares—
  Each comrade yields him to a wife.
And henceforth epaulette or sash,
  Or chapeau-bras, or baldric bright,
Are nothing more than empty trash—
  Their rank and file (not wives) to fight.

For higher than all flags that float,
  Or all the stars on straps conferred,
Is woman's deathless petticoat,
  And woman's last appealing word!
In vain they strive—our comrades old—
  Against the sway when first 'tis felt,
'Tis beauty's dower as slaves to hold
  The heart that once her power could melt.

And so they fall—the young, the proud,
  The gay and festive cusses fall—
An orange wreath instead of shroud,
  A ring in lieu of Minié ball;
The men who faced a battle's roar
  Now yield to broidered chemisettes,
And lion hearts bow down before
  Some twilled, frilled pair of pantalettes.

ONLY SOME RELICS.

A ring she wore—a jewel that pressed
The maiden beauty of her breast.

A glove our happy hands once drew
From her small fingers veined with blue.

A ribbon that around her throat
Loved in the dallying winds to float.

A golden clasp, that once had known
The silken pressure of her zone.

A little slipper with blue rosette,
In which her fairy foot was set.

And one brown tress, through happy years
Shading the shell-films of her ears—

These, and an ivorytype's dull stain,
Are all of our dear one that now remain;

All the dear relics that are left
Of her by whose loss our hearts are cleft;

Leaving the world a dim, dead space
Of cares and duties with little grace—

A dull, dead level of weary years,
In which no blossoming joy appears;

No girl with teeth like the rows of corn
When you strip the ear as the summer is born;

And tresses of changing gold and brown,
Over shoulders of ivory shaken down;

And lips in whose arched and crimson bow
All the flushing balms of the tropics glow;

And over whose dimpled cheeks, like light
And shade over meadows, the thoughts take flight;

Winged by her innocent, dancing eyes,
With coyness and coquetry, smiles and sighs.

Her voice was the hum of a summer wind
When it breathes through a lattice with roses twined:

Her soul was as pure, as unsullied and white,
As the chanting seraphs in robes of light;

And the kindness that dwelt in her heart, I deem,
Of the heaven she now dwells in was some stray gleam.

Oh, loved and lost! our soul's adored!
Our dove with silver wings—our bird!

Beauty embodied, and joy, and peace,
Whose breath had a charm bidding sorrow cease.

Best gift that heaven to bless us gave,
We cast this chaplet on thy grave.

PHILADELPHIA.[11]

VOICE OF THE BOYS IN BLUE.

Be merciful to the South—
Not with the empty word in your mouth,
But merciful be—let your actions tell—
To the men who were beaten, but fought so well:
Be merciful to the South!

Be generous to the South,
Gentle in deed, and in word of mouth;
For no craven brand on the forehead shines
Of the men who met us in volleying lines,
And fought for the flag of the South.

Be tender and just to the South,
For famine, and slaughter, and hunger, and drouth
They have suffered, who made such a gallant fight
For a cause that was wrong—but they thought right—
Be just to the beaten South!

Be just, and be something more,
Now that the hot days of battle are o'er;
For brothers we were in the glorious past,
And brothers again we must be at last—
Be merciful to the South!

We are all here once more,
The terrible days of our conflict o'er;
And again the old flag floats elate
O'er the capital dome of each sister state
In the East, North, West, and South!

Let us join hands once more,
Renewing the vows that our fathers swore;
Forgetting all strife save the lesson it taught,
And meeting as reconciled brothers ought—
A reconciled North and South.

Errors on both sides were,
But for these—they are past, and we have no care;
Let a sponge glide over the hideous years
Of terror and bloodshed, havoc and tears,
Dividing the North and South.

One destiny holds us yet,
We have common hopes and a common debt;
For England was false to us both alike,
And against her power with strong arms should strike
The reconciled North and South.

Oh, 'tis a glorious hour,
That joins us again in imperial power;
And long o'er the land of the free and the brave
May the Pine and Palmetto united wave—
Fit emblems of North and South.

Again, like two parted friends,
With our quarrel fought out, the hatred ends;
And none more welcome this happy day
Than the Boys in Blue and the Boys in Gray,
Who fought for the North and the South.

THE HOUSEHOLD TOMB.

The shafts of disappointment fall
Where most we build our pride,
And now the dearest loved of all
Their little ones had died;
The tears they shed in silence fell
Like rain-drops through the gloom,
And unto him they loved so well
They reared this household tomb.

The little bird whose tender wing
Grew weak in winter tide,
Who seemed to strengthen in the spring,
And soared in summer's pride—
Grew fainter as the autumn fell
On summer's withering bloom,
And unto him they loved so well
They built this household tomb.

He had a trick in sunny hours
To seek the garden walks,
And pluck from out the radiant flowers
The withered buds and stalks;
He bore them in as if to tell
That canker-worms consume,
And soon to him, beloved so well,
They reared this household tomb.

The church hath massive iron gates,
  Six days 'tis cold and dim,
Till Sabbath fills the silken seats,
  And the organ swells the hymn;
Shall there a blazoned pillar tell
  A child's so common doom?
Ah! no; for him, beloved so well,
  They built a household tomb.

On the mantle-piece all old and worn,
  Where his childish toys are laid,
Where the withered buds he plucked were borne,
  In the room where oft he played—
A kneeling statue sheds a spell
  Of prayer around the room,
And the little boy they loved so well
  Has thus a household tomb.

Oh, friend, I've seen the tear-drops shine,
  And watched your quivering lip,
I've felt your arm clutch closer mine
  When a bright boy chanced to trip
Across our path, and though there fell
  No tear, nor word of gloom,
I knew your spirit bowed before
  That little household tomb.

But, comfort! There's a higher sphere
  Where the earth-lost reunite;
The spirit of your boy seems near,
  To prompt each word I write;
He says he shares the loved ones' mirth
  When they gather in the room,
And smiles down on the silent hearth,
  Even from the household tomb.

IRELAND AND THE SOUTH.

THE BOYS IN GREEN TO THE BOYS IN GRAY.

Air: "The Wearing of the Green."

Ring out from every steeple,
  Call the clans from every fold,
We're a democratic people,
  And our faith we mean to hold;

We're for mercy to the beaten foe,
For brothers we have been,
And what oppression is we know,
All we who wear the Green—
Ay, what oppression is we know,
All we who wear the Green—
In our very bones what it is we know,
We boys who wear the Green.

We have felt it in our sire-land,
With its whip our backs are scored;
Of the South we'll make no Ireland
Scourged with famine and the sword;
'Tis true they tried the rebel game,
But punished they have been,
And I rather think we've done the same,
All we who wear the Green—
We ourselves have done the very same,
All we who wear the Green,
And we hope again to do the same,
We boys who wear the Green.

Oh, manhood's proudest duty
Is to fight for manhood's faith;
And true courage has a beauty
That not even crime can scathe;
Into chaos they plunged headward, boys;
Their guilt we do not screen;
But our Emmet and Lord Edward, boys,
Did likewise for the Green—
Ay! Sheares, and Orr, and Edward, boys,
Were rebels for the Green;
Wolfe Tone, and Bond, and Edward, boys,
Did likewise for the Green!

And the day is not far distant
When our equal boast shall be
That our country's crown is glistened
With Grant, Farragut, and Lee;
By Stonewall Jackson's front of flame,
And Sherman swift and keen,
And Meagher, who led on to fame
Us boys who wear the Green—
Tom Meagher, whose brigade of fame
All wore the plumes of Green;
And Sheridan, whose deathless name
Proclaims he wears the Green!

So "Mercy" be the countersign,
 And "Hoffman" the parole—
Let the bugles ring along our line,
 And the drums for battle roll.
And the cry shall swell from every mouth,
 And on our flags be seen,
We're for mercy for the rebel South,
 "We rebels of the Green"—
We've a fellow feeling for the South,
 We rebels of the Green—
The boys who wore the Gray down South,
 We boys who wore the Green.

A LITTLE RHYME OF LITTLE THINGS,

FOR VERY LITTLE PEOPLE.

A curious thing it were to know,
 And knowledge worth the winning,
How very big a fact may grow
 From quite a small beginning;
Tom treads on Freddy's tender toe,
And gives a curse, and then a blow
 That sets poor Tommy spinning;
Next knives are drawn, and blood must flow,
And Freddy to the gallows go
 For homicidal sinning;
And yet a corn upon the toe—
 A corn was the beginning.

A ripened apple fell one day
 Where a wise man was walking—
An accident, as some would say,
 Not worth a moment's talking;
But—in a philosophic way—
That apple called a mind in play
 That was not easy balking;
The secret of mechanics lay
Enshrined therein—'twas heaven's own ray
 To us in darkness walking:
Yet trifles such as these, we say,
 Scarce merit serious talking.

An idle man sat down one night
 Before a boiling kettle,
And plugged the spout exceeding tight
 With some soft kind of metal;

Off went the lid! a common sight,
But unto him 'twas different quite,
For he resolved to settle
What force this boiling water might
Possess? and so there came to light
The steed of tireless mettle;
The locomotive lay that night
Within a tap-room kettle.

A Yankee youth—a sturdy chap—
Was partial to kite flying,
And just to see what chance would hap,
A fork he took, and tying
The prongs above the peak, the trap
Caught, caged, and tamed the thunder-clap!
A fact now patent, lying
In the electric wires which lap
Our country, and will soon enwrap
All climes and oceans lying
Upon the broad earth's mighty map—
So much for his kite flying!

So don't despise the little things
Which happen daily round us,
For some of them may chance take wings
To startle and astound us.
Trace back the greatest deed—it springs
From trifles which no poet sings—
Some trifling change, which found us
Prepared to grasp and mount its wings;
Then with our fame the wide earth rings,
And Fate's high hand hath crowned us,
Because we watched those little things
Which she made happen round us.

THE BETTER CHOICE.

Too little do we gaze on Nature's face—
Too much have dwelt in colleges and towns,
Where man pursues the miserable race
Of wealth and mere book-learning. The muse frowns
On him whose footsteps o'er the breezy downs
Seldom have pressed; our need is solitude,
For the harsh dissonance of the city drowns
Those dreams of virtue, loveliness, and good,
Which in the breast of youth, however stifled, brood.

Let us arise, and shake away the dust
  Of brick and pavement from our flying feet,
All former visions from remembrance thrust,
  And even forget that once we trod the street.
  Up in the mountains haply we may meet
Those glorious fancies that still shun the throng;
  The rill's wild music, tremulous and sweet,
Will lend a softer cadence to our song,
The cataract's curbless strength may teach us to be strong.

And flowers, and perfumes, and untainted air,
  And forest green with dark cathedral glooms,
And the fleet birds, whose mission is to bear
  Nature's true music on their outspread plumes,
  And mossy banks, and overhanging blooms
Of trailing honeysuckle—these shall teach
  Our tongues to breathe the passion that consumes
The inmost spirit; and we shall learn a speech
Wide-general enough all human hearts to reach.

All forms of art are transient, and they die
  Even with the folly which conferred their birth.
Fashion deceives, but Nature can not lie
  While the wide ocean cradles the green earth.
  False are the echoes of conventional mirth,
Falser the semblance of conventional woe,
  Mere puppet feelings cherished in the dearth
Of genuine passion; for a while they glow
Like paint on death's shrunk cheek—there is no life below.

The couch of velvet and the damask fold
  May give luxurious languor some brief ease,
And mirror'd walls and cornices of gold
  Afford good shelter, and a while may please;
  But look again, and tell me where are these?
A heap of tatters and a tottering wall!
  Not so this mossy bank, these sheltering trees;
Nor fades the sun, nor does the green hill fall,
Nor fails the bright still pool to mirror back the whole.

Forms, books, and customs are the chains that bind
  Our hearts to wretchedness. Whoe'er would be
Strong in himself, these fetters cast behind
  And seek the desert—limbs and reason free!
  There let him ponder of his destiny,
Survey the mountain shrine, the starlit dome,
  Hear Nature's prompting voice: "All this for thee
Was made and is sustained; it is thy home;
Be true to your own life, and here earth's monarch roam!"

Oh, false conceit! self-baffling avarice!
  That strives to grasp the mental riches earned
By former toilers! Be assured of this—
  No ray of thought that erst in Goethe burned,
  Through pedant-channel can to you be turned.
Each hand must pluck its individual fruit.
  Books are the grave where knowledge is inurned;
No second blossom from their clay can shoot;
Yourself must sow the seed—let them manure the root.

And we have idled our best years away
  In gathering dead leaves. There yet is time
To plant a better harvest, such as may
  In part compensate for wasted prime.
  And though no forest, leafy and sublime,
Our wintering sun can hope to shake abroad,
  Still may we graft some creepers that will climb
Round our old age, enlivening the green sod,
And breathing grateful praise to the benignant God.

Oh, mother earth! to us estranged too long
  Have been thy beauties—not by our own will,
For with a passion blind as it was strong
  Have we adored thy purity, and still
  Would, ere the years our destiny fulfill,
Drink thy inspiring eloquence; nor thou
  This tardy homage to thy throne repel—
Clouds may not always linger on heaven's brow,
And let the future speak the fervor of our vow.

DUET FOR THE BREAKFAST-TABLE.

ROMANTIC HUSBAND.

Thou art my love! I have none other
  But only thee—but only thee.

SENSIBLE WIFE.

Now, Charles, do stop this silly bother,
  And drink your tea—your cooling tea.

ROMANTIC HUSBAND.

Your eyes are diamonds, gems refined,
  Your teeth are pearl, your hair is gold—

SENSIBLE WIFE.

Oh nonsense now! I know you'll find
  Your cutlets cold—exceeding cold.

ROMANTIC HUSBAND.

Where'er thou art, my passions burn;
I envy not the monarch's crown—

SENSIBLE WIFE.

Put some hot water in the urn,
And toast this bread, and toast it brown.

ROMANTIC HUSBAND.

Had I Golconda's wealth, I say,
'Twere thine at will—'twere thine at will—

SENSIBLE WIFE.

Then let me have a check to pay
The dry-goods bill—that tedious bill!

ROMANTIC HUSBAND.

Oh, heed it not, my trembling flower;
If want should press us, let it come—

SENSIBLE WIFE.

And, apropos, the bill for flour
Is quite a sum—an unpaid sum.

ROMANTIC HUSBAND.

So rich in love, so rich in joy,
No change our cup of bliss can spill—

SENSIBLE WIFE.

Now do be quiet! You destroy
My cambric frill—my well-starched frill.

ROMANTIC HUSBAND.

Ha! senseless, soulless, loveless girl,
To sympathy and passion dead!

SENSIBLE WIFE.

A moment since I was your "pearl,"
Your "only love"—at least you said.

ROMANTIC HUSBAND.

I spoke it in the bitter jest
Of one his own deep sadness scorning—

SENSIBLE WIFE.

Well, candor is at all times best:
I wish you, sir, a fair good morning!

THE NYMPH OF LURLEIBERGH.

In Lurleibergh's deep shadowed vale,
  Where all the Rhine's blue waters meet,
A maiden sat, as fair and pale
  As were the lilies at her feet;
Her hair in wild profusion flowing
  From roses richly wreathed above
To hide the gentle bosom, glowing
  With mingled thoughts of fear and love.
Oh, Nymph of Lurleibergh! thy lute,
Why stands it thus untouched and mute?
What pensive shadows cloud thine eye,
And cheat the moments as they fly?
Thou art too young, too fair for pain
To dim the smile or wring the brain;
Too pure thou seem'st for thought of ill,
Yet sad thou art, and pensive still.

Yea, thou art sad, although no tear
  Bedews thy silken-fringed lid,
And all the more will sorrow sear
  When thus in mute endurance hid.
Thine eyes are fixed upon the river,
  As past thy feet its waters roll,
And, swift as are its ripples, quiver
  The tides of feeling in thy soul.
Oh, Nymph of Lurleibergh! the crown
Of flowers you wear will wither soon,
The lute's harmonious chords will slack,
And youth, once flown, comes never back;
The gushing waters, pure and sweet,
That pour their tribute to thy feet,
Soon pass the bowers of trellised vine,
And perish in the stormful brine.

We should not waste in tears the hours
  Of youth, that all too fleetly flow;
In spring the fields are decked with flowers,
  And wintry age is capped with snow;
And thou art in the spring of being,
  And thou shouldst be as light and gay
As is the lark when upward fleeing
  To bathe his pinions in the ray
That calls the bluebell from the meadow,
And steeps the hill in sultry shadow;

That bathes the morning lake in fire,
And tips with gold the village spire.
I too have felt the hopeless void
Of pleasures lost when most enjoyed,
And learned, alas! that tears are vain
To wash such memories from the brain.

THE PARTING KISS.

JULIET.

One kiss before you go, love,
  One kiss before we part,
Indeed you do not know, love,
  The sadness of my heart.
The dawn that wakes the birds, love,
  To joy, is pain to me;
I hear your farewell words, love,
  Nor care how bright it be.

Oh, softly down the stream, love,
  Let your light oars be driven,
For I have dreamt a dream, love—
  Perchance a warning given!
I dreamt my brother stood, love,
  And saw our parting kiss;
It can not bode us good, love,
  Be sure, forget not this!

Nor must thou yet forget, love,
  At nightfall to return,
When o'er the parapet, love,
  You see my signal burn.
Adieu! we may not stay, love;
  Cease not to think of me;
And through the weary day, love,
  I'll pray for night and thee.

ROMEO.

Oh, hush! your fears are vain, love,
  Nor sire nor brother near;
Indeed I may remain, love,
  There is no danger here.
The prying dawn delays, love,
  As loth to break our bliss;
He did but peep to win from thee
  The fond, the parting kiss.

The willows, bending deep, love,
  In prudent awe look down;
They will not raise their heads to peep
  Lest you, my love, should frown.
The birds are all asleep, love—
  Oh, chide not my delay;
For where thou art not is my night,
  Where'er thou art, my day.

Alas! the spell is riven, love,
  I hear the bells afar;
Dost thou not see in heaven, love,
  Yon dimly-fading star?
When in the dewy eve, love,
  It rises o'er the hill,
You'll see my shallop on the stream,
  And hear my bugle shrill.

Adieu! it is the dawn, love,
  I must—I must away;
The fading star hath gone, love,
  The birds awake the day.
To part at all is pain, love,
  To thee and me; I wish—
But, till we meet again, love,
  Oh, keep my parting kiss.

ORIGINAL SIN.

RECOLLECTIONS OF A SERMON ON THIS TEXT BY THE REV. DR. BELLOWS, SENT TO A LADY EQUALLY REMARKABLE FOR HER BEAUTY, WIT, BENEVOLENCE, AND THE INTEREST SHE TOOK IN FAST HORSES AND DEMOCRATIC POLITICS.

My dear Mrs. Blank, for the excellent sermon
  You led me to hear, I your debtor remain;
And revolving the subject has made me determine
  To sift the discourse into language more plain.
Your pastor in me has now found a disciple
  Who means to go into religion and win;
But, in case he should fail, in the words of the Bible,
  Impute his mishap to "original sin!"

That "man is not perfect" the excellent Bellows
  Undoubtedly proves, and I boldly maintain;
Whenever you show me "a prince of good fellows,"
  His sins will keep pace with the size of his brain.

Your men of small natures are prim and decorous,
  To prudery's domain their brief steps they confine,
While the "big hearted Indians" who truly rule o'er us,
  Can't bring down their strides to the limiting line.

But woman! dear woman! the excellent Bellows,
  In all his discourse, breathed no word about her;
He was fearful, perhaps, Mrs. B. would grow jealous,
  And therefore thought better that point to defer.
But that woman is perfect in all things becoming
  A womanly nature, he could not deny,
And assuredly not, if this sermon while humming,
  He chanced on our pew to direct his staid eye.

I heard his discourse with a kind of mixed notion
  That "the bliss" he described was allied to our pew;
And whenever he spoke of "the need of devotion,"
  I felt most devoutly—attracted to you.
That heaven has rewards "both in here and hereafter"
  For those who 'tend meeting, I felt to be plain;
For a pleasanter goblet of dreams than I quaffed there
  Was never poured out—labeled "Fancy's Champagne."

Oh, ne'er while I live be that sermon forgotten—
  It made an impression no years can efface;
Your parson's the best horse I know of to trot on,
  When girdling our loins for eternity's race.
"Two thirty" we got it—the dull nags we "dish 'em,"
  Ne'er turning a hair, and ne'er casting a shoe;
And the "Bloomingdale Road" which leads up to Elysium,
  I am firmly convinced has its start from your pew.

STAMPING OUT.[12]

Ay, stamp away! Can you stamp it out—
  This quenchless fire of a nation's freedom?
Your feet are broad and your legs are stout,
  But stouter for this you'll need 'em!
You have stamped away for six hundred years,
  But again and again the old cause rallies,
Pikes gleam in the hands of our mountaineers,
  And with scythes come the men from our valleys;

The steel-clad Norman, as he roams,
  Is faced by our naked gallowglasses,
We lost the plains and our pleasant homes,
  But we held the hills and passes.

And still the beltane fires at night,
  If not a man were left to feed 'em,
By widows' hands piled high and bright,
  Flashed far the flame of freedom.

Ay, stamp away! Can you stamp it out,
  Or how have your brutal arts been baffled?
You have wielded the power of rope and knout,
  Fire, dungeon, sword, and scaffold.
But still, as from each martyr's hand
  The fiery cross fell down in fighting,
A thousand sprang to seize the brand,
  Our beltane fires relighting.
And once again through Irish nights,
  O'er every dark hill redly streaming,
And numerous as the heavenly lights
  Our rebel fires were gleaming.
And though again might fail that flame,
  Quenched in the blood of its devoted,
Fresh chieftains rose, fresh clansmen came,
  And again the old flag floated.

That fire will burn, that flag will float,
  By virtue nursed, by valor tended,
Till with one fierce clutch upon your throat
  Your Moloch reign is ended.
It may be now, or it may be then,
  That the hour will come we have hoped for ages,
But, failing and failing, we try again,
  And again the conflict rages.
Our hate, though hot, is a patient hate,
  Deadly and patient to catch you tripping,
And your years are many, your crimes are great,
  And the sceptre is from you slipping.
But stamp away with your brutal hoof,
  While the fires to scorch you are upward cleaving,
For with bloody shuttles, the warp and woof
  Of your shroud the Fates are weaving.

THE LISPER AND BOOTH.

"Come tell me, girls, and tell me truth,
Why are you all so in love with Booth?

"Has he given you filters, or mixed love-powders
In your breakfast coffee or luncheon chowders?"

Fast came the answer, clear and crisp,
From a young, plump blonde with a lovely lisp:

"I'm thure, Mither Mileth, we love him tho,
Becauth he ith Booth-iful, you know!"

I caught the lisper and kissed her there:
"Kith me muth ath you pleath, but don't wumple my hair;

"And fondle me, Mileth, juth ath muth ath you will,
If you only won't wuffle my Bwuthells fwill!"

So I drew her aside, and, with kiss and whisper,
There were high old times between Miles and the lisper;

And—let Booth be "boothiful" or no,
'Twas a beautiful girl that called him so.

THE OLD GREEN FLAG.

"The Fenian cause is dead," they say;
"Clean crushed by Seward's craven sway!"
'Tis dead—that is, for the present day—
'Twill rise again.

That cause, in Irish lore appears
Has lived for full seven hundred years—
Oft quenched in blood, and quenched in tears,
It rose again.

The dying sire bequeathed his sword
To sons who then their life-blood poured,
And o'er their sons the Green Flag soared—
'Twill soar again.

The Irish mother, as she pressed
The warm, full nipple of her breast,
Thus lullabied her babe to rest—
"'Twill rise again."

Despite rope, dungeon, famine, chains,
And bills of penalties and pains,
For all with Irish in their veins,
It rose again.

From Silken Thomas trace its flow
To Hugh O'Neil and Owen Roe;
And though Lord Edward felt the blow,
It rose again.

And though Wolfe Tone in prison died,
And Emmet was slain on Liffy's side,
Despite all England's power and pride,
It rose again.

It crossed the sea. The Irish race,
Uprooted from their dwelling-place,
Came here new destinies to face—
It rose again.

"Eternal hatred of the foe—
Eternal warfare, blow for blow,
Till England's power in the dust lies low"—
This rose again.

"While Irish blood through our veins is led,
For the Cause and Flag shall our blood be shed,
Till the Green, high soaring above the Red,
Floats free again."

Despite of Seward's truckling fears,
And Irish slaves, with mocks and jeers
For those who hold the faith of years,
'Twill rise again.

By suffering taught to help the weak—
For all the oppressed of earth we speak—
For all the oppressed some hope we seek
To rise again.

Oh, generous, proud, and gallant race—
So often rash, so rarely base—
Sure as the bright sun holds her place,
'Twill rise again.

The old Green Flag, the good old Cause,
Despite the check of cramping laws,
Shall yet obtain the world's applause
When risen again.

Wherever England's flag may float,
Or slaves may wear her scarlet coat,
Leap, Fenians! at the tyrant's throat,
And try again.

The great heart of the land, we claim,
Is thrilled with sympathetic flame,
For they, as we, hate England's name—
'Twill rise again.

For perjured faith—for foulest blows
Struck when the rebel standard rose—
England, even here, a deep debt owes:
'Twill rise again.

Let Seward curve his craven knee,
Yet, while America is free,
The flag we bore across the sea
Shall rise again—

Will rise despite all human power—
Will flame abroad in time's full hour—
Till, high in air, o'er field and tower,
It floats again.

But, brethren, till that hour shall come,
Be busy with your hands—but dumb;
Nor speak till told by the rolling drum
"It floats again."

"It floats—the good old Green Flag floats
Once more in the face of the scarlet coats"—
Then fiercely and full at your foemen's throats
Spring once again.

God of our Fathers! God of Peace!
Grant us from factious feuds release,
For never until these shall cease
Can the old Flag rise again.

LINES ON THE RUSSO-TURKISH WAR.

So far as I can reason down
The complex Eastern question,
A Turkey done exceeding brown
Would suit the Czar's digestion.
Be trussed it must with bayonets first,
And peppered well with powder,
Then, sliced out into provinces,
'Twill make a famous chowder.

Poor Turkey can not bear a yolk,
Though turkey-eggs bear pullets,
Nor can the sultan see the joke
Of making his eggs bullets.
Though he has got a hundred wives,
He dearly loves Moll Davia,
And Galatz is the kind of "gal"
He wouldn't part to save you.

Though men-shake-off the Russian wiles,
  Still Men-tshi-koff is great, sir,
And the Dardan-elles are crooked miles,
  Although they call them "Strait," sir.
The sultan in his harem sits
  While things go harum-scarum;
He gets in-sultin' messages,
  And can not choose but bear 'em.

The Turk appeals to God and Truth,
  But suffers ne'ertheless he,
For Gortschakoff, beside the Pruth
  At Jassy, gives him Jessy.
With Gortscha-koff and Mentschi-koff
  His breast has got a-stuffin',
And, if he can not shake them off,
  These koffs will nail his coffin.

The czar is clad in costly furs
  From Vashka and Yakaka,
While Turkey's sole defense from koffs
  Is Redschid Ali Pacha.
The sultan to the Prophet prays—
  No profit comes a-near him;
And though his Porte be called sublime,
  It has no strength to cheer him.

He prays to Mecca, but he finds
  The mecha-nism rusty;
His prayer can not unlock the gate,
  And so the Porte grows crusty.
His viziers put their visors down,
  And will not face the tussle;
Alas! the faithful Mussulmans
  Have neither brain nor muscle.

Dis-turbin' hands his turban touch,
  His hookah it is hooked, sir,
And soon before a Cossack fire
  Will Turkey's goose be cooked, sir.
His Mamelukes to mammy look,
  Nor are for battle pressing;
His pachas of a dozen tails
  Have tales the most distressing.

His dragomans can't drag a man
  To fight—the Turks ain't stupid;
His eunuchs are as impotent
  For Mars as eke for Cupid.

There's not a man in his divan
  In honor's van will die, sir;
Before the storm that Bruin brews
  The Turkey soon must fly, sir.

The Turks gave shelter to Kossuth—
  For this esteemed their souls are:
May they ne'er know a Hungary day,
  Partitioned as the Poles are.
May Allah and the Christian's God
  Confound unchristian czars, sir,
And may the Turkish moon be girt
  With bright Columbian stars, sir.

TO LAURA.

We must not show the hidden bower,
  Where love's high feasts are holden;
We must not let another see
  The secret flower, perfumed and golden,
That twinkles on the shadowy lea
  For thee and me,
                Dear Laura.

We must not show the priceless gem
  That gleams in pleasure's casket;
No jealous eye its light may see,
  Lest those who envy us should ask it,
Or question how it came to be
  With thee and me,
                Dear Laura.

We must not show the hidden spring
  Where passion cools its fever;
We must not let the slightest sound
  Betray our joy, but be forever
Mute as the woods that wave around
  Our hallowed ground,
                My Laura.

Oh, could we flee, like doves, afar
  From custom's iron bondage,
To some rich isle in the Southern Sea,
  There, in the wood's enwoven frondage,
With all our beings linked, to be
  Unwatched and free,
                Dear Laura.

Still, in the world be cold, reserved,
With social fetters laden;
The humble minstrel, what were he
To win the heart of this proud maiden?
But there are hours—thank heaven there be—
For thee and me,
My Laura.

I would not change my pride of song
For all a prince's treasure;
Not all the wealth beneath the sea
Could yield its lord such passionate pleasure
As when, upon the shadowy lea,
I pluck the golden flower with thee,
And kiss the gem which none may see
Save thee and me,
My Laura.

AT THE SEA-SIDE.

The bay lay sobbing at our feet,
The night was dark, and warm, and calm,
We felt the throbbing pulses beat
Each in the other's palm.

Behind us, crested on the bank,
Were great hotels a-gleam with lights,
Where youth and beauty, wealth and rank,
Held revel through the nights.

But round us all was hushed and dark—
No sound except the sobbing bay—
No light, save when some phosphor-spark
Flashed upward in the spray.

There on the rocks we talked of love—
An old, lost love—till on my breast
Her head, like some o'erwearied dove,
Came fluttering down to rest.

Between us and the anchored light
That marks the shoal beneath its lee,
We watched the white and ghostly flight
Of schooners out to sea.

We talked of freighted ships, that sailed
From bays like this with no return;
We talked of many hopes that failed
To reach the promised bourne.

We sat, recalling all the past—
   The march and camp in prairie lands,
Our canvas cities rising fast
   Along the Southern sands.

Our canters through the scented pine,
   The halts in many an orange grove,
The wreaths of yellow jessamine
   That round our heads we wove.

And then came up, in sad review,
   Full many a friend in battle slain,
And all the war that either knew
   Before us passed again.

And tremulous grew the clasping palm,
   And gentlier sank the fair dear head,
And o'er our souls a deeper calm
   Than o'er the bay was spread—

A calm of pained and softened thought,
   A tender trance of vanished years—
A ghostly mirror, quaintly wrought,
   In which the past appears.

And still, as sadder grew the theme,
   Her hand crept closelier into mine,
And on my breast, in deeper rest,
   I felt her head decline.

Oh, dark blue bay, with your anchored light,
   Your belt of hills and your silver shore,
For the freighted hearts relaunched to-night,
   What harbor has Fate in store?

WASHINGTON'S BIRTHDAY, 1865.[13]

AN APPEAL TO THE PATRIOTIC AND BENEVOLENT FOR A SOLDIER'S HOME.

Forever past the days of gloom—
   The long, sad days of doubt and fear—
When woman, by her idle loom,
Heard the dread battle's nearing boom
   With claspéd hands and straining ear;
While each new hour the past pursues
   With farther threat of loss and pain,
Till the sick senses would refuse
To longer drink the bloody news
   That told of sons and brothers slain.

The days of calm at length are won,
  And, sitting thus, with folded hands,
We talk of great deeds greatly done,
While all the future seems to run
  A silvery tide o'er golden sands.
With pomp the votive sword and shield
  The saviors of the land return,
And while new shrines to peace we build,
On our great banner's azure field
  Yet larger constellations burn.

Who bore the flag—who won the day?
  The young, proud manhood of the land.
Called from the forge and plow away,
They seized the weapons of the fray
  With eager but untutored hand;
They swarmed o'er all the roads that led
  To where the peril hotliest burned—
By night, by day, their hurrying tread
Still southward to the struggle sped,
  Nor ever from their purpose turned.

Why tell how long the contest hung,
  Now crowned with hope, and now depressed,
And now the varying balance swung,
Until, like gold in furnace flung,
  The truth grew stronger for the test?
'Twas our own blood we had to meet;
  'Twas with full peers our swords were crossed,
Till in the march, assault, retreat,
And in the school of stern defeat,
  We learned success at bloody cost.

Oh, comrades of the camp and deck,
  All that is left by pitying Fate
Of those who bore through fire and wreck,
With sinewy arm and stubborn neck,
  His flag whose birth we celebrate—
Oh, men, whose names forever bright
  On history's golden tablet graved—
By land, by sea, who waged the fight,
What guerdon will you ask to-night
  For service done, for perils braved?

The charging lines no more we see,
  No more we hear the din of strife,
Nor under every greenwood tree,
Stretched in their life's great agony,
  Are those who wait the surgeon's knife;

No more the bloodied stretchers drip,
  The jolting ambulances groan;
No more, while all the senses slip,
We hear from the soon silent lip
  The prayer for death as balm alone.

And ye, who on the sea's blue breast,
  And down the rivers of the land,
With clouds of thunder as a crest,
Where still your conquering prows were pressed,
  War's lightnings wielded in your hand—
Ye too, released, no longer feel
  The threat of battle, storm, and rock—
Torpedoes grating on the keel,
While the strained sides with broadsides reel,
  And turrets feel the indenting shock.

Joint saviors of the land, to-day
  What guerdon ask you of the land?
No boon too great for you to pray—
What can it give that could repay
  The men we miss from our worn band?
The men who lie in trench and swamp,
  The dead who rock beneath the wave—
The brother-souls of march and camp—
Bright spirits—each a shining lamp,
  Teaching how nobly die the brave.

And thou, Great Shade! in whom was nursed
  The germ and grandeur of our land—
In peace, in war, in reverence first,
Who taught our infancy to burst
  The tightening yoke of Britain's hand—
Thou, too, from thy celestial height
  Will join the prayer we make to-day—
"Homes for the crippled in the fight,
And what of life is left made bright
  By all that gratitude can pay."

Teach these who loll in gilded seats,
  With nodding plume and jeweled gown,
Boasting a pedigree that dates
Back to the men who swayed the fates
  When thou wert battling Britain's crown,
That, ere the world a century swims
  Through time, this poor blue-coated host,
With brevet rank of shattered limbs,
Will swell to fame in choral hymns,
  And be of pride the proudest boast.

Homes for the heroes we implore—
  The brave, who limbs and vigor gave
That—North and South, from shore to shore,
One free, rich, boundless country o'er—
  The flag of Washington might wave;
The flag that first—the day recall—
  Long years ago, one summer morn,
Flashed up o'er Independence Hall,
A meteor-messenger to all
  That a new nation here was born.

Oh, wives and daughters of the land,
  To every gentler impulse true,
To you we raise the invoking hand:
Take pity on our stricken band,
  These demigods disguised in blue.
More sweet than coo of pairing birds
  Your voice when urging gentle deeds,
And power and beauty clothe her words—
A west wind through the heart's thrilled chords
  When woman's voice for pity pleads.

To you I leave the soldier's doom—
  Your glistening eyes assure me right;
Oh think, through many a night of gloom,
When round you all was light and bloom,
  And he preparing for the fight,
The soldier bade his fancy roam
  Far from the foe's battalions proud—
From camps, and hot steeds' charging foam,
And fondly on your breast at home
  The forehead of his spirit bowed.

Oh, by the legions of the dead,
  Whose ears even yet our love may reach—
Whose souls, in fight or prison fled,
Now swarm in column overhead,
  Winging with fire my faltering speech—
From stricken fields and ocean caves
  I hear their voice and cry instead:
"Gazing upon our myriad graves,
Be generous to the crippled braves
  Who were the comrades of the dead."

Our cause was holy to the height
  Of holiest cause to manhood given;
For peace and liberty to smite,
And while the warm blood bounded bright,
  For these to die, if called by heaven.

The dead are cared for: in the clay
  The grinning skull no laurel seeks;
But for the wounded in the fray,
It is through my weak lips to-day
  The Order of the Legion speaks.

HURRAH FOR GORDON GRANGER.

Come, boys, a toast! our pride and boast—
  To friends a joy, to fear a stranger;
Brim every glass, and let it pass—
  The health of Gordon Granger!

His manly grace of form and face
  Made women bless our stalwart ranger;
Her sparkling eyes, her tenderest sighs
  Were all for Gordon Granger.

Each rebel lass, to see him pass,
  To loyalty the sight would change her;
For "Union" she would henceforth be
  With winsome Gordon Granger.

We turned to hear his voice of cheer
  On many a field of death and danger;
The rebel foe soon came to know
  Our yells for Gordon Granger.

No finer clay, for feast or fray,
  Since the Babe Divine lay in the manger,
Has blessed the earth, than had its birth
  With General Gordon Granger.

So here's his health! Long life and wealth,
  And years of peace exempt from danger
Forevermore—so prays his corps—
  Be round our Gordon Granger.

MA NORMANDIE.

FROM THE FRENCH OF BERANGER.

When hope buds forth in vernal prime,
  And winter flies on sunny wings
Far from our country's lovely clime,
  And June her fresh, warm radiance flings;

When Nature's bloom again we see,
And swallows skim the jocund earth,
I love to visit Normandie—
It is the country of my birth.

I have seen the Switzer's scenery,
His cottage home and glaciers;
The unclouded skies of Italy,
Sweet Venice and her gondoliers:
Where'er I roamed or chanced to be,
I cried, "There is no place on earth
So dear to me as Normandie—
It is the country of my birth."

There comes a time to all, alack!
When every day-dream flies away,
And when the wearied soul falls back
To memories of a brighter day.
When my cold Muse nor warbles free
Her songs of love or songs of mirth,
I'll seek fresh fire in Normandie—
It is the country of my birth.

THE MIDNIGHT WATCH.

'Tis late—but thus I mused and read,
While all around in slumber nod;
O Night! to those who will but heed,
Thou art the sermon-time of God!
Our house is hushed—a smouldering fire
Burns low within the glowing grate,
And one by one the lamps expire—
Fit time to meditate.

How hushed! The morning breeze evokes
A thrill of terror—ghostly—dim!
The grim clock deals some fearful strokes
On Time's outspreading cherubim.
The muffled Hours, with hurrying feet,
Still bear to the eternal gate
Reproachful thoughts—an offering meet—
From those who meditate.

No sound save when the wainscot mouse
Or crumbling cinder bids us start—
Sepulchral silence in the house,
And turmoil in the sleepless heart.

Oh, dreams of youth! ye seem to creep
 In formless vapors from the grate
Round one to whom the eternal sleep
 Comes welcome, if not late!

MILES ON THE WHITE FAWN.[14]

A fairy scene of colored light,
 Of gorgeous dress and magic changes,
Where still the gazer's dazzled sight
 From beauty to new beauty ranges.
Now rings the music clear and high,
 Now seems to die—now swells in clangors;
Voluptuous visions fill the eye,
 And thrill the pulse with tropic languors.

A dream grotesque, supremely warm,
 A whirling swarm of fancies devious;
The central figure—woman's form—
 Elastic, languishing, lascivious.
The arching thigh, the rounded calf,
 Ankles and feet of tapering lightness—
Plump bosoms, too unveiled by half,
 And waving arms of marble whiteness.

THE PARTING.

Sadly from my host I parted,
Stiff he was, but genial-hearted,
And a tear unbidden started
  As I lingeringly delayed.
There the mother stood before us,
Prim as ever, and decorous,
But her eye a meaning bore us
  Kinder than her tongue conveyed.

Round the supper-room the glowing
Logs a fitful light were throwing,
While the night-breeze, hoarsely blowing,
  Murmured through the circling trees.
"Friends, adieu! I must oppose you;
Ill repaid the debt he owes you,
If your guest should now expose you
  Unto drafts so rude as these."

Cruel Laura seemed delighted
At my leaving—"Ill requited
Love," I thought, and yet she lighted
    Me, departing, to the door.
Suddenly—of no use saying
How—the breeze, a frolic playing,
Blew the light out, and delaying
    Grew more pleasant than before.

Dank and cold the midnight drizzle—
"One adieu! I hear the whistle!"
Something seemed to strive and wrestle,
    And we tore ourselves apart.
What took place I have an inkling,
For my ear was smartly tingling,
And another soul seemed mingling,
    Lip-conducted, through my heart.

A MORNING SERENADE.

FROM THE FRENCH.

Rose, the red sun peeps o'er the hill,
  Oh quit your couch's soft retreat;
Dost thou not hear the village bell
  Chime forth the hour when we should meet?
The crowded town no pleasure yields,
  Then hie with me—oh, hie away,
And, wandering through the flowery fields,
  We'll pass in love the summer's day.

Come, Rose, the fields with flowers are crowned,
  My arm thy gentle prop shall be;
With loving nature all around,
  We too will love more tenderly.
The woodbine bower the linnet shields,
  And there it sings the livelong day;
Then haste—oh, haste thee to the fields,
  Where hours, like moments, glide away.

In rustic form our life to mould,
  We'll rise when dawn's first glances peep,
And evening's shadows on the wold
  Shall herald our untroubled sleep.
Perchance to thee this prospect yields
  But tedious days and weary hours;
Or dost thou love the scented fields,
  The song-birds and the breezy bowers?

She comes! the town no more appears;
  Oh, hateful city, fare thee well;
Where Art her lifeless beauty rears,
  But genuine passion dare not dwell.
Rose, let us quit Parisian noise
  For sweet seclusion far away,
Our moments crowned with rustic joys,
  Our love increasing day by day.

THE LAST APPEAL.

Brethren, 'tis the last appeal
  Of human woe to outraged heaven;
God witness for us that we feel
Reluctant all to draw the steel,
  But what hope else to us is given?
  The bonds of social concord riven,
    We try the last appeal.

Brethren, on! one stubborn fight,
  And peace for evermore shall be;
The red sea's wave will soon unite
Above the vanquished hosts of Might,
  And conquest lead us into thee,
  Dear Canaan of liberty,
    Where God protects the Right.

Brethren, Power's triumphant heel
  Hath struck us oft, but now we turn,
And they who wronged us soon shall feel
The spell that lies in patriot zeal
  Their bonds to break, their threats to spurn:
  The victor's wreath and martyr's urn
    Await this last appeal.

THE MINER'S DREAM.

I lie all cold and lonely
  Beneath an elm at night,
When the stars are shining only,
  And the glow-worm twinkles bright;
I sleep where the star-gleams quiver,
  And my restless memories roam
Away from the golden river
  To my boyhood's happy home.

The golden dream is fleeting
  Away from my troubled sight,
And my heart with hope is beating
  As I see the cottage light;
My old rude cot before me,
  Where in by-gone hours I dwelt
Ere the clouds of life came o'er me,
  When no care my bosom felt.

And I see my mother smiling
  With a faint, uneasy mirth,
While my father's hands were piling
  The fagots on the hearth;
And they whisper ever lowly—
  Yea, I think I hear my name;
It was breathed in accents holy,
  And a tear-drop with it came.

The golden sands are gleaming
  In the ruddy flush of dawn,
The golden sun is beaming,
  And my mighty dream is gone;
But ever and forever
  In my sleep my wild thoughts roam
Away from the golden river
  To my boyhood's happy home.

THE WIDOWER'S CHRISTMAS.

Oh Christmas night! thy spectral hand outreaches,
  Drawing aside the curtain of the years;
Let us give gifts, let us make happy speeches,
  If but to hide—to hide the blinding tears.

Oh Christmas night! again the table glistens
  With gold and crystal, and the wine is red;
But my heart's ear in throbbing silence listens
  For her sweet voice—my beautiful, my dead!

Oh Christmas night! the children, gladly screaming,
  Dance in young rapture round the lighted tree;
And thus I watch them while my soul is dreaming—
  Dreaming of her mine eyes no more may see.

Oh Christmas night! again thy feast returning,
  Darker by contrast makes my darkness be,
And all thy lamps seem funeral torches burning
  For the dear face I never more may see.

BLACK LOYALTY.

LET THE TRUTH OF HISTORY BE PRESERVED.

Nigh a million of lives we have spent,
And three billions of dollars or more,
That each fetter in twain should be rent,
And the slave-horn be heard never more;
Full six years we have given to the Black,
And the thing was undoubtedly right;
Now suppose, just to alter the tack,
We devote half an hour to the White?

When the South, in its hour of mad pride,
At Fort Sumter let drive the first shot,
Neck and heels our poor Sambo was tied,
And the North held one end of the knot;
But our hold we let go at the sound,
For both hands we required in the fight,
And the war for the Black was then found
Quite a tough job of work for the White.

Well, we fought—ay, for four years we fought,
Pouring out lavish treasure and life—
Did the Black then arise as he ought,
Cleaving northward with torch and with knife?
All his masters were far from his track,
Under Johnston and Lee in the fight;
There was nothing to hold the Black back
From assisting his champion, the White.

Did he aid us when bleeding we stood
To chase from him slavery's dreams,
Or to Lee sent he clothing and food,
Harness, powder, equipments, and teams?
We all know that in one single state
A revolt would have ended the fight,
So no more of their "loyalty" prate,
For the Black rebs were worse than the White.

The White rebels came with a cheer,
Their bayonets aslant and aglow,
While the Black rebels slunk in the rear,
Assisting (and freely) our foe;
Phillips, Sumner, and men of that school,
May click-clatter from morning till night,
But if Black or White rebels must rule,
Then, by heaven! count me in for the White.

It would sicken a dog, this vile cant
  That we hear of "Black loyalty" now,
And I notice the twaddlers who rant
  On the subject were far from the row;
But since cold has been Lee's latest gun,
  And since Johnston stacked arms after fight,
We are told "by Black valor we won"—
  'Tis all humbug to laurel the White.

To the Black rebel glory and power,
  To the White rebel chains and disgrace;
Oh, madness, and worse, rules the hour—
  We are false to faith, wisdom, and race!
To my heart with you, Longstreet and Hill,
  Johnston, Lee—every man in the fight—
You were rebels, and bad ones, but still
  You share my misfortune—you're White.

THE QUAKER COQUETTE.

Dear coy coquette, but once we met—
  But once, and yet 'twas once too often,
Plunged unawares in silvery snares,
  All vain my prayers her heart to soften;
Yet seemed so true her eyes of blue,
  Veined lids and longest lashes under,
Good angels dwelt therein, I felt,
  And could have knelt in reverent wonder.

Poor heart, alas! what eye could pass
  The auburn mass of curls caressing
Her pure white brow, made regal now
  By this simplicity of dressing.
Lips dewy, red as Cupid's bed
  Of rose-leaves shed on Mount Hymettus,
With balm imbued they might be wooed,
  But ah! coy prude, she will not let us.

No jewels deck her radiant neck—
  What pearl would reck its hue to rival?
A pin of gold—the fashion old—
  A ribbon-fold, or some such trifle;
And—beauty chief! the lily's leaf
  In dark relief sets off the whiteness
Of all the breast not veiled and pressed
  Beneath her collar's Quaker tightness.

And milk-white robes o'er snowier globes,
  As Roman maids are drawn by Gibbon,
With classic taste are gently braced
  Around her waist beneath a ribbon;
And thence unrolled in billowy fold
  Profuse and bold—a silken torrent—
Not hide, but dim each rounded limb,
  Well turned, and trim, and plump, I warrant.

Oh, Quaker maid, were I more staid,
  Or you a shade less archly pious;
If soberest suit from crown to boot
  Could chance uproot your Quaker bias,
How gladly so, in weeds of woe,
  From head to toe my frame I'd cover,
That in the end the convert "friend"
  Might thus ascend—a convert lover.

BLESSING THE SHAMROCK.

God's blessing and his holy smile
On the emblem-leaf of Erin's Isle,
  Our green immortal shamrock.
From Irish hills, though far away,
Through this bright Western land we stray,
From every leaf there comes a ray
Of the olden light—of the olden day,
  While gazing on the shamrock.

Saint Patrick found upon the sod
This emblem of our triple God,
  And taught us by the shamrock
The mystery of our creed divine,
How one in three distinct may shine,
Yet three in one, as leaves, combine,
And their joint blessings intertwine—
  'Tis a lesson from the shamrock.

And the three virtues which are dear
To Irish hearts are emblemed here
  Within our three-leaved shamrock:
Fidelity, that knows no end
To country, sweetheart, faith, or friend;
Courage, that no reverse can bend;
And hospitality—all blend
  Their types within the shamrock.

So may Heaven's blessings, choice and chief,
Bedew each petal of thy leaf,
  Our own immortal shamrock;
And mayest thou, in this Western clime,
As long ago, in Ireland's prime,
Be emblem of a faith sublime
In God and Country, through all time,
  Our green and glorious shamrock.

And may our proud and ancient race,
Uprooted from the dwelling-place
  Where grew this votive shamrock,
Still keep this night, where'er they fly,
Sacred to memories dear and high
Of the land where all our kindred lie
In the green graves, made beauteous by
  Thick verdure of the shamrock.

God bless the old dear spot of earth—
God bless the green land of our birth,
  Where grew this bunch of shamrock;
And blessings on this generous land,
Which welcomes with a lavish hand,
Each year, the sad and stricken band
Of exiles from the silver strand
  Where grows the saintly shamrock.

THE LAST RESORT.

WRITTEN DURING A FRESHET OF STEAM-BOAT EXPLOSIONS.

A dramatist declared he had got
So many people in his plot
That what to do with half he had
Was like to drive him drama-mad.
  "The hero and the heroine
Of course are married—very fine!
But with the others what to do
Is more than I can tell—can you?"

His friend replied: "'Tis hard to say,
But yet I think there is a way.
The married couple thank their stars,
And half the 'others' take the cars;
  The other half you put on board
A racing steam-boat—take my word,
They'll never trouble you again."
The dramatist resumed his pen.

LOAFING AS A FINE ART.[5]

My friend, my chum, my trusty crony,
We were designed, it seems to me,
To be two happy lazzaroni,
On sunshine fed and maccaroni,
Far off by some Sicilian sea.

From dawn to eve in the happy land,
No duty on us but to lie—
Straw-hatted on the shining sand,
With bronzing chest, and arm, and hand—
Beneath the blue Italian sky.

There, with the mountains idly glassing
Their purple splendors in the sea—
To watch the white-winged vessels passing
(Fortunes for busier fools amassing),
This were a heaven to you and me.

Our meerschaums coloring cloudy brown,
Two young girls coloring with a blush,
The blue waves with a silver crown,
The mountain shadows dropping down,
And all the air in perfect hush—

Thus should we lie in the happy land,
Nor fame, nor power, nor fortune miss—
Straw-hatted on the shining sand,
With bronzing chest, and arm, and hand—
Two loafers couched in perfect bliss.

A MAINE-LAW LYRIC.

With thickest growth of beard his face
Was matted in a ghastly smile;
His hat preserved the faintest trace
Of what was once a shapely tile;
His elbows glimmered through his coat,
His trowsers needed tailor's care,
His boots they were not of a pair,
And through them you his toes might note.
He only said, "It is the tipple,
The tipple 'tis," he said;
He murmured, "Go it like a cripple,
And go it till your dead."

He raised his hand at dewy morn,
  He raised it far into the night,
And, in a tone of maudling scorn,
  The temperance party he would slight;
He drank his glass, and called for more,
  With trembling fingers searching out
  For dimes within the tattered clout
Which once the name of pocket bore.
    He only said, "It is the tipple,
      The tipple 'tis," he said;
    He murmured, "Go it like a cripple,
      And go it till you're dead."

And ever as the lamp grew dim,
  And brandy lay beyond his reach,
He saw pale spectres glare at him,
  And mutter fiercely each to each.
Oh, they were hours to freeze the soul,
  When those blue corpses o'er him bent,
  And to convey the moral meant,
Each fiend upheld a glittering bowl.
    He only said, "It is the tipple,
      The tipple 'tis," he said;
    He murmured, "Go it like a cripple,
      And go it till you're dead."

There is within some granite walls
  A high and hideous wooden thing,
And in its floor a door that falls
  Obedient to a secret spring;
Ay, groan and shriek! With cries and tears,
  Mercy of earth and heaven demand,
  A wife's red blood is on your hand—
Your kindest gift to her for years.
    So ends the ballad of the tipple:
      Be warned, and pray, and think;
    The tap is Mother Murder's nipple—
      You suck blood as you drink.

JANETTE'S HAIR.

"Oh, loosen the snood that you wear, Janette,
Let me tangle a hand in your hair, my pet,"
For the world to me had no daintier sight
Than your brown hair veiling your shoulders white,
  As I tangled a hand in your hair, my pet.

It was brown with a golden gloss, Janette,
It was finer than silk of the floss, my pet,
'Twas a beautiful mist falling down to your wrist,
'Twas a thing to be braided, and jeweled, and kissed—
'Twas the loveliest hair in the world, my pet.

My arm was the arm of a clown, Janette,
It was sinewy, bristled, and brown, my pet,
But warmly and softly it loved to caress
Your round white neck and your wealth of tress—
Your beautiful plenty of hair, my pet.

Your eyes had a swimming glory, Janette,
Revealing the old, dear story, my pet—
They were gray, with that chastened tinge of the sky,
When the trout leaps quickest to snap the fly,
And they matched with your golden hair, my pet.

Your lips—but I have no words, Janette—
They were fresh as the twitter of birds, my pet,
When the spring is young, and the roses are wet
With the dew-drops in each red bosom set,
And they suited your gold-brown hair, my pet.

Oh, you tangled my life in your hair, Janette,
'Twas a silken and golden snare, my pet,
But, so gentle the bondage, my soul did implore
The right to continue your slave evermore,
With my fingers enmeshed in your hair, my pet.

* * * * * * *

Thus ever I dream what you were, Janette,
With your lips, and your eyes, and your hair, my pet;
In the darkness of desolate years I moan,
And my tears fall bitterly over the stone
That covers your golden hair, my pet.

LES HIRONDELLES.

A captive on Africa's shore,
A warrior laden with chains,
Cried aloud, "I behold ye once more,
As ye fly from the frozen plains,
Ye swallows, whom Hope, in despite
Of this fierce-glowing climate, pursues;
From France ye have taken your flight—
Of my home do ye bring me no news?

"Three summers I've begged that ye might
  Recall the fond wishes that stray
To that vale where in dreams of delight
  My youth glided swiftly away;
To the river whose winding waves foam
  'Neath lilac bowers, scenting the breeze;
Ye have perched on my old cottage-home—
  Have ye nothing to tell me of these?

"Perchance your young nestlings were born
  'Neath the roof where I welcomed the day;
Ye have pitied my mother's heart torn
  By the love which can never decay:
Though dying, she hopes that each hour
  My step on the silence will break;
She listens, and fast her tears shower—
  Of her love have ye nothing to speak?

"My sister! perchance she is wed;
  Have ye seen the gay youth who in throngs
At the feast of her bridal were met,
  And welcome her marriage with songs?
And those, my companions of yore,
  Who lived through the combats we fought—
Do they dwell in the village once more?
  Oh, of so many friends know ye naught?

"It may be the stranger's foot presses
  The graves in the vale where they sleep;
My home a new master possesses,
  My sister but living to weep;
No prayers that for me wing to heaven,
  And torture and fetters below:
Your silence perchance is but given
  To spare me this burden of woe."

TO AZRA.

We meet once more: the early bloom
  Of passion perished in its pride,
And slumbers in a foreign tomb,
  Beyond a dark and stormy tide;
The young Evangel faded fast
  From its ethereal form of clay;
That sea of anguish—but 'tis past,
  And we have met once more to-day.

Thy cheek with paler tinge imbued—
  Thine eyes—ah! where their mirthful glance?
A sense of former pain subdued
  Breathes o'er thy gentle countenance.
My heart! how bright, in older days,
  The smile that played from brow to chin.
But now, as through a setting haze,
  The sun peeps sadly from within.

Thy voice is changed: no more its tone
  From music's ocean may emerge;
Thy laugh is mingled with a moan,
  Thy words of hope resound a dirge;
And ever through thy gay discourse
  Some thread of suffering winds along—
A clew that leads with mystic force
  To the deep fount of sadder song.

Love lives—perhaps in purer form—
  But ah! the magic thrills no more;
The shipwrecked pilgrim of the storm
  May prize his chance-directed shore,
But from its desolate cliffs his eye
  Will range in vain the circling seas,
And picture a more brilliant sky,
  A lovelier land, that once was his.

Thy hand! time was its faintest touch,
  Like sacred fire, lit up my frame;
Those dreams of youth, those hours had much
  That memory fondly loves to claim.
I dreamed my soul lay soft and hushed
  As was the sod beneath thy feet;
It gave its flowers, and they were crushed—
  And once again, once more we meet.

Henceforth the world may smoothlier pass,
  But life's one star shines cold and dim;
Though Fortune prove a sea of glass,
  O'er which our lives uninjured swim,
Far better were the storm, the strife
  Which overcast our earlier suns:
There is a record kept in life
  Where love but stamps his signet once.

The lip that quickest wings the jest
  Is first to breathe the secret sigh;
The laugh that rings with freshest zest
  But chokes the floodgates of the eye;

The heart, like Egypt's queen of old,
Ne'er lets its misery see the light;
But o'er the deadly asp we fold
The garments of the gala night.

And months—ay, long, unsolaced years
Have found me reckless, loveless, wild—
A man who is not, but appears
The living jest at which he smiled.
There is a pleasure born of pain,
When all its outward signs depart,
A triumph when the steadfast brain
Floats calmly o'er the struggling heart.

Forbear thy early fire to feign,
Nor weep that I am colder grown;
With less of joy and less of pain,
The heart assumes a temperate tone;
Can prayers or tears revive the flowers
Which in the past have shrunk and died?
Can we recall the golden hours
Whose waves are in the eternal tide?

The Hand that wrote the Persian's fall,
"Weighed, wanting, worthless, cast aside,"
The dark hand on the glittering wall
Was but the touchstone of his pride;
Adversity—another hand—
Revealed thy falsehood and my fate;
Long years of sorrow, a strange land,
And a reunion given too late.

THE STARS OF MEMORY.

In retrospection's dream we see
The waste of years that stretch afar
Into the dim eternity,
With here and there a shining star;
Sweet stars of memory beaming o'er
The sepulchres of perished hope,
And backward turn we more and more,
As gloomier paths before us ope.

We turn to see the memoried sky
Grow ruddy in the youthful dawn;
We watch the glorious shadows fly
Across the lake and o'er the lawn;

The evening clouds are turned to gray,
  Though streaked by many a crimson bar,
And darkness comes, yet, in its way,
  Lifts up to heaven full many a star.

It lifts—but not the star of morn,
  Whose pale beams merge in fuller light,
When flowers and birds seem newly born,
  And freshened by the dews of night;
That loveliest light, forever set,
  No second morrow bids arise,
And sadly, vainly, we regret
  The lustre that has left our skies.

The Past was as an easy road
  That led us down a hill of flowers,
Where every opening vista showed
  But brighter streams and greener bowers.
We reach at length the barren plain
  Where man contests the race of life;
We join the struggle, feel the pain,
  Yet love the excitement of the strife.

We love the strife that makes the tide
  Of passion swell within the heart;
Nor deem we, in our youthful pride,
  Ambition's pulse can e'er depart;
We love it while our hearts are strung
  With high romance and ancient love;
We love it while our hopes are young,
  And paint a brighter scene before.

But, as we wander on and on,
  And weary of the loveless life,
We turn to find the flowers are gone
  Beneath the mailéd hoofs of strife;
We wake to know that manhood brings
  The pain that finds no balm in tears;
We wake to know that memory stings;
  We wake to mourn the by-gone years.

The stubborn soul is loth to quit
  The dream that it hath made its god,
And—forced to own its misery—yet
  Pursues the path it once hath trod;
Looks round it, with a careless eye,
  On others equally unbless'd,
And pinions every struggling sigh
  Within the portals of the breast.

We wander on: the early hope
  In which, beyond the sultry plain,
We saw serener vistas ope,
  Experience proves is false and vain;
Forever with a lengthening chain,
  Forever with a darker pall,
We journey to the grave in pain,
  And see our fellow-bondsman fall.

Pride checks the tear, and with a frown
  Would chase the phantom Grief away;
The snows of age come thickening down,
  And chill and bleaker grows the way;
We speak what we would fain unsay,
  But pride steps in with ready art,
And in a semblance of the gay
  We veil the sorrows of the heart.

Amid the gloom, we gladly turn
  Where none may mock our silent tears,
To where the stars of memory burn
  Above the joys of other years;
And Fancy in the dusk uprears
  The radiant forms of perished worth,
Which we have borne on flowery biers,
  And laid within the lap of earth.

O stars of Memory! ever shine,
  And brighter as our years decay;
Still shed your influence divine
  To cheer us on our lonely way.
Bright stars of Memory! shine forever,
  Like beacons o'er the troubled main,
Until in Lethe's tranquil river
  We have ablution of all pain.

SPIRIT RAPPING.

ON THE INTRODUCTION INTO THE MASSACHUSETTS LEGISLATURE OF A BILL FOR THE "SUPPRESSION OF SPIRITUAL MANIFESTATIONS."

"De par le Roi! Defense a Dieu
De faire miracles en ce lieu."

What! pass a statute to dispatch 'em!
  It is a proposition rare;
Imprison—hang—when you first catch 'em,
  The bodiless spirits of the air?

Despise all reason—hear no question—
  The scourge of legal power is thine;
Condemn—and then ('twill aid digestion)
  Say grace before you dine.

Of old, when glorious Galileo
  Announced the planetary plan,
A pope—a sacerdotal Leo—
  Declared his doctrine under ban;
But, though the Church affirmed his error,
  The world has since his truth averred;
And, in despite of condign terror,
  The spirits will be heard.

When Franklin raised his brawny arm
  To rob the lightning's callow nest,
When little thunder-gods did swarm
  Beneath the electric mother's breast,
Why did no Yankee pope arise
  To bid the impious hand withdraw,
Spreading an ægis o'er the skies
  Of Massachusetts law?

O Liberty! thou splendid word,
  We do adore thy clap-trap name;
'Tis reverenced wheresoever heard,
  But violated just the same.
Shall men with narrow brows and hearts
  Forbid our spiritual faith?
Rap! rap! from the dull table starts—
  It lends a spur to death.

No! by the hallowed rights we wrung
  In years of blood from Britain's hand—
No! by the stars—heaven's cressets—hung
  In the blue dome that spans our land,
We will not yield to Yankee drill—
  We scorn and hate its idiot ban—
With force of intellect and will,
  We claim the rights of man.

The right to hope, the right to pray,
  The right of conscience and of rest,
The right to choose whatever way,
  Unhurting others, suits us best.
We reaffirm, in reverent awe,
  This heresy which Knox began,
That conscience towers o'er human law—
  That God is more than man.

AN OLD MAXIM REVERSED.

"Et arma cedunt togæ,"
  Said a Roman of renown;
"When the din of war is over,
  Arms yield unto the gown."

But this motto Jeff reverses;
  For, arrayed in female charms,
When the din of war is over,
  In his gown he yields to arms.

THE ISLANDS THAT AWAIT US.

Come, brothers, fill! To-night we will
  Give joy its longest tether;
Take hands around—let music sound—
  We're exiles here together.
For fatherland we draw the brand—
  We failed, but do not falter;
Some other day again we may
  Fling fire on Freedom's altar.
    The toast to-night is one of light,
      Let's drink ere time belate us;
    Come, brim the glass, and let it pass—
      "The islands that await us!"

There's Cuba lies in sunniest skies,
  By Spanish thraldom trampled,
Her treasure spent, and blood besprent,
  Her wrongs are unexampled;
But exiled sons with Yankee guns
  Can make the tyrants vanish,
For once we'll teach these grandees each
  The way to "walk it Spanish!"
    The one Lone Star shall not be far
      From our unsullied cluster,
    The Southern queen shall yet be seen
      Arrayed in Northern lustre.

There's Ireland, too—'tis vain to rue
  The doom imprinted on her;
Some day we'll make, or we mistake,
  That very curse her honor.

The green shall spread above the red
  When Saxon blood is under,
And old John Bull, at Liverpool,
  Be waked by Yankee thunder.
    The Eastern queen in starry sheen
      With her of the Antilles,
    The Yankees' banner floating high
      O'er shamrocks and o'er lilies.

Then, brethren, fill—pledge heart and will—
  Our cause we'll try and gain, too,
The exile's name shall reach a fame
  No king's could e'er attain to.
In France at first was freedom nursed,
  But there, so wild and skittish,
She fell a prey one luckless day
  To Spaniards and the British;
    But here with growth surpassing both,
      Majestic in her status,
    And to her sod, so help us God!
      We'll bring the "isles that wait us."

FOND AND FOOLISH.

My Lydia, do you never miss,
  Since grown of late so prim and mulish,
The drive, the dinner, and the bliss
  Of being very fond and foolish?
The game we played was one of cost—
  Good cause, no doubt, for your retreating;
But, ah! the joys forever lost—
  The dear, wild, passionate thrills of meeting!

I always went an hour too soon—
  The clocks were wrong, my head was dizzy;
Your whispered words, "The square at noon"—
  Each object kept my fancy busy.
That mantle—yes, it is her own;
  I run—oh, pooh! my eyes deceive me;
That bonnet—it is hers alone;
  Not hers! good heavens! my senses leave me.

The air grew dense, my pulse was high,
  I counted steps or plucked at brambles;
The exulting fountain seemed to cry,
  "No more shall Lydia share your rambles."

A thousand shooting hints of fear
  Suggest—but no, they can't discover;
And yet, past noon, and she not here—
  Was ever such unhappy lover?

This surely is her step, her height,
  The same white Cashmere round her flowing;
She nears—ah! lovelier to my sight
  Than Venus with her locks out-blowing.
I fly to meet her at the gates—
  "Welcome, and welcome beyond measure;
Our carriage at the corner waits,
  And now for five dear hours of pleasure."

The fields were green, the flowers were sweet;
  Each rose—you gave a kiss to win it,
And said, "Our cottage was as neat
  As any nest of any linnet;"
The silver tray—a flask of wine,
  Then, all too soon, your visit over,
And back to town, your hand in mine,
  Again you parted from your lover.

These pleasures do you never miss,
  My Lydia, now so prim and mulish,
The drive, the dinner, and the bliss
  Of being very fond and foolish?
The game we played was one of cost—
  Good cause, no doubt, for your retreating;
But, ah! the bliss forever lost—
  The dear, wild, passionate joys of meeting.

A HYMN TO THE TYPES.

Oh silent myriad army, whose true metal
  Ne'er flinched nor blenched before the despot Wrong!
Ye brethren, linked in an immortal battle
  With time-grown Falsehoods, tyrannous and strong!
Fragments of strength and beauty lying idle,
  Each in its place, until the appointed day;
Then, swift as wheels the squadron to the bridle,
  Ye spring into the long, compact array.

Obedient, self-contained, and self-contented,
  Like veteran warriors in the mingled broil,
Each giving help where just his help is wanted,
  Nor seeking more than his due share of toil;

Striving not, vainly, each to be a leader,
  Your capitals are captains of the file,
The crown you aim at, to inform the reader,
  And help old Truth on for another mile.

What wondrous dreams of beauty may be flying
  Unwinged, unuttered, through your silent mass!
Even as a prism, in some deep grotto lying,
  Until the informing soul of Genius pass,
Filling the cavern with a light as tender
  As that which breaks from Love's half downcast eyes;
Then the cold gem awakes to rainbow splendor,
  Where, couched in moss, beside the fount it lies.

Oh what a burst of glory when ye mingle
  Your bloodless hands in the support of truth—
When to your banded spell the pulses tingle
  Of tottering age and fiery-visioned youth!
What power and strength when ye stand up united
  Beneath the master-spirits' guiding sway;
A thousand lamps at one lone star lighted,
  Turning the night of error into day.

Ye are the messengers, all earth pervading,
  Who speak of comfort and communion still—
Planks of a mighty ship, whose precious lading
  Is man's just reason and his heart's fond will—
Launched on the stream of time, our thoughts are drifted
  Far, far adown our children-peopled shore,
And the gay pennon of our hope is lifted
  When him it cheered through life it cheers no more.

Unmarshaled army! earth is still a wonder—
  A bright God's wonder, all too little known;
Star-eyes above us and the green sod under,
  Oceans of beauty girdling every zone;
And man himself, whose deep heart throbs forever
  With passionate longings, and the fierce unrest
Of hopes that struggle in a vain endeavor
  To hear themselves by other lips confess'd.

Ye are the mightier tongues we have invented
  To bear our utterance ever and allwhere;
Our hearts into a thousand hearts transplanted,
  A multiplied existence ye confer.
Falsehood, with bloodshot eyes, awoke from slumber,
  And glared in baleful terror on your birth;
Meek-fronted Truth enrolled you in her number,
  And cried, "I am not without swords on earth!"

Ye are true types of men. When disunited,
 The world has nothing feebler or more vain;
But when one animating thought has lighted
 The dim recesses of each heart and brain,
The mass rolls onward with a steady motion,
 Warned by your beacon from the rock of Death,
The breath of Knowledge sweeps the stagnant ocean,
 And men rise up like billows at its breath.

Ye are the swords of Truth—the only weapon
 That Truth should wield in this protracted war;
Ye are the rocks of Knowledge that we step on,
 In thought's bright firmament, from star to star!
I see an angel winged in every letter,
 Even as man's soul is hid within his clay:
I see a prisoner with his broken fetter
 Emerging out of darkness into day.

Unspeakable ye are! We have created
 A new existence than our own more firm;
Our life and hopes into your life translated,
 Enjoy a being that shall know no term.
The plowman's frolic song still kindles gladness
 Within the heart, though care has gnawn its core,
And bright eyes weep at his recorded sadness
 Who sleeps where pride and envy sting no more.

Even as the marble block contains all beauty
 Enshrined in darkness and the outward husk,
Which the warm sculptor, with love-prompted duty,
 Shall make to shine, through darkness and through dusk,
Into the day of loveliness, ye treasure
 All forms of thought and song in your mute sphere;
Our pen the chisel, and our rhyme the measure
 By which we make the inborn god appear.

Would that my heart were wider-tongued and deeper,
 Nor moved involved in cares of meaner place,
Then would I mow down, like a sturdy reaper,
 The crop of thought that rises from the "case."
Flowers of bright songs, and fruit of mellow reason,
 And many a peeping bud of infant Truth,
My soul should garner in its summer season,
 And steep in dews of a perpetual youth.

But ah! mute types, are ye not all too often
 Constrained to serve at some unsolaced toil—
To harden hearts that ye would love to soften,
 And help to swell where ye would still the broil?

Even so with me! My dreams of song are hurried
  Like moon-ray flashes through the drifting storm,
And all that God made noble in me buried
  In wants I share in common with the worm.

OUR CZAR AND THE SULTAN.

A LYRIC OF "CIVILIZATION."

Why should we love the heathen Turk,
  And hate the Christian czar,
While Russia is in wealth and work
  "More civilized" by far?
Her banner bears the Holy Cross
  Wherewith our creed is signed,
While Turkey's pachas only toss
  Their horse-tails to the wind.

Why hate the czar, and pray for him
  Whose grim seraglio walls
Hold beauties that are growing dim,
  His concubines and thralls?
Why hate the czar, and wish success
  To one who dares to libel
Our telegraph and printing-press,
  Our cotton goods and Bible?

The czar is "civilized," of course—
  He writes it on his banner—
A Christian praying till he's hoarse
  In the devoutest manner;
One wife alone he has to kiss,
  As in church members seemly,
And in his walk of life he is
  "Respectable—extremely."

The sultan hath a stud of wives,
  And sultans have, they tell us,
An awkward trick of taking lives
  From all obnoxious fellows.
Their headlong passions will not brook
  To mingle farce with fury,
And wring from death the killing joke
  Of "murder done by jury."

The "march of intellect" is quite
  A march beyond their drilling;
They never made a "proselyte"
  By one judicious shilling;

Deficient much in legal skill
  And "organized starvation,"
They never mixed a patent pill
  For Turkish "melioration."

In fact, we say, with deep regret,
  But truth must be our sure hope,
The sultan is some ages yet
  Behind the kings of Europe;
He has not got the royal blood
  Which festers so divinely
In men not made of common mud,
  But porcelain, painted finely.

He has not got the Russian knout
  Wherewith the nuns were beaten,
Nor Austria's axe—grown fat, no doubt,
  On all the flesh it has eaten;
No guilt-extracting guillotine,
  As France has got to cure hers;
But, worst of all, and deadliest sin,
  He has no "British jurors."

He thinks kings should, against all taste,
  Have nothing underhand meant,
Whereas all know the crown is placed
  Above the tenth commandment;
For we believe that monarchs are
  Exempt from keeping promise,
Especially the queen and czar—
  God keep their armies from us.

Then why, we ask—what mysteries lurk
  That we are so excited,
While burglar Nick and goodman Turk
  Are getting matters righted?
A friend suggests some twaddling cant
  Of "justice and humanity!"
Such trifles ought not, and they sha'n't,
  Impede our Christianity.

We mean to save the Turkish souls
  By cleaving skulls asunder,
Destroy them as we did the Poles,
  And profit by the plunder;
We mean to give them Gospel light
  By piercing lights and livers,
When dead and at the judgment seat
  They'll then be "true believers."

But if, with merely human hearts,
  We ask, "How goes the war?"
One hoarse-tongued execration starts
  Against the butcher czar;
There reeks a cloud from Poland's sod
  That takes a giant form,
A mangled though immortal god,
  Much wasted, but yet warm.

And from the plains of Hungary
  Another cloud ascends—
Heaven! what a fury-frenzied eye
  Upon the North it bends!
A woman form—a Juno shape—
  Queen mother of the gods—
A woman! but her shoulders drip,
  Plowed red with Russian rods.

Lo! watch them—watch them evermore
  Until the rite be done;
High up in air their lips converge—
  That kiss hath made them one.
From that embrace they quickly turn,
  Their cloud-hands pointing north,
And in their eyes the lightnings burn
  Which soon shall thunder forth.

God speed the union, sealed in blood,
  Of Freedom and Despair!
God speed the cause of human right
  Whenever and where'er!
God speed the Turk! God speed the Pole!
  God speed who'er will fight
With sword and word, heart, brain, and hand,
  For man's eternal right.

ROMANCE AND ECHO.

It rains—it rains—the slimy street
Is silent, though a hundred feet
In eager hurry homeward beat—
    (Coz why? they all wear rubbers.)
We hurry homeward, there to meet
The tender ones, who long to greet
Papa and husband—oh! 'tis sweet!
    (Wife scolds, and baby blubbers.)

The skies have all their clouds amassed,
But sunshine waits us, and will last
When we into our homes have passed.
  (I wouldn't like to risk it!)
No rain-tears there, no cutting blast
Of angry words; the hours as fast
As moments fly; we find at last—
  (Weak tea and leathern biscuit.)

What tongue describe, what pen portray
The transports which, at close of day,
The working head and hand repay?
  (Due bills, sour looks, and twaddle!)
O Seraphina! soon I pray,
With thee to bless my onward way,
Our home, though humble, shall be gay—
  (There was a man called "Caudle!")

I do not smoke, was never "tight,"
And, while your beauties charm my sight,
I'll find the marriage burden light—
  (As soldiers find their knapsacks!)
And home returning night by night,
Your eyes, the hearth, and all things bright,
Oh, will you not my toils requite?
  (With pickled pork and flapjacks!)

THE WELL-DRESSED MAN.

My poor old coat, my holy coat,
  But not like that of Treves,
With pain ineffable I note
  Your frayed and wasted sleeves.
Time was, my coat, that I in you
  Right daintily began
To take of life a jovial view—
  I was a well-dressed man.

My laundress called, her pay required,
  I paid—my morning call;
Attired in thee, till fairly tired,
  I danced at rout and ball;
The ladies smiled, and, as I passed,
  The pleasing whisper ran,
"That's Mister Miles, he's rather fast,
  But such a well-dressed man!"

My tailor's bill was much behind,
  And I for board was bored,
But still the landlady was kind,
  And still mein schneider scored;
"He feared to press, but could I pay?"
  'Twas thus the rogue began;
She "really could not turn away
  So sweetly dressed a man."

I drove abroad and drank my wine,
  Match-making mothers sought me,
And many a maiden fair and fine
  Flushed red to think she'd caught me.
With tongue and pen I played my part,
  To dazzle was my plan;
None e'er could deem an aching heart
  In such a well-dressed man.

But ah! it is the utmost pound
  That kills the patient camel,
And to my terror soon I found
  My debts I could not trammel.
My tailor's "tick" grew short, and quick
  A hundred duns began;
One suit of clothes had saved all suits
  Against the well-dressed man.

I'm beggared now, but you'll allow
  It was a sad temptation
Obscure to live, while clothes can give
  Respect and social station.
It could not last, my folly's past,
  I've learned a wiser plan—
By hand and brain I'll be again
  A (paid for) well-dressed man.

SPECIAL ORDERS, A., No. 1.[16]

Headquarters Department of the South,
Hilton Head, S.C., March 25, 1863.

With her charming looks
  And all her graces,
Miss Mary Brooks,
  Whose lovely face is
The sweetest thing we have seen down here
On these desolate islands for more than a year,

Is hereby appointed an extra aid
On the staff of the general commanding,
With a captain of cavalry's strap and grade,
And with this most definite understanding—
That Captain Mary,
Gay and airy,
At nine each day, until further orders,
To Colonel Halpine shall report
For special duty at these headquarters;
And Captain Mary
(Bless the fairy!)
Shall hold herself, upon all occasions,
Prepared to ride
At the adjutant's side,
And give him of flirting his regular rations;
And she sha'n't vamoose
With the younglings loose
Of the junior staff, such as Hay and Skinner,
But, galloping around, she shall sing
Like an everlasting lark on the wing;
And she sha'n't keep the adjutant late for dinner.

The chief quartermaster of department
Will give Captain Mary a riding garment—
A long, rich skirt of a comely hue—
Shot silk, with just a suspicion of blue—
A gipsy hat, with an ostrich feather,
A veil to protect her against the weather,
And delicate gauntlets of pale buff leather;
Her saddle with silver shall all be studded,
And her pony—a sorrel—it shall be blooded;
Its shoes shall be silver, its bridle all ringing
With bells that shall harmonize well with her singing;
And thus Captain Mary,
Gay, festive, and airy,
Each morning shall ride
At the adjutant's side,
And hold herself ready, on all fit occasions,
To give him of flirting his full army rations.

By command of
MAJOR GENERAL D. HUNTER.
ED. W. SMITH, Assist. Adjt. General.

Official copy:
CHAS. G. HALPINE, Lieut. Col. and Assist. Adjt. General Tenth Army Corps and Dept. of the South.

ROOSEVELTIANA.[17]

OUR BOY BOB.

He angles in all sorts of ways
  For fish and lobby operators,
Now hooking speckled trout he strays,
  Now spearing railroad corporators;
At times with worms he baits his hook,
  Or trolls along with whirling gudgeons,
Then gives the wondering world a look
  At Brennan, Blunt, and such curmudgeons.

His rod hath slain full many a carp,
  His line hath played full many a salmon,
And, though our aldermen are sharp,
  They can't bluff him with any gammon.
His art the scaly prey commands,
  His landing-net they enter gayly,
And then, backed up by Mr. Sands,
  He hunts for politicians scaly.

His specs are bright, his eyes are blue,
  He knows all kinds of flies and hackles,
He knows the Hackley contract too,
  And each new scheme of plunder tackles;
To Boole a blight, and—bitterer yet—
  The Tammany folk would like to flay him;
All's fish that comes within his net,
  And when they're hooked he likes to play 'em.

His barb hath stuck in Southern "drums,"
  He knows the pulling force of turbot,
And each new civic fraud that comes,
  It gives him pleasure to disturb it;
The ravenous pikes he doth pursue,
  Taking, when baked, on plates their measure;
And the still more rapacious crew
  Of councilmen have felt his pressure.

He makes the deadly fox-fly swing
  On silken line in circles o'er us,
Or sings—as only he can sing—
  Leading the new reforming chorus!
The triple brass of Blunt gives way
  Before his pen's two-hundred-pounder;
Then, rocking in some quiet bay,
  He picks up cod, bass, bream, and flounder.

The portly and white-chokered throng
  Opposed to Brennan and such cattle,
For once, we say, have not gone wrong
  In choosing him to fight their battle;
All scaly fish with baited bribes
  He oft hath struck with barbed incisions,
And of all scaly, slimy tribes,
  The slimiest are the politicians.

RIME OF YE SEEDIE PRINTEERE MAN.

It is a seedie printeere man,
  And he stoppeth one of three—
"By thy unshorn beard and fevered eye,
  Now wherefore stopp'st thou me?

"For Jullien's band doth play to-night,
  And I must hence away;
The fiddles they are deftly tuned—
  Dost hear Herr Koenig play?"

He holds him with his grimy hand—
  "More copy" he doth cry;
"Hold off! thou grizzly printeere man,"
  The victim makes reply.

He holds him with his fevered eye—
  "More copy! it must come;
My printeeres they are standing still"—
  The editeere is dumb.

The editeere he sat him down,
  His tears they quickly ran,
While thus spake in the seedie one,
  The red-eyed printeere man:

"The papeeres must to-morrow out,
  To-morrow be on hand,
And you are our chief editeere—
  More copy we demand.

"The Times comes out at early dawn,
  The Tribune follows soon,
The Evening Post, and the Express,
  They will be out by noon."
The editeere let fall a tear
  As he heard the loud bassoon.

Lo! Jullien to the daïs mounts—
  A bearded wight is he;
With bugle-blow before him go
  The merrie minstrelsy.

But still the steadfast printeere man
  "More copy" cries aloud,
And ye broken-hearted editeere
  Withdraws him from the crowd.

"God save thee, wretched editeere!
  What 'devils' plague thee thus?"
He ground an answer through his teeth—
  It sounded like a cuss.

All night that wretched editeere
  Before his desk did sit;
In vain for him had Mr. Brough
  A free admission writ.

"More copy" still the "devils" cry—
  He can not choose but make it;
And when his weary task is done,
  He bids the "devil" take it.

Next morning, when the sheet appeared,
  The public laughed amain;
They little thought the little jokes
  Had cost such mickle pain.

He wrote like one that had been dunned
  For copy, all forlorn;
A less harmonious Democrat
  He rose the morrow morn.

THE RHYMER'S RITUAL.

Of all the kinds of snobbish rhyme
  That fail to please or tickle us,
  The worst and most ridiculous
  Is when young bards be-tickle us
Whith "tears" they shed "in early time."

The poet's task, when understood,
  Is not with pain to fetter us,
  And dolefully be-letter us;
  It is to touch and better us
With glintings of a gentler mood.

What cares a steam-electric age
For narratives Byronical?
It rather loves to chronicle
Some witty thing laconical,
Flung lightly down upon the page.

We all have griefs enough to spare
Without a man inditing 'em,
And metrically writing 'em;
The wiser plan is slighting 'em—
A hearty laugh can conquer care.

A grain of Burns is worth a mint
Of Byron's dolorosity;
Tom Hood's immense jocosity
Beats Milton's ponderosity—
True wit has always wisdom in't.

In youth each inexperienced fool
Adores the hyperbolical,
The Sue-Dumas-Sand-Gaulical
Creations melancholical—
The writings of the "thrilling school."

'Tis strange that while of real grief
We all have such immensities,
Men still should have propensities
For reading wild intensities
Of agonies beyond belief.

For me, I will not read the stuff
Of German tales—too deep a bit,
That will not let me sleep a bit;
If e'er we want to weep a bit,
Our lives are tragical enough.

I'd rather think the lines I penned
Made one hour pass more cheerily,
More lightly and less wearily,
Than know that readers drearily
Went blubbering on from end to end.

MINNIE, MY DOLL-WIFE.

She is fair as a peach,
She is light as a feather,
And more tuneful her speech
Than all song-birds together;

Her face is delicious,
  Bright, modest, and clear,
And she fills all the wishes
  Of eye, heart, and ear.

O'er her brow, in the wind,
  Little curls toss and clamber,
While the thick hair behind
  Is of chestnut with amber;
Her dark eyes are seen
  Ever kindling or dimming,
As a falcon's now keen,
  Now in tenderness swimming.

Then her lips—ah! mon Dieu!
  Curving, crimson, and scented,
As if made with a view
  But to drive us demented.
Little chin, rosy cheek,
  Each hath got its own dimple,
And her whole features speak
  A soul arch and yet simple.

How slender her throat,
  And how white beyond telling!
While her bust you may note
  Into womanhood swelling—
Like a bud, newly graced
  As the sun-rays unfold it;
While so small is her waist,
  In spanned hands you may hold it.

In her little doll's boot—
  At least such is my notion—
Her superb Arab foot
  Seems a poem of motion;
Like a deer in her pace,
  And in beauty abounding,
Every motion a grace,
  As if music were sounding.

My little doll-wife,
  Had we two come together
When the year of my life
  Was in early spring weather,
Not a doll-wife wert thou,
  But a wife warm and glowing,
To whose young heart, even now,
  My soul's currents are flowing.

To a little doll's cot,
  Set in flowers, I would sue you—
Even the sunlight should not
  Too unguardedly woo you;
There, with ribbons and toys,
  Roses, jewels, and dances,
I would ask for no joys
  But to bask in your glances.

So, when weary my life—
  Heart and brain, ear and vision—
Of the long, paltry strife
  Which we think is ambition,
In my little doll's cot
  And her arms I might hide me,
And, while brightening her lot,
  Find the peace else denied me.

TO THE CHIEF JUSTICE: FROM MILES O'REILLY.[18]

"Incedimus per ignes, suppositos cineri doloso."

Guardian of liberty and right,
  Of law and justice in the land,
  Hold the scales firm with even hand;
  For thou must either greatly stand,
  Calm as a Fate, with purpose grand,
Or sink beyond all reach of light.

Down to the deep foundation-stones
  On which our country's pillars rest,
  Propping the roof once brightly pressed
  By stars—beneath which many a guest
  Came in to share the banquet bless'd
Of liberty—our temple groans.

Groans in this earthquake's helpless loss
  (The war was nothing, and is past);
  But the temple groans with tremors vast,
  Seeing the sacred things, amassed
  By our great fathers, rudely cast
Down to the dust as worthless dross.

'Tis thine to bid the storm be o'er—
  A right almost too great for speech—
  'Tis thine the sacred vessels each
  To lift again; 'tis thine to teach
  Lessons of love that yet may reach
And knit all sections as of yore.

High towering o'er the vulgar train,
  By rage and greed of gain debased,
  Thy lines in loftier planes are placed;
  And with thy heart to justice braced,
  Faction may all her thunders waste
Against thy calm decrees in vain.

It is no common thing to sit,
  Clothed as thou art with power so great,
  Balancing points of subtlest weight
  Between the ruler of a state
  And a cabal's unscrupling hate:
Thy place in history here is writ.

I know thee well: thy life's proud lot,
  A struggle vehement and long,
  With soundest heart and judgment strong,
  Against whate'er to thee seemed wrong:
  Now raised by virtue o'er the throng,
Thy record must receive no blot.

Hold the scales even; firmly stand
  In thy great office, guarding law;
  Round thee thy sacred ermine draw;
  Pluck Justice from Hate's ravening maw;
  And, grandest sight the world e'er saw,
Let one man's firm soul save the land.

TO FENTON.[19]

AN EARNEST CRY AND PRAYER FOR OUR ENDANGERED TAX LEVY.

That bill, O Fenton! spare;
  Let not thy veto fly;
The child of many a prayer—
  Say, would'st thou have it die?
Brittle and bright as glass,
  It is both "rich and rare;"
But, Fenton, let it pass—
  Thy veto pray forbear.

For months, when short of cash,
  We've dreamed about this bill,
Hoping—perhaps 'twas rash—
  That it our fobs would fill.
When tailors pressed us hard,
  Or we for board were bored,
We did all fears discard—
  This bill would swell our hoard.

But now, in ghastly fear,
 We hear dark rumors fly—
Forgive this foolish tear,
 But let that bill go by.
Ten thousand humble men
 Depend on it for bread,
And should it fail—oh! then
 Their woes be on thy head.

The nabobs of the League,
 Their purses dense with gold,
Weave round thee an intrigue
 That levy to withhold;
But think, ere flies the dart
 Making that bill a corse,
How shrill through many a heart
 The barb its way will force.

Grant that there are some "steals"—
 Some "big steals," if you will—
Which Greeley's pen reveals
 In this unhappy bill;
Yet think of all the poor,
 Unpaid-for, honest toil,
And what they must endure,
 If you this bill shall foil.

Let thy assent be given—
 Sign, sign thy potent name,
And to the gates of heaven
 Our tongues shall waft thy fame.
Sign that financial bill,
 No single item touch,
And, by thy bounteous will,
 Save us from Famine's clutch.

{5 ct. stamp, canceled.} Given this 1st day of May, 1868, from our royal seat on the chains in the City Hall Park,

MILES O'REILLY,

Special Pleader and Spokesman for the great Unpaid of our City Government.

WEBSTER.

Gone! and the world may never hear again
 The grand old music of thy wondrous speech.
Striking far deeper than the mind can reach
 Into the hearts and purposes of men.

Gone! and the helm that in thy Roman hand
  Drove the stout vessel through the blinding storm,
Scarce to a feebler guidance will conform
  When waves beat high, and ropes break strand by strand.

Gone! we are like old men whose infant eyes
  Familiar grew with some vast pyramid;
Even as we gaze, earth yawns, and it is hid—
  A long, wide desert mocks the empty skies.

NOT A STAR FROM THE FLAG SHALL FADE.

Air: "Oh! a rare old plant is the ivy green."

Och! a rare ould flag was the flag we bore,
  'Twas a bully ould flag, an' nice;
It had sthripes in plenty, an' shtars galore—
  'Twas the broth of a purty device.
Faix, we carried it South, an' we carried it far,
  An' around it our bivouacs made;
An' we swore by the shamrock that never a shtar
  From its azure field should fade.
    Ay, this was the oath, I tell you thrue,
    That was sworn in the sowls of our Boys in Blue.

The fight it grows thick, an' our boys they fall,
  An' the shells like a banshee scream;
An' the flag—it is torn by many a ball,
  But to yield it we never dhream.
Though pierced by bullets, yet still it bears
  All the shtars in its tatthered field,
An' again the brigade, like to one man swears,
  "Not a shtar from the flag we yield!"
    'Twas the deep, hot oath, I tell you thrue,
    That lay close to the hearts of our Boys in Blue.

Shure, the fight it was won, afther many a year,
  But two thirds of the boys who bore
That flag from their wives and sweethearts dear
  Returned to their homes no more.
They died by the bullet—disease had power,
  An' to death they were rudely tossed;
But the thought came warm in their dying hour,
  "Not a shtar from the flag is lost!"
    Then they said their pathers and aves through,
    An', like Irishmen, died—did our Boys in Blue.

But now they tell us some shtars are gone,
  Torn out by the rebel gale;
That the shtars we fought for, the states we won,
  Are still out of the Union's pale.
May their sowls in the dioul's hot kitchen glow
  Who sing such a lyin' shtrain;
By the dead in their graves, it shall not be so—
  They shall have what they died to gain!
    All the shtars in our flag shall still shine through
    The grass growing soft o'er our Dead in Blue!

FEMININE ARITHMETIC.

LAURA.

On me he shall ne'er put a ring,
  So, mamma, 'tis in vain to take trouble,
For I was but eighteen in spring,
  While his age exactly is double.

MAMMA.

He is but in his thirty-sixth year,
  Tall, handsome, good-natured, rich, witty,
And should you refuse him, my dear,
  May you die an old maid without pity.

LAURA.

His figure, I grant you, will pass,
  And at present he's young enough plenty;
But, when I am sixty, alas!
  Will not he be a hundred and twenty?

LA SUISSESSE AU BORD DU LAC.

The flowers have breathed their sweetest perfumes here,
  And night approaches us with noiseless feet;
The lake is sparkling, and the air is clear—
  The peace of evening shadows our retreat.
    Oh, dearest home—oh, happy, happy lot—
    Sweet home, in our hearts thou shalt never be forgot.

Come, my companions, let us dance and sing—
  A lovely evening crowns the glorious day—
Come, let us make the mountain echoes ring
  With songs of joy and many a tender lay.
    Oh, dearest home—oh, happy, happy lot—
    Sweet home, in our hearts thou shalt never be forgot.

By the moon shimmering through the silent woods,
 I know my love will not be absent long;
Hark! from across the bright lake's silent floods
 I hear his voice re-echo back my song.
  Oh, dearest home—oh, happy, happy lot—
  Sweet home, in our hearts thou shalt never be forgot.

ADIEU TO THE PRINCESS PICCOLOMINI.

ON AN ACTION AGAINST THE PRINCESS PICCOLOMINI FOR HER BOARD BILL.

The wonderful Princess Piccolomini
Ought to have paid for her hog and hominy;
Ought to have paid for her beer and brandy,
Mutton, and beef, and molasses candy;
Either herself should have paid for her victuals
(This shirking your board bill much belittles),
Or the dandy snobs who her favor prayed for—
These should have seen that her grub was paid for.

Yes, the enchanting Piccolomini
Should have shelled out for her hog and hominy,
And never compelled Mr. Hawley Clapp
To pull and haul up the fishy chap,
Who was seized on a writ "ad satis cap,"
Though 'tis certain that he never owed a rap—
Nary a red for the hog and hominy
Munched and crunched by the Piccolomini;
Nary a cent for the beer and brandy,
Oysters, and eggs, and molasses candy,
Puddings, and pies, and lobster salads,
Gorged by our fat little queen of ballads!

Large in her feet was the Piccolomini,
Fat were her feet, and her hog and hominy;
Waddling around with a lazy looseness,
Lavishing smiles with a rank profuseness,
Doing snobs out of gigs and ponies,
Quizzing them next to her bosom cronies—
A very dear lady was Piccolomini,
And dear to Clapp was her hog and hominy;
Dear to the public her dubious singing,
And dear were the bouquets her friends kept flinging.
She looked like a dropsical female Jew sick,
And scaly, indeed, was her scale of music.
One victim still wanders around the Academy,
Sighing, "Alas! all the gifts she had of me."

IN PLEASANT HOURS.

In pleasant hours, the merriest toy
That e'er made time roll lightly—
A living, animated joy,
That flitted round us brightly;
We thought not courage lay beneath
Those lips of pouting coral—
We little guessed that beauty's wreath
But hid the heroine's laurel.

Yet, in the hour of peril tried,
The gentle heart grew fearless;
Her eyes still beamed with hope and pride
When all looked dark and cheerless.
Then loudly let her praises ring,
And may her name be legion,
Who soared on love's unfaltering wing
Through sorrow's darkest region.

PAREPA ROSA.

AS SUNG BY JUDGE JOHN R. BRADY—WITH IMMENSE EFFECT!

Air: "The Groves of Blarney."

Och! of song a fountain,
An' of charms a mountain,
There's no prima-donna
Can wid her compare;
For she is the sweetest,
An' the most completest,
From her golden girdle
To her nut-brown hair.
She's the gorgeous sposa
Of the Signor Rosa,
An' she does outvalue him
By a hundred pounds.
Sure her smile is gracious,
An' her bust is spacious,
Like a milk-white reservoir

[An', throth! that's what it is, the darlint—an' may God bless her an' it for the same! An' may he look down upon her, an' be good to her!]

Of all silvery sounds.

Hear her voice a minute!
Like a lark or linnet,
How the warble bubbles up
From her purty throat;
An' now hear it fallin',
Like an echo callin',
Flickerin' gently downward
From some hills remote.
Then again it rises,
An' wid joy surprises,
For her love an' rapture
Find in song relief;
An' it now sinks lowly
Into prayer most holy,
Or now swells in rondeaux
[Though I don't meself rightly know, upon me conscience! what sort of a thing a "rondeau" is, whin it's at home]
Of melodious grief.

When I think o' dyin',
An' me sperit flyin'
To that high Olympus
Where good gossoons go—
Where, their harps a-holdin',
An' wid cymbals golden,
All the proud immortals
Into music flow—
Och! the future taskin',
It is then I'm askin',
"Shall we hear Parepa
In that shinin' throng?"
For if her sweet singin'
Through all heaven's not ringin',
Earth can whip the Nine Muses
[Ay, faix! an' a dozen or two of them little cherubims and seraphims who "continually do cry," as poor Father Mulcahy—God rest him!—tould me long ago at Sunday-school]
In the line o' song.

Philharmonic Night, Academy of Music.

THE BROKEN HEART.

FROM THE FRENCH.

Her heart was broken; day by day
She wasted silently away,

And o'er her large dark eyes there grew
A film of leaden-colored hue;
Her step was languid, slow, and weak,
A hectic fever flushed her cheek,
Seldom and little did she speak.

And he to whom her faith was vowed,
Her husband—by the world allowed
A kind, good-natured, easy man—
O'er all his present conduct ran
To see if he had given her aught
To cause this apathy of thought,
This tearful silence, sorrow fraught.

At length she spake one dewy morn:
"Adolphe, you wonder why forlorn
I pensive sit from day to day,
And pine in solitude away;
Dear husband, I will tell thee all:
My neighbor, Madame D'Argental,
Has got—I have not—a new shawl."

NEW YORK IN A SNOW-COAT.

In Gotham, though no more it rained,
Full ankle deep the slush remained,
Till all our pants, with mud engrained,
  Flapped round our insteps heavily.

But Gotham saw another sight
When the snow fell at dead of night,
Enrobing noiselessly in white
  The squalor of her scenery.

For soon the wind began to blow,
And drifting fell the virgin snow,
'Till, white as Greeley's coat, the row
  Of streets diverging mazily.

By dextrous blacks and grooms arrayed,
Was harnessed every equine jade,
While bells a merry music made,
  And sledges slipped on ringingly.

Then wheels rolled off from every 'bus,
Then rose to heaven the cry and "cuss,"
While Bowery boys enjoyed the muss
  In Broadway raging fearfully.

Then shook the street with sledges riven,
Then rushed the eight in tandem driven,
While faster than the bolts of heaven
  Flashed the snow-ball artillery.

Full many a bonnet, pink and blue,
Full many a nose of ditto hue,
Changed color as the missiles flew
  And hit them—oh! so stingingly.

But pleasure dies when keenest felt,
And snow, when most enjoyed, will melt,
And they who ride, and they who pelt,
  Beneath the drift lie peacefully.

THE TURQUOIS BROOCH.

They tell us of a precious stone
  Which changes with the wearer,
And, moved by sympathy alone,
  Grows lustreless or fairer;
Thus, if the loved one's bosom grieve,
  Its azure glory flies,
But if to joy that bosom heave,
  'Tis bright as summer skies.

So, Mary, is my soul to thee,
  By thee illumed or saddened,
O'ercast if thou look'st moodily,
  And bright if thou art gladdened;
Thou, like the turquois to my pain,
  Unlike to my unrest,
For, Mary, thou hast never ta'en
  My spirit to thy breast.

A PALPABLE PARODY.

'Tis the last golden dollar,
  Left shining alone;
All its brilliant companions
  Are squandered and gone.
No coin of its mintage
  Reflects back its hue,
They went in mint-juleps,
  And this will go too.

I'll not keep thee, thou lone one,
  Too long in suspense;
Thy brethren were melted,
  And melt thou to pence.
I ask for no quarter,
  I'll spend and not spare,
Till my poor empty pocket
  Lie centless and bare.

So soon may I follow
  When friendships decay,
And from beggary's last dollar
  The dimes drop away.
When the Maine law has passed,
  And the groggeries sink,
What use would be dollars
  With nothing to drink?

THINE EYES OF BLUE.

FROM THE FRENCH.

Thine eyes of blue, the heaven's own hue,
  Thy soft eyes thrill my fevered pulse;
The light that lies within thine eyes
  Hath blinded me to all things else.

Love at a single word may bloom,
  The quick heart blossoming fair and free;
One glance may gild the future's gloom,
  And now thy bright eyes shine on me.
    Thine eyes of blue, etc.

And canst thou ask me why my cheek,
  Where thou art not, grows pale and wan?
Why sadness that I can not speak
  Surrounds my path when thou art gone?
    Thine eyes of blue, etc.

And, farther, canst thou wish to know
  What change comes o'er me when we meet,
And why my pallid brow will glow,
  And why my quivering pulses beat?
    Thine eyes of blue, the heaven's own hue,
      Thy soft eyes thrill my fevered pulse;
    The fire that lies within thine eyes
      Hath blinded me to all things else.

SOME WISDOM IN DOGGEREL.

We know not why nor how it is,
  Yet find it every hour,
'Twixt Fortune and her sister Mis
  There's most unequal power.
How quickly in our noon of pride
  May clouds obscure the sun;
How rapidly we fling aside
  The wealth so hardly won.

'Tis so where'er we turn our foot,
  And sad it is to write it;
A whole long summer plumps the fruit,
  An hour of frost can blight it.
What are Dame Fortune's thousand smiles
  Against Miss Fortune's frown?
The ship has sailed a thousand miles—
  One shock—she settles down.

'Tis so in love, 'tis so in fame,
  In all we prize on earth;
The priceless jewel of a name
  Untarnished from our birth,
One moment's folly, passion, haste—
  The name is ruined—gone!
So easy 'tis—so quick we waste
  The wealth so hardly won.

Even love—the sweetest flower that stirred
  In all life's gloomy vale,
An angry breath, a hasty word—
  It sickens in the gale.
O Life! to Death thy hour-glass toss,
  Let all its sands outrun;
We can not daily bear the loss
  Of joys so dearly won.

CHANT OF THE NO-KAMI.

TO BE LEARNED BY ALL ADMIRERS OF THE JAPANESE PRINCES.

To pronounce the name of a Japanese,
Give a cough and hiccough, a grunt and sneeze,
Then finish the whole with a whistle, and, blame me!
If that ain't the name of some grand No-Kami.

They are clad in petticoats made of silk,
And they drink no lager, but whey and milk;
Their money goes down to the tenth of a cent,
And they carry two swords—one straight, one bent.

Namoo Amida they call their God,
And they enter his churches with feet unshod;
But their God of Wealth is called Dai Gak,
And his altars never full worshipers lack.

At Nagasaki their foreign trade
With Dutchmen and Chinamen long was made;
Camphor, and coffee, and porcelain rare,
And trays of their much-vaunted lacquer-ware.

Copper, and wax, and rice they sell;
In heavy silk goods they bear the bell;
And whenever they chance to fall into disgrace,
Then they rip themselves open before your face.

For this they carry the second sword;
And whene'er they're in debt, or default, or bored,
Or get a toothache, or make a slip,
They open their bowels, and let things rip.

So honor the Japanese night and day,
With congenial blacking-pots strew their way.
And if to admire them you fail, don't blame me,
For this is the song of a Jap No-Kami.

THE BACCHANTES.

Say, art thou sad? our golden cup
  With precious balm is laden;
A world of joy in every drop
  For man, and, eke, for maiden.
Its scent outvies the rosy ties
  That in our tresses cluster;
The light that lies within our eyes
  Grows pale beside its lustre.

Our zones ungirt, our pulses warm,
  Our thoughts at random roaming,
Wilt thou refuse the fragrant charm,
  Wilt thou refuse it foaming?
Its scent outvies the rosy ties
  That in our tresses cluster;
The light that lies within our eyes
  Grows pale beside its lustre.

INDIFFERENCE.[20]

Through days, and nights, and weary years
I struggle on, through hopes and fears,
If "hopes" are called those spectres gaunt
That, like bog-lanterns, flare and flaunt
  Before the way-worn trav'ler's face,
    Yet vanish as he nears.

And for her sake, whose lightest breath
Could give me strength to cope with death,
And overcome where now I die—
Whose face downlooketh like the sky,
  While trembling I await her grace,
    Yet not a word she saith.

She knows the purposes I frame,
And sees them fail me, aim by aim—
She sees wild passions tear my heart,
While foes and snares around me start,
  Yet her sweet breath,that might me save,
    But serves to fan the flame.

She sees me captured by their wiles,
And tortured till my soul reviles
The God who made me—sees me when
The demons drag me down; and then,
  While in their toils I writhe and rave,
    Looks calmly on—and smiles.

ADIEU.

Oh, heed him not, if rhymer prate
  Of parted love and endless woe:
  True love would scorn to babble so,
And grief is inarticulate,
  Or with a hoarse and broken flow
It rushes, murmuring, to its fate—
That ocean which, or soon or late,
  Receives the wreck of all we know,
  Or be it love, or be it hate.
Oh, heed him not. The spirit bowed
With grief sincere was ne'er so loud.

But if to say in simple praise
  That I will ne'er forget you, friends,
  Though at the earth's remotest ends
I pass my long unsolaced days;
  That, when the evening shade descends,
And high and bright the fagots blaze,
My faithful heart your forms shall raise,
  While memory the curtain rends
That Time would drop o'er earlier days—
If this content you, 'tis sincere,
Though vouched by neither oath nor tear.

ONE DEAD SURE THING.[21]

Air: "The Groves of Blarney."

It is John B. Haskin
Will hereafter bask in
The smiles of Johnsing, who is named An-drew;
For 'twas John B. Haskin
Did succeed the task in
Of the "Ninth Resolution" putting squarely through.
And whatever you ask in
The name of Haskin—
Be it place in the Customs, or what else he begs—
There's no need of maskin'
That; if axed by Haskin,
You'll be sure to get it—just as sure as eggs!

MOTTO OF THE MASS.[22]

I've seen enough of life, although
  Not yet beyond my prime;
With men of all sorts, high and low,
  I've mingled in my time.
When but a boy it came to pass
  That, thrown upon the town,
I found the motto of the mass
  Was, "Kick him when he's down."

And every year since then hath given
  Fresh proofs of this decree,
But, whether made in hell or heaven,
  The doctors disagree.

I only know the fact is so,
  And—smile at it or frown—
The art of life seems in the strife
  To kick whoever's down.

Young Leon in his twentieth year
  Had friends, God wot! a heap;
Their friendship may have been sincere—
  It surely was not cheap;
He came of age, spent all he had,
  And, wandering through the town,
Neglected, hungry, well-nigh mad,
  Was kicked when he was down.

Poor Edith, too, the loveliest girl
  That ever charmed our sight,
Of beauty's crown the fairest pearl,
  And good as she was bright—
Alas! she fell; let scandal tell
  The tale to all the town;
Aloud proclaim a sister's shame,
  And kick her when she's down.

With high and low, but chiefly so
  Among the vulgar great,
This motto rules, and all are fools
  Who dare its truth debate.
Oh, brothers! Earth were paradise,
  And heaven without a frown,
Could we uproot such social lies
  As "Kick him when he's down."

TIME.[23]

Time rolls away, and bears along
A mingled mass of right and wrong;
The flowers of love, that bloomed beside
The margin of his summer tide;
The weeds of passion, drenched and torn
From dripping banks, and headlong borne
Into that unhorizoned sea
Which mortals call eternity.

Noiseless and rapid as a dream
Forever flows the widening stream,
While every wave or transient hour
Heaves up a weed and takes a flower.

The Isle of Life, that seemed to be
A continent infinity,
Grows bleaker, narrower, day by day,
And channeled by a salter spray.

Like shipwrecked men, who closelier flock
To the bare summit of the rock
When the loud storm that wrecked them flings
Some loftier billow from his wings,
We climb from youth's wave-rippled strand,
With heavier heart and feebler hand,
Up the gray rock of age, whose peak
Time's hungry billows, mounting, seek.

There, from the barren top, espy
A girth of tears—an ashen sky;
Bowed heads, cold hearts, and palsied feet
To Age's pinnacle retreat,
While the dull tide that swells below
Pursues them with a sullen flow—
The rock is hid, the waves beat high,
And, lo! an Ocean and a Sky.

FIERY ELOQUENCE.[24]

THE PICTURE OF ONE WE KNOW.

His mind throws out its own discourse,
Not checked nor helped by rule or form;
He utters by instinctive force
An eloquence deep, terse, and warm;
He is not fanciful, nor strains
For words or thoughts beyond his reach—
A molten fury of the veins
Glows through his lens of crystal speech.

He grasps and crushes into mould
Whate'er can serve his headlong need,
The weapon may be brass or gold,
But it must make the victim bleed.
Imagination's powers of flight
Are harnessed to his glowing wheel—
Sunward or hellward, wrong or right,
He will not think—he can but feel.

He lives in pain, in fierce desire,
Or vain regret for perished joy;
His aspirations have the fire
Which tortures, but will not destroy;

He is Prometheus chained again
  Amid the elemental strife—
The scourges and the crowns of men
  Are emblemed in his fitful life.

His joys are full luxuriant flowers,
  Though nurtured on a mouldering root,
Though watered by the bitterest showers,
  And bearing a most bitter fruit.
Keen shafts of sarcasm now he hurls,
  Now pathos trembles in his tone,
And, in his passionate tide, he whirls
  All souls that hear him with his own.

FAUGH AN BEALLACH.[25]

SONG OF THE IRISH BRIGADE.

Where glory's beams are seen, boys,
  To cheer the way, to cheer the way,
We bear the emerald green, boys,
  And clear the way, and clear the way.
Where life-blood torrents gush, boys,
  In battle fray, in battle fray,
The bold brigade-men rush, boys,
  And clear the way, and clear the way.

That home where valor first, boys,
  In all her charms, in all her charms,
Roused up the souls she nursed, boys,
  And called to arms, and called to arms—
That home was surely worth, boys,
  The years we've known, the years we've known,
Since treachery drove us forth, boys,
  To fight alone, to fight alone.

Oh who, while memory's given, boys,
  That hour forgets, that hour forgets,
'Tis like the sun in heaven, boys,
  That never sets, that never sets;
When England's legions, dying,
  Oh day of joy, oh day of joy,
Before our flag were flying
  At Fontenoy, at Fontenoy.

And what is Sarsfield's meed, boys,
  Whose conquering smile, whose conquering smile,
Inspired each martial deed, boys,
  To right our isle, to right our isle?

His memory still is bright'ning
From day to day, from day to day,
As when his sword of lightning
Led on the fray, led on the fray.

Then here's to Sarsfield's glory—
A bumper round, a bumper round—
And may his deathless story
For aye be found, for aye be found
A star our country's tomb in—
A star of light, a star of light,
Whose radiance may illumine
Her final light, her final light.

MATRIMONIAL COMPLACENCY.[6]

Since Grace and I were double,
I'd have the world to know,
We've been a goodish couple,
As goodish couples go;
To no ecstatic passion
Our present hearts respond,
But you know 'tis out of fashion
For couples to be fond.

I thought her once angelic—
A fairy she did seem—
There is not now a relic
Of that diviner dream;
Her dress is more than costly,
Her taste in music fine,
She eats—and it is vastly,
As other people dine.

Nor am I now her hero—
The worshiped one alone;
A matrimonial Nero
She seems to think me grown;
A brute, should I refuse her
That dear, sweet Cashmere shawl;
Worse than a brute I use her
If kept in town the fall.

Cigars are her abhorrence,
She hates the sight of wine,
And no presumption warrants
A friend brought home to dine;

She won't believe 'tis business
  That keeps me late at night,
And on the slightest dizziness
  I am condemned as "tight."

But still, despite this trouble,
  These little puffs of woe,
We make a goodish couple,
  As goodish couples go;
To no ecstatic passion
  Our present hearts respond,
But you know 'tis out of fashion
  For couples to be fond.

"OH, YOUNG GEORDIE SANDERS."

Oh, young Geordie Sanders came over the sea,
And of all the good consuls the goodest is he;
And, save his credentials, he letters had none—
He sailed on a sudden, and sailed all alone;
So faithful to truth and his country was he,
No "harder" American e'er crossed the sea.

He staid not to see would the Senate conform,
But crossed the Atlantic through shine and through storm:
And when the new consul at London arrived,
He showed his credentials, and then was received;
For never before did America send
A consul unworthy the name of a friend.

So boldly he entered upon his new place,
That we thought that our Senate would never disgrace
Its fame and traditions by raising its voice
Against our executive's favorite choice;
But when in the Senate his name was received,
The Cabinet party arose and upheaved.

But Sanders, we know, is an excellent "Hard,"
And the Cabinet "Softs" did him therefore discard;
And, when he was named, all the Senate arose
Like a parcel of Turks at the sight of their foes.
"There are Soft Shells in Gotham, done utterly brown,
Who would gladly be consul to famed London town."

The Cabinet issued its orders to vote,
And the Senate reluctantly opened its throat;
It took down the pill, and it threw up its eyes,
And "No" to the name of George Sanders replies,

Though the Democrats whispered, "The slaves of Freesoil
Have resolved to take e'en this last bit of spoil."

But Marcy and Cushing, 'twas they pulled the wires,
And 'tis Marcy, we know, that the Senate inspires;
For he hates even more than he hates me, the bard,
The welfare or name of a "national Hard;"
And so they refused—though the vote was absurd—
While the poor craven Cabinet said not a word.

There was reveling that night 'mid the Cabinet clan—
Davis, Cushing, and Marcy concocted the plan—
There were oysters for all, and Champagne for the crowd
Who the name of the consular "Hard" disallowed;
So luckless was Sanders sent over the sea,
Have you e'er heard of consul was treated as he?

IRISH ASTRONOMY.[27]

A VERITABLE MYTH, TOUCHING THE CONSTELLATION OF O'RYAN, IGNORANTLY AND FALSELY SPELLED ORION.

O'Ryan was a man of might
  Whin Ireland was a nation,
But poachin' was his heart's delight
  And constant occupation.
He had an ould militia gun,
  And sartin sure his aim was;
He gave the keepers many a run,
  And wouldn't mind the game laws.

St. Pathrick wanst was passin' by
  O'Ryan's little houldin',
And, as the saint felt wake and dhry,
  He thought he'd enther bould in.
"O'Ryan," says the saint, "avick!
  To praich at Thurles I'm goin',
So let me have a rasher quick,
  And a dhrop of Innishowen."

"No rasher will I cook for you
  While betther is to spare, sir,
But here's a jug of mountain dew,
  And there's a rattlin' hare, sir."
St. Pathrick he looked mighty sweet,
  And says he, "Good luck attind you,
And, when you're in your windin' sheet,
  It's up to heaven I'll sind you."

O'Ryan gave his pipe a whiff—
  "Them tidin's is thransportin',
But may I ax your saintship if
  There's any kind of sportin'?"
St. Pathrick said, "A Lion's there,
  Two Bears, a Bull, and Cancer"—
"Bedad," says Mick, "the huntin's rare;
  St. Pathrick, I'm your man, sir."

So, to conclude my song aright,
  For fear I'd tire your patience,
You'll see O'Ryan any night
  Amid the constellations.
And Venus follows in his track
  Till Mars grows jealous raally,
But, faith, he fears the Irish knack
  Of handling the shillaly.

TO A FRIEND.[28]

Dear friend and honored, though thy words be rough,
  I take them kindly, for I know them true;
  And that thy heart, an icicle to view,
Is warm, and made of penetrable stuff.

Little, perchance, had the world cause to chide,
  Had I, emerging from youth's glittering gate
  Into the riotous strength of man's estate,
Found such a friend to cheer me and to guide.

'Tis easy to condemn, and hard to spare;
  And blood is hot, and pleasures will allure;
  And cloaked hypocrisy would fain insure
Its own good name by branding those who err.

I have my sins as thick as April showers—
  Some virtues also, if I know my heart;
  And something tells me that my latter part
Of life may choke the weeds and feed the flowers.

I have been grateful for whatever good
  Was strewn along my path—not overmuch!
  I never yet with acrimonious touch
Probed the diseases of another's blood.

My hand was free while it had aught to give;
  I ne'er oppressed when chance conferred the power;
  And I have struggled many a prayerful hour
A worthier and more useful life to live.

If wrong were offered me, I never stopped
To curse my foe, to grumble, or to writhe,
Although beneath misfortune's glittering scythe
My dearest hopes, like crimson poppies, dropped.

Still struggling on to a diviner goal,
Though gored by thorns and tumbling into quags.
Nor ever hesitates, nor ever flags
The fixed resolve that centres in my soul;

For life is but a struggle of weak will
With intellectual purpose, and the rod
Which chastens pride is in the hands of God,
Who does not always smite nor wholly kill.

From the high hope which filled my boyish heart
Ne'er have my eyes been lured, nor have I lost
Faith in the future, and, though tempest-toss'd
I still steer firmly by the early chart.

Should that be right, my voyage prospers well;
Should that be wrong, I perish, and no more—
Another wreck upon a thankless shore;
But of the issue let the future tell.

WEARIE PEN.

I weary of my pen,
And write not of mine own accord;
It was my slave, and I was happy then;
'Tis now my lord.

I weary of the themes
Which the gross multitude pursue;
Who writes for bread must bid all higher dreams
His last adieu.

Harness the antelope,
Burden his back until it bleeds—
Trample his fiery spirit, and then hope
His former speed.

Bid the lush country yield
Not annual gift, but daily boon—
A fungus growth defiles the morning field,
And rots ere noon.

We squander sterling thought
  On frivolous feuds and foolish cares;
The harvest of our life becomes inwrought,
  And choked with tares.

Oh for song's dædal prime,
  When, wandering o'er the plains afoot,
The shepherd minstrel tuned the spear of time—
  His shield, a lute.

Ay, there were giants then,
  Gentle as strong, and good as bold—
A stalwart race of freedom-loving men
  Were those of old.

Their blood ran red and warm
  Through healthy pulses, and they found
Infinite loveliness of hue and form,
  Of taste and sound.

Their souls in music bathed,
  Freedom inspired their highest hymns;
No mummy-cloths of a dead custom swathed
  Their vigorous limbs.

And yet in every age
  There must be themes to touch the heart:
We have the self-same passions, joy and rage,
  But lack their art.

We pore o'er books. They trod
  Mountain, and vale, and sounding shore;
They make their spirits intimate with God
  And nature's lore.

As falls the levin-scaith
  On the young oaks that clothe a hill,
We have been stunted by our want of faith
  And resolute will.

To Nature false, our eyes
  See nothing beautiful; we warm
And stamp with social currency the lies
  Of fraud and form.

Where passion throbbed high words,
  With beggar whine the age complains;
Gone the red glory of controlling swords,
  And Mammon reigns.

Life grows a stagnant pool,
  Green with the dregs of trade and toil,
Youth's pure ideals of the beautiful
  Are Lucre's spoil.

I weary of the pen,
  And write not of mine own accord;
It was my slave, and I was happy then:
  Alas! 'tis now my lord.

A PICTURE IN WATER-COLORS.

'Twas a bright expanse of water
Where the Quaker's gentle daughter
Every summer morning sought her
  Bath of beauty, light, and grace;
Quite a fleet of drifted lilies
Danced above the mimic billows,
And a screen of drooping willows
  Curtained close the bathing-place.

In my skiff at random floating,
Rod and line but nothing noting—
Ah! what subtle charm had boating
  Since the bathing-place was known;
I across the lake was drifted,
While with life my fancy gifted
Every lily-shoulder lifted,
  White and dimpled as her own.

"Ah! how clear!" I muttered, eying
Many a colored pebble lying
Far below, and vainly trying
  On some book to fix my thought;
"Now some good breeze hither winging,
Set yon silver curtain swinging,
Coolness to the bather bringing,"
  But the good breeze answered not.

Homeward o'er the meadows tripping,
All the lovelier for her dipping,
Soon I saw the maiden skipping,
  Who said archly, when we met,
"Friend, thou hast grown fond of boating;"
And my weak heart quailed on noting
The malicious laughter floating
  In the eyes of my coquette.

EPIGRAM

TO A YOUNG LADY WHO ASKED FOR HIS NAME IN HER ALBUM.

You ask for my name! Ah! dear madam, you palter
 With the hopes I have felt, as you well understand.
If you wish for my name, it is yours at the altar:
 I'll give you my name when you give me your hand.

THE OLD YEAR AND THE NEW.

The good Old Year hath run his race,
 And the latest hour draws near;
The cold dew shines on his hoary face,
And he hobbles along with a listless pace,
To his lonely and snow-covered resting-place
 In the northern hemisphere.

See how his stiff joints faint and shrink
 As the cold breeze whistles by;
He hath a bitter cup to drink
As he watches the sand in his hour-glass sink,
Standing alone on the icy brink
 Of the gulf of eternity.

His scanty robe is wrapped more tight
 As the dim sun dwindles down;
And no stars arise to cheer the night
Of him whose temples they once made bright,
When crimson roses and lilies white
 Half hid his golden crown.

He reels—he slips—no power at hand
 To check him from tumbling o'er;
The hour-glass clicks with its latest sand,
And each movement falls like the stroke of a brand
On one already too weak to stand—
 He falls—he is seen no more.

And, lo! in the east a star ascends,
 And a burst of music comes—
A young lord, followed by troops of friends,
Down to the broad equator wends,
While the star that travels above him bends
 O'er a sea of floating plumes.

And Hope springs up from the couch of Care,
  Her eyes are full of the softest fire,
A light burns round her golden hair,
And her bosom is soft, and oh, how fair!
As she clasps the boy, and presses him there,
  As once she had pressed his sire.

On every hill the bonfire glows,
  And clarions blend with the beating drums;
The yellow crocus disparts the snows,
And the river, freed from its bondage, flows,
While sparrows chirp, and the shrill cock crows
  As the New Year hitherward comes.

His glittering mail he flings aside,
  And we see a robe of the brightest green;
And the velvet green but serves to hide
The crimson vest of the richer pride
He dons in the brilliant summer tide
  When he weds his Harvest Queen.

But time rolls on; and the New Year turns
  His wearying feet to the frozen north;
The sun each day more dimly burns,
And the mother earth each day inurns
Her summer brood, while the cold winds spurns
  The victor it heralded forth.

And again the Old Year treads alone
  To the north, bereft of friends:
He totters along to the frozen zone,
With an icicle in each marrowless bone,
And the hoarse wind buries his dying groan
  As another star ascends.

Then kindly think of the dying year—
  The joys, the hopes, and the love he nursed;
Let fall a tear on his narrow bier;
For, although not perfect, yet much I fear
That he was the best we shall ever see—
  God grant he may prove the worst.

A BROADWAY BELLE.

I saw her in the window—
  She was fairest of the fair;
I thought it was no sin to
  Kneel down before her there.

Her dress was brightest, fullest,
  That e'er by zone was bound;
And her fan—it was the coolest
  That e'er shed fragrance round.

She turned around—but slowly,
  With a cold, unfeeling grace,
Although a hundred lowly
  Adored her radiant face;
Her hair was dark as the winglets
  By the raven's brood unfurled,
And pearls were mixed in the ringlets
  Above her bright brow curled.

There were brilliant toys around her
  Of velvet and of silk,
As fair as those which bound her
  White shoulders—white as milk;
Her eyes were bright, but rayless;
  They lacked the vital spark;
And lovely—could I say less?
  The mind—the soul was dark.

"Oh, loveliest of the gentle
  And fair!" I did repeat,
"Behold me! I have bent all
  My passions to thy feet;
Grant—and the boon entrances
  Your poet, bard, and slave—
One of the kindly glances
  For which all lovers crave."

Thus rapt in mystic wonder
  I stood before the shrine,
When a voice like summer thunder
  Disturbed this dream of mine.
It cried, "I am astonished
  That to gain her smile you strive;
Henceforward be admonished—
  That thing is not alive!"

"Oh, creature of wax and leather,
  Of pulleys, and wheels, and bran,
Changeless in change of weather,"
  It was thus my answer ran—
"No blame to you, not being human,
  For your eyes of unpitying blue;
But I've knelt to a score of live women,
  Brainless, lovely, and heartless as you."

THINGS THAT I SEEN AND HEERD IN BUCKIN'HAM PALICE

WHILE CLANIN' THE WINDIES IN THE RED DHRAWIN'-ROOM.

BY GARLAND O'HALLORAN, DEPUTY ASSISTANT SUB-DEPUTY GLAZIER.

I was clanin' the windies
In Buckin'ham Palice,
An' I thought o' the shindies
O' Russians and Allies,
Whin into the room, wid a brow full of gloom,
An' a bottle of goold—it was filled with perfume—
Held up to her nose—pop! past me she goes—
The queen! an' I thrembled in, undher me toes,
But she didn't perceive I was undher the eave,
So I thought I'd just watch her a while, ere I'd leave,
For it struck me as odd that her queenship should grieve.
She flopped in a chair
Which the flunky put there,
An' she "pished" an' she "pshawed" wid a wanderin' air,
That was half of it anger an' half was despair;
An' the great Koh-i-noor, that was fixed on her brow,
Wid the rubies set round it, flashed blood-like enow;
An' over her soul, in that dark hour of dole,
The red hand of Care dhrove his merciless plow,
While she thought of her sins an' the big Russian row;
An' the gem on her brow grew too hot to retain it
Whin she thought of the millions she butchered to gain it;
An', through the thick mist that was chokin' her eye,
The ghost of her famine-killed sisther went by.
In Ireland 'twas famine—in India 'twas slaughter,
An' every where, every where blood ran like wather.

Well, still, while I looked—shure I thought I was booked
To that place where there's nothin' but kangaroos cooked,
For an ould man came in—he was ugly as sin,
Wid the dismalest grin round his fat double chin;
An' he tucked up his coat-tails an' backed to the fire,
An' he looked at the queen half in pity, half ire;
An' she rocked in her chair, an' she tapped wid her toes
On the carpet of velvet that blushed like a rose,
An' she didn't seem plaised with the double-chinned man,
But he talked quite familiar, and thus his words ran:

"Good-day, my Queen Vic. Have you suffered a thrick?
For you're lookin' by no means good-naychured or slick."

"Och! indeed an' I'm sick, an' I can't ate a pick,
An' I'm perishin' quick; my legs isn't as thick
As your highly respectable goold-headed stick."

"No, nor more nor a half—not a sign of a calf?"
An' I knew by his laugh he was tippin' her chaff
(For she's fat as a puncheon: an' dinner, an' luncheon,
An' breakfasht, an' supper, it takes beef to stop her,
An' plenty of that—gravied, spicy, and fat;
An' rich wine and porther must flow at her ordher—
I'm tellin' no lies, sir, 'tis the doctors advise her).

"Now tell me what's wrong," sez he;
"Don't keep me long," sez he,
"For I'm dhry, an' I think
That I'd much like a dhrink."

"Take your time, my ould brick," sez she;
"Don't be so quick," sez she,
"An' I'll make a clane breast, for my throubles is thick," sez she;
"I ordhered the pick of my sojers to lick,
Bate, wallop, an' kick that ould thievin' rogue Nick;
I thought he'd cut his stick whin he heard the first click
Of my bombs, an' my rifles, an' other such thrifles;
But he didn't do it, an' I'm like to rue it,
An' God knows at all how I'll ever get through it."

"Och! conshume the ould rogue, wid his Cossacky brogue;
Him an' Prussia'll collogue, as wid kings 'tis the vogue,
An' the Austriches too—they'll be into the stew,
An' ferment in the brew; an', 'tis every way thrue,
My lady, your queenship, that things does look blue,
An' no wondher you feel just as bad as you do."

"Och! that ain't the worst of it—
Only the first of it.
Come, I'll tell all, or I fear I shall burst of it.
There's wan Lewy Nap—
He's a hang-gallows chap,
An' the likes of him, rightly, should take off his cap
To the likes of meself; but that's not like to hap,
For he cribbed at a throne, an' has made it his own,
An' has gathered an' keeps at a place called Boolone
(From whence they can see Dover Lights an' Folkstone)
An army of men that are just wan to ten
(I mane ten to wan—but my senses is gone)
Of the whole of my force—cannon, footmen, an' horse;
An' that ould Aberdeen—he's a dirty spalpeen—
But keep (an' she winked) what I tell you between
Yourself and the bedpost—you know what I mean.

Well, he came in wan day," sez she,
"Wrigglin' his way," sez she,
"An' I knew by his mug that he meant no child's play," sez she.
"Sez he, 'Mrs. Vic,' sez he,
'Dhress yourself quick,' sez he;
'I've asked Lewy over, wid his wife—"fammy cover,"
As at Paris we say—an' they'll soon be at Dover.
They're now on their way,
So look afther the tay,
For you know we must make a most sumpshis display.
Get some nice oysther stews, bully-beef and ragoos,
Wid a bushel of frogs for the d—d parley voos!
They're fond of what's nice—must I bid you go twice?'
An' his thin fingers clutched themselves up like a vice.
'Conshumin' the bit,' sez I,
'At the table I'll sit,' sez I,
'Wid the beggar-born chap
That they call Lewy Nap;
If he come, he must dine at the scullery tap.
But who axed him to come?' sez I;
'Why, are you dumb?' sez I.
'Do you know, my ould buck, that you're undher my thumb?' sez I.
'Your majesty—why,' sez he, 'he's your ally,' sez he;
'Besides, though to get them away I did thry,' sez he,
'In the camp at Boolone, in that wan camp alone—
Which looks so convayniently over Folkstone—
He has ten times ten thousand of French flesh an' bone;
An' the French flesh an' bone is all weaponed and ready,
Its thrainin' is good, an' its practice is steady,
An' London is richer, an' not half so far,
As that murdherin' Cronstadt that's owned by the Czar.'
'My ally he is not,' sez I,
For my blood it was hot; sez I—
'An' as for Eugenie,' sez I, 'is she fit to be seen,' sez I.
'Wid a regular queen?' sez I—'it's meself I mean,' sez I.
Then he flew in a rage, an' he made me engage
To take all soorts of thrubble for the parley-voo couple:
An' whin Lewy is come, we must bate the big dhrum,
An' play thrumpet an' fife in an emulous sthrife,
To do honor to mounseer an' his thrallop of a wife."

"Then how goes the fightin'?" sez he;
"Have you done the inditin'," sez he,
"Of thim notes that took nine men a month in the writin'?" sez he.
"Have thim ould diplomats," sez he,
"That's as cunnin' as cats," sez he,
"Scared the Bear of the North wid their parchment flats?" sez he.

"Och! good luck to their souls, wid their protocoals!
Shure their rigmaroles were so full o' holes
That the rats and the bats slipped in it an' out,
An' the Austriches echoed the Prussians' shout,
An' it gives me the gout to think what they're about;
For, to my eyes, its every where jumble and rout.
They're all tellin' lies, throwin' dust in my eyes,
An' the man that lies deepest 'tis him that is wise."

"What started the war? What are you fightin' for
Wid your highly respectable cousin the Czar?
Do your sympathies lurk wid the infidel Turk?
An' why, wid ould Nick, don't you make it short work?
Shure each school-boy repeats that Britannia, she beats
All creashin to smash wid her sojers and fleets?"

"Nabocklish! No!" sez she; "I wanst thought so," sez she;
"The historians blow," sez she; "but it ain't no go!" sez she,
"As I feel very keenly, an' much to my woe," sez she.
"I sent Charley Napier, who knows how to steer
First rate, as I hear, an' he wint very near
To the Cronstadt pier; but he thought it looked queer,
An' he cum back here wid a flay in his ear.
An' he swears it was all the Reform Club beer
That muddled his head whin he solemnly said
That he'd pull the Czar's lug in St. Petersburg,
Or be off to hell
In a three weeks' time.
An', indeed, 'twould be well
If he'd make the fact chime
Wid his plighted promise. A good riddance from us!
Thin there's ould Dundas," sez she; "to my thinkin' an ass," sez she;
"Not worth his grass," sez she; "but let that pass," sez she.
"Shure he talked like a Nelson, or some other red-hell-son,
Of tundher and blood," sez she, "whin he swore that he could," sez she,
"Take some jaw-breakin' town," sez she,
"I could never get down," sez she.
"It was built by a basthard, I think,
An' called afther the dasthard, I think;
It ends wid a 'pol,'" sez she,
"An' is girt wid a wall," sez she;
An' up to this time we're not shure of its fall," sez she;
"So I sent Lord Raglan, wid the juke for his flagman—
Not the 'Iron Juke,'" sez she, "wid a nose like a hook," sez she,
"Whose ould brazen cloak an' whose murdherin' look," sez she,
"Upon Hyde Park corner, is a caution and warner
To any dead nigger not to swell any bigger

Than his breeches will hould," sez she, "lest he burst and get cowld,"
sez she,
"As ould Boney did do at the famed Watherloo," sez she.
"Arrah! what 'ud he say, could he only look through
From the high place or low place he's now gone unto,
An' find us allied to the young Parleyvoo?
It was Cambridge's juke for the scrimmage I took;
An' now here's a saycrit—but swear on the book
That you'll never divulge it by hook or by crook—
For you'd ruin me sthraight, an' my throne 'ud be shook.

"Shure to fear I began
That they'd ax my ould man—
He's field-marshal, they say," sez she,
"An' I know he's dhrawn pay," sez she,
"This many a day," sez she.
"An' he made a new hat from the skin of a cat,
An' I've heerd, an', indeed, even Punch owns to that,
That the hat bids defiance to milithary science
To pass or to peer it, or even come near it,
In the way of a shed," sez she, "for a sojer's head," sez she;
"But he's tendher an' weakly," sez she,
"An' of late somewhat sickly," sez she,
"Wid a bad rheumatiz," sez she,
"In that sword-arm of his," sez she.
"He tuk ill the first night that we heerd of the fight;
An', since Inkermann," sez she, "no mortal can," sez she,
"Describe what he feels from his head to his heels;
He's in a cold sweat till it makes his sheets wet,
An' he's shiv'rin an' shakin', and his bones they are achin',
An' he's thremblin' an' sore to his very heart's core,
An' he's worn out intirely, an' worried what's more.
He's a soldier thrue," sez she,
"An' at Chopham Review," sez she,
"I seen him to do," sez she,
"Things to make you look blue," sez she.
"An' he's ravin' quite, by day and by night,
To be into the fight, as is proper an' right;
An' he swears that he'd kill," sez she—
"If it worn't for the accident that he happens to be ill," sez she—
"Ould Mentschikoff an' the Prince Pop-em-off,
Liprandi, an' Luders, an' Count Orloff;
But he says he can not think of it until he cures his cough.
Och! his pains is cruel; he's as wake as wather gruel;
An' should any wan hint—in speeches or print—
That the man who does quartherly dhraw," sez she,
"In accordions wid milithary law," sez she,

"The highest pay
Should take part in the fray,
Och! he'd faint away
From the blessed light of day!
Me poor Albert 'ud fall, rowled up in a ball,
His bowels 'ud turn into wather an' gall—
An' I know widows' caps don't become me at all."

"Well, now, Mrs. Vic"—
An' his eye had a thrick
As cunnin' an' knowin' as a cat's that is goin',
Whin the cook's asleep, wid the softest creep,
To lick fresh butther—"if you let me, I'll utther
Some good advice," sez he, "an' think over it twice," sez he.
"Go an' make your ould man," sez he,
"Just as soon as he can," sez he,
"Cure the rheumatiz," sez he,
"In that sword-arm of his," sez he,
"Or he'd betther resign," sez he,
"His uniform fine," sez he,
"An' fall out o' the line," sez he.

"Och! but, thin, the pay?" sez she,
"It 'ud go asthray," sez she,
"An' that's not at all afther Albert's way," sez she.

"Resign that too," sez he,
"For, betune me an' you," sez he,
"Whin the people see," sez he,
"(Betune you an' me)," sez he,
"Their gallant field-marshal to rheumatiz partial
Whin colors are flyin', an' thousands are dyin'
For a shillin' a day round Sevastopol's Bay,
They'll begin to compare the sick gentleman's pay
Wid the throoper's who dashed through the thick of the fray,
Where bullets were whizzing an' sabres did play
On casque an' cuirass, an' the min fell like grass,
While the field-marshal—Balaam-like—sat on his ass,
An' prayed for the foes he was bound to oppose
From the top of his head to the root of his toes.
Let him give up his place wid whatever of grace
Can be possibly lint to so dirty a case,
Or the very ould wimin will spit in his face,
An' the childher, God bless 'em! throw dirt at his grace.
Inniskilling's an' Grays, Irish Lancers and Bays—
Whatever poor wreck of them's left in these days—
The men, not of rank, who dhrove spurs in the flank
Of their chargers, an' dashed up the cannon-plowed bank,
While the grape an' cross-fire mowed them down rank by rank;

Never haltin', though reelin', but formin' and wheelin'
Again an' again, wid diminishin' min,
While the pulks of the Cossackry crowded the glin.
No end to their labors—no rest for their sabres—
Blood-spatthered, they could not be known by their neighbors.
An' still by sheer steel, strength of hand, heart, an' heel,
Though shatthered, disordhered, invincible still,
Through a long lane of fire—through a laygion of foes—
Grimly forced to retire—the Light Cavalry goes.
They've left—an' what thin?—just three fourths of their min
To fat the next harvest in Inkermann's glin;
But the colors they bore, though bedabbled with gore,
Still wave o'er the remnant returnin' once more.
What a sight there will be, should they ever come back,
An' the field-marshal—partial to a timely attack
Of the rheumatic fayver—should fall in their thrack!"

What more there was said,
Shure, no more than the dead
Do I know, for I chanced to lane forward my head,
An' the queen gave a scream an' the man gave a start,
An' I judged it was best for meself to depart.

Deputy Glazier's Room, Buckin'ham Palice,
London, December 4, 1854.

WOMAN'S RIGHTS.

Oh, ladies, will you hear a truth,
Of late too seldom told to you,
Nor deem—he begs it of your ruth—
The writer over-bold to you;
For, by the pulses of his youth,
He never yet was cold to you,
And therefore 'tis in sober sooth
That he would now unfold to you
What may—apart from rhythmic flights—
Be called the sum of "Woman's Rights."

For you the calm sequestered bowers,
For us to kneel and sue to you;
Your feet upon the path of flowers
We struggle still to strew to you;
For you to drop the healing showers
Of kindness—gentle dew to you—
On failing health and wasted powers—
The task is nothing new to you—

"Oh, these, indeed"—'tis Love indites—
"These are unquestioned Woman's Rights."

All hail! we cry, the stormiest hours,
  If thus a joy we woo to you;
For us, of life's drugged bowl, the sours,
  If so the sweets ensue to you.
When many a heavy hap was ours,
  Fond retrospection flew to you;
Good husbands and unstinted dowers,
  And smiling babes accrue to you;
And, let me ask, what maiden slights
These latter-mentioned "Woman's Rights?"

The faithfulness, the grace, the high,
  Pure thoughts of life we gain by you;
The vision of a softer eye,
  The finer touch attain by you;
Weak hopes that unto death are nigh
  Out-leaning, we sustain by you;
And when misfortune sweeps the sky,
  Our anchored hearts remain by you.
Long days of toil and feverish nights
Would ill repay these "Woman's Rights."

Why quit the calm and holy hearth
  That is heaven's antepast to us,
To face the sterner scenes of earth,
  The troubles that are cast to us?
Why change your soul's unsullied mirth
  For woes that rush so fast to us,
That we would daily curse our birth
  Were not your sphere at last to us—
That sphere of home, which well requites
The loss of these unsexing rights.

AN OLFACTORY ODE IN PRAISE OF NEW YORK CLEANLINESS.

BY OUR POET WITH A COLD IN HIS HEAD.

Thank heaven! the crisis,
  The terror is past,
And the sense they call smelling
  Hath perished at last;
And the anguish of smelling
  Is over at last.

Sadly I know
  Of one sense I'm forlorn,
But with pleasure and profit
  The loss may be borne;
With profit and pleasure
  That loss may be borne.

And I walk so composedly
  Now through the street,
That any beholder
  Might fancy my feet
Were treading on roses
  All fragrant and sweet.

The stifling and choking,
  The odors and stenches,
Are quieted now;
  The olfactory wrenches,
That maddened my brow,
  Are gone. Ah! those horrible,
    Horrible stenches!

The sickness—the nausea—
  The pitiless pain,
Have ceased with the smelling
  That maddened my brain;
With the smell of the garbage
  That rose to my brain.

And, oh! of all odors,
  That odor the worst—
The odor commingled
  Of sauerkraut accursed;
The odors of fish
  And of sauerkraut accursed—
That torture no more
  In my nostril is nursed.

And, ah! let it never
  Be foolishly said
That I am regretting
  The cold in my head;
The cold whence this numbness
  Of smelling is bred.

For now I walk happily,
  Fearless of any
Diversified odors—
  Although there are many;
For my nostril is choked,
  And I care not for any.

And happy am I with
  A cold in my head!
The dank exhalation
  From garbage-heaps bred,
The sewerage and filth
  Upon which hogs are fed,
Never trouble me, bless'd
  With a cold in my head.

A PUNGENT CONSIDERATION OF THE VARIOUS TRADES AND CALLINGS.

Of all the trades that men may call
  Unpleasant and offensive,
The editor's is worst of all,
  For he is ever pen-sive;
His leaders lead to nothing high,
  His columns are unstable,
And though the printers make him pie,
  It does not suit his table.

The carpenter—his course is plane,
  His bit is always near him;
He augers every hour of gain,
  He chisels—and none jeer him;
He shaves, yet is not close, they say;
  The public pay his board, sir;
Full of wise saws, he bores away,
  And so he swells his hoard, sir.

St. Crispin's son—the man of shoes,
  Has awl things at control, sir;
He waxes wealthy in his views,
  But ne'er neglects his sole, sir;
His is, indeed, a heeling trade;
  And when he comes to casting
The toe-tal profits he has made,
  We find his ends are lasting.

The tailor, too, gives fits to all,
  Yet never gets a basting;
His cabbages, however small,
  Are most delicious tasting;
His goose is heated—happy prig!
  Unstinted in his measure;
He always plays at thimble-rig,
  And seams a man of pleasure.

The farmer reaps a fortune plump,
  Though harrowed, far from woe, sir;
His spade forever proves a trump,
  His book is I've-an-hoe, sir;
However corned, he does not slip;
  Though husky, never hoarse, sir;
And in a plowshare partnership
  He gets his share, of course, sir.

The sailor on the giddy mast—
  Comparatively master—
Has many a bulwark round him cast
  To wave away disaster;
Even shrouds to him are full of life,
  His mainstay still is o'er him,
A gallant and a top-gallant crew
  Of beaux esprits before him.

The sturdy Irish laborer picks
  And climbs to fame—'tis funny!
He deals with none but regular bricks,
  And so he pockets money;
One friend sticks to him (mortar 'tis)
  In hodden gray, unbaffled,
He leaves below an honest name
  When he ascends the scaffold.

The printer, though his case be hard,
  Yet sticks not at his hap, sir;
'Tis his to canonize the bard,
  And trim a Roman Cap, sir.
Some go two-forty—what of that?
  He goes it by the thousand;
A man of form, and fond of fat,
  He loves the song I now send.

The engine-driver, if we track
  His outward semblance deeper,
Has got some very tender traits—
  He ne'er disturbs the sleeper;
And when you switch him as he goes,
  He whistles all the louder;
And should you brake him on the wheel,
  It only makes him prouder.

I launched this skiff of rhymes upon
  The trade-winds of the Muses,
Through pungent seas they've borne it on,
  The boat no rudder uses;

So masticate its meaning once,
And judge not sternly of it—
You'll find a freight of little puns,
And very little profit.

THE FERRY-BOAT.

Let them rave of the bowers that are beaming with roses,
Where young lovers whisper the moonlight away,
But the scene that I fix for my courtship discloses
Attractions, though public, more brilliant and gay.
What care I for walks in the leaf-shaded alleys,
For kisses in hay-fields, and sighs on the hill;
For love is but love in the streets or the valleys,
And all that it needs is an intimate will.
Oh, give me a merry short trip on the ferry,
With I and my fair in a corner ensconced;
'Mid the hustling and bustling, the jostling and tussling,
We sit unobserved, in our own dreams entranced.

It is exquisite, very, that trip on the ferry—
The roar of the wheels in a fine double bass
To the tenor of whispers from dear rosy lispers,
With love in their hearts, but reproof on each face.
What countless sensations! What men from all nations
Are crowded and jammed in the one little boat!
There are German and Spanish, Dutch, Irish, and Danish—
Our ark is a species of Babel afloat.
But still it is merry, that trip on the ferry,
With I and my fair in a corner ensconced;
'Mid the crowd of stock-brokers and Joe Miller jokers,
We sit unobserved, in our own dreams entranced.

The chains rattle loudly, the steam whistles proudly,
The wheels beat the water, the furnaces flame;
Some laggards, belated, are gibed at and rated,
While some make a jump, but fall short of their aim;
And there on the ferry, like straws in iced sherry,
They stick half way up, calling fiercely for aid;
While the lucky ones, laughing, and sneering, and chaffing,
Are straight to New York from the Fulton conveyed.
'Tis dangerous, very, that jump for the ferry,
But what's it to us in our corner ensconced;
If a fool likes to do it, why then let him rue it—
We sit unobserved, in our own dreams entranced.

What is life but a ferry—a dismal one, very—
  It starts from the cradle, its goal is the grave;
And yet we can make it, if rightly we take it,
  A sweet, pleasant trip o'er a sun-gilded wave.
With a partner to cheer us, a friend sitting near us,
  With Truth for our pilot and Fame for our fire,
We can make it as pleasant as this is at present,
  And what more delightful could mortal desire?
    A transient, but merry trip over the ferry—
      The joy that it gives from its briefness enhanced—
    With the hustling and bustling, the jostling and tussling,
      We'll sit unobservèd, in our own dreams entranced.

COMPOSITION DUETT.

ROMEO (*the romantic man*).

In my dreams beneath a willow,
  I heard thee cry "Depart!"

FUBBS (*the matter-of-fact individual*).

"And an ice-cream of Vanilla
  Was not colder than thy heart."

ROMEO.

Ah! Love's fever, how imperious—
  How the passionate pain exalts!

FUBBS.

"Fever, really! Are you serious?
  Try a dose of Epsom salts."

ROMEO.

Laura Liddowe! Laura Liddowe!
  Thou hast ta'en thy lover's life.

FUBBS (*indignantly*).

"Would you make the maid a widow
  Who has never been a wife?"

ROMEO.

When I'm dead, I pray thee gather
  Flowers to deck my lowly bed—

FUBBS.

"Pooh! I say—the girl would rather
  One live beau than fifty dead."

ROMEO.

Laura Liddowe, might a flowery
Band our hearts together bind—

FUBBS (*urgently*).

"Say you'll fix a handsome dowry,
And I guarantee her kind."

ROMEO.

Shine, ye stars—ah! shine above her;
Bear my passions in your beams—

FUBBS (*indignantly*).

"Tell her plumply that you love her,
And have done with idle dreams."

ROMEO.

Wilt thou have me? Say, my fairest
Queen; for thus my fancy dubbs—

FUBBS (*gloriously*).

"I would simply say, 'My dearest,
Will you be my Mrs. Fubbs?'"

LE PRINTEMPS.

FROM THE FRENCH OF DESANGIER.

Youths and maidens, come,
The skies are bright above,
Blow the fife and strike the drum—
Let us sing of love.

The thick leaves overhead
Will fling a shadow deep
Over the ferny bed
On which we sit or sleep.

Thanks to their pulses high,
And the high sun, bright as gold,
Phillis becomes less shy
As Colin becomes more bold.

Agnes would believe
That love's delicious glow
Her breast will never heave
When violets cease to blow.

Spurning the restraint
  Imposed by fashion's goddess,
Hearts their bondage break,
  Heaving breasts the bodice.

Season, sweetly strung,
  How thy genial charm
Makes the mother young,
  And makes the daughter warm.

Now the dotard feels
  A thrill of new desire,
O'er the husband steals
  The lover's former fire.

The river, murmuring on,
  The lambs that frisk and fling,
The sky, whose clouds are gone—
  All nature seems to sing.

Every hour that rolls
  Leads us near the time
When to our wintry souls
  The year will have no prime.

Therefore, youths and maidens, come,
  While the skies are bright above—
  Bright, and warm, and vast above—
Blow the fife and strike the drum,
  And let us sing of love.

MY SOUTHWARD WINGING ORIOLE.

The fading sunset's golden light
  Was glancing over town and river,
When flashed a vision on my sight,
  One moment seen, yet fixed forever.

On memory's retina still glows
  That picture, all my heart entrancing;
The rosy mouth—the brow of snow,
  The blue eyes in sweet dalliance dancing.

The dimples in her soft chin set,
  Her maiden smile serene and peaceful,
And those brown locks—ah! never yet
  Were tendrils of the vine more graceful.

She came in robes of Quaker hue,
  Such livery as the fawns inherit;
But then her bonnet's dazzling blue
  Gave hint of her celestial spirit.

"Great heavens!" I cried; "sweet sunny South,
  Your praise—all poets well may rhyme it,
If such bright flowers as yonder mouth
  Are native to this glowing climate?

"But no; this fresh and joyous face,
  This eye, from which gay fancy sallies,
This artless and yet winning grace
  All speak of Northern hills and valleys.

"The languid beauties hereaway,
  Who half the year for cool air stifle,
Their features lack the subtle play
  Which leaves this face without a rival."

And thus I thought, and thus I dreamed,
  Your life in various colors painting;
Now Hope's blest ray upon me beamed,
  Now left me in the darkness fainting.

Ah! well, these dreams are idle all—
  Mere shadows—and we chase them blindly;
But yet my pulses rise or fall
  Just as I find you cross or kindly.

And still on memory's retina glows
  Thy picture, heart and brain entrancing;
The rosy mouth—the brow of snow,
  And those small feet just made for dancing.

Ne'er may the future bring regret
  For these bright dreams which now caress me,
But, long in golden circle set,
  May this fair image smile to bless me.

BARON RENFREW'S BALL.[29]

'Twas a grand display was the prince's ball,
A pageant or fête, or what you may call
    A brilliant coruscation,
Where ladies and knights of noble worth
Enchanted a prince of royal birth
    By a royal demonstration.

Like queens arrayed in their regal guise,
They charmed the prince with dazzling eyes,
Fair ladies of rank and station,
Till the floor gave way, and down they sprawled,
In a tableaux style, which the artists called
A floor-all decoration.

At the prince's feet like flowers they were laid,
In the brightest bouquet ever made,
For a prince's choice to falter—
Perplexed to find, where all were rare,
Which was the fairest of the fair
To cull for a queenly altar.

But soon the floor was set aright,
And Peter Cooper's face grew bright,
When, like the swell of an organ,
All hearts beat time to the first quadrille,
And the prince confessed to a joyous thrill
As he danced with Mrs. Morgan.

Then came the waltz—the Prince's Own—
And every bar and brilliant tone
Had music's sweetest grace on ;
But the prince himself ne'er felt its charm
Till he slightly clasped, with circling arm,
That lovely girl, Miss Mason.

But ah ! the work went bravely on,
And meek-eyed Peace a trophy won
By the magic art of the dancers ;
For the daring prince's next exploit
Was to league with Scott's Camilla Hoyt,
And overcome the Lancers.

Besides these three, he deigned to yield
His hand to Mrs. M. B. Field,
Miss Jay, and Miss Van Buren ;
Miss Russell, too, was given a place—
All beauties famous for their grace
From Texas to Lake Huron.

With Mrs. Kernochan he "lanced,"
With Mrs. Edward Cooper danced,
With Mrs. Belmont capered ;
With fair Miss Fish, in fairy rig,
He tripped a sort of royal jig,
And next Miss Butler favored.

And thus, 'mid many hopes and fears,
By the brilliant light of the chandeliers,
Did they gayly quaff and revel;
Well pleased to charm a royal prince—
The only one from old England since
George Washington was a rebel.

And so the fleeting hours went by,
And watches stopped—lest Time should fly—
Or that they winding wanted;
Old matrons dozed, and papas smiled,
And many a fair one was beguiled
As the prince danced on, undaunted.

'Tis now a dream—the prince's ball,
Its vanished glories, one and all,
The scenes of the fairy tales;
For Cinderella herself was there,
And Barnum keeps for trial fair
The beautiful slipper deposited there
By his highness the Prince of Wales.

THE CRUSADER SONG.

FROM THE RUSSIAN.

Before the holy image
I thrice have bent to-night,
And, having paid my orisons,
Now rush to join the fight;
The fight of faith and fatherland,
For this I rush afar—
My life and lance for Russia,
My fealty to the Czar.

My sword—the only heritage
My valiant fathers left,
Hath bit the flesh of Sweden,
And many a Tartar cleft.
Too long in shameful idleness
The rusting blade hath lain,
And now it longs for blood to cleanse
The dull, corroding stain.

From the summit of the Balkan
Our brethren stretch their hands;
They pray to us to rescue them—
Their prayers become commands.

We feel for them, we'll fight for them,
  For God and us they bleed;
The weaponed strength of Russia goes
  To strike for Russia's creed.

The memories of our Church are twined
  Round Kiew's white-bastioned crest,
The loveliest and the brightest town
  That ever Turk oppressed.
Those memories are consecrate,
  And shadow forth the doom
Which gathers strength in silence,
  And will quickly burst in gloom.

The cross of pain, the spear of might,
  On these our strength we cast;
The hand of God protected both
  In ages long o'erpast;
Think you our hearts so soon forget
  The sires for whom we mourn?
Their sons shall bear the flag of faith
  As it by them was borne.

We go to break the Moslem's pride,
  To crush his creed accursed;
Then welcome be the Holy War,
  And let its tempest burst.
Be this our victor battle-cry
  As east and south we press—
"The God that blesses Russia,
  And the Czar the Russians bless!"

SONG: PHILANTHROPIC AND PIRATICAL.

We've borne too long the idiot wrong of Cuba's tyrant masters,
And tamely ta'en from shattered Spain dishonors and disasters.
The camel's back at length will crack—nor are we like dumb cattle:
Our patient strength has failed at length—peace only comes by battle.
Ring out the bells! our banner swells, in Freedom's breezes blowing;
To arms and up! this bitter cup is filled to overflowing.

Nor pray nor speak, but let us seek redress in tones of thunder;
They slew our brave who went to save the land they rob and plunder.
Around the Moro's grim façade the soul of Lopez wanders,
And Crittenden—a glorious shade—beside him walks and ponders.
O God of Peace! that such as these like dogs should be garroted—
Choked out of life by Spanish beasts—fierce, bloody, and besotted.

To arms and up! we brim the cup to vengeance and to glory!
By Western zeal let "Old Castile" be taught a different story;
Let Spanish Dons now learn for once how great the power they've slighted;
By guns and swords, not pens and words, must Cuba's wrongs be righted.
They've chained our men, they've seized our ships, their yoke around us twining;
Our "stars" are in a long eclipse—we'll bring them forth more shining.

What pulsing starts from youthful hearts to hear the tocsin pealing!
Their glittering eyes, their fierce replies, betray the inward feeling—
The hidden thirst of vengeance, nursed through years of mute, restraining.
Hurra! that torrent forth has burst, no more in meek complaining.
The "One Lone Star" shall not be far from our immortal cluster;
The Southern Queen shall soon be seen arrayed in Western lustre.

Then, brethren, up! one parting cup to Washington and Jackson;
Our sprouting tree of liberty no Spaniard lays an axe on.
By Freedom's God! our lavish blood shall water it to blossom;
No foul garrote shall press our throat, though balls may pierce our bosom.
Ring out the bells! our banner swells, in Freedom's breezes blowing;
To arms and up! this bitter cup is filled to overflowing.

A WALL STREET USURER ON RUSTIC BLISS.

SECOND ODE—FIFTH BOOK OF HORACE.

"Beatus ille qui procul negotiis."

He is bless'd who, far from city toil,
  As those who lived in elder time,
Furrows his own paternal soil,
  Unstained of all usurious crime.
The trumpet's voice he will not heed,
  Nor billows raging fierce and loud;
He shuns the bar where suitors plead,
  He shuns the portals of the proud.

Around the poplar's lofty tops
  He twines the creepers of the vine,
Or with his pruning sickle lops
  The boughs that yield no generous wine;
Or in the lonely valley sees
  His herds of cattle wandering far,
Or stores the honey of his bees
  In chestnut bowl and crystal jar.

Or shears his sheep, or, in the hours
  When her bright brow old Autumn rears,
Adorned with mellow fruits and flowers,
  How gladly will he pluck the pears,
And the rich, gushing grape, that vies
  With purple, as a gift and charm
To those benignant deities
  Who guard from blight his little farm.

He sleeps beneath some aged oak,
  Or in the tangled meadow lies,
While waters leap from rock to rock,
  And woodland song-birds fill the skies,
And fountains flow with murmuring streams,
  Inviting sleep and blissful dreams.

But when old Winter, grim and hoar,
  With rain and snow o'erfloods the soil,
With dogs he hunts the savage boar
  Into his interwoven toil;
The hungry thrush may vainly seek
  To shun his net; the timorous hare,
And the wild crane, whose pinions seek
  A foreign clime, reward his care.

Amid such tranquil sports as these
  We might forget—oh! blissful rest—
Those harassing anxieties
  Which love entails on every breast.
Children, a wife to tend the house
  (Such as the Sabine mothers give),
A sunburnt and industrious spouse—
  Even such in old Apulia live—
Who piles the hallowed hearth on high
With blazing fagots, bright and dry,
As home her weary husband turns
To where the cottage beacon burns.
In wicker sheds she shuts the kine,
  Their milk delicious to the taste,
And, drawing forth her finest wine,
  Prepares the unbought and temperate feast.

Oh! not the richest feast that e'er
  For king was spread could please me more;
Nor dainty fishes, sweet and rare,
  Nor pheasants brought from India's shore;
Not all the banquet wealth allows
  A keener relish could attain
Than olives gathered from the boughs,
  And sorrel growing on the plain,

Or mallows—food of all the best
  To keep us free from inward harm;
Or the young lamb, with which I feast
  The guardian god who shields my farm.

In such a life, how sweet to see
  The well-fed sheep returning home,
And weary oxen, droopingly,
  With an inverted ploughshare come,
While numerous laborers join their mirth
  Around our happy household hearth.
The usurer Alpheus, sick of gain,
  To turn a country farmer bent,
Thus sang the pleasures of the plain,
  And vowed to quit his cent per cent;
But Avarice comes—the sweet dream flies,
And back once more to Rome the veteran usurer hies.

LETTER FROM JOHN BULL, ESQ., TO JEREMIAH SLY, ESQ., COTTON BROKER, NEW YORK.

We are fighting for the Turks, Jerry Sly, Jerry Sly;
We are fighting for the Turks, Jerry Sly;
    We are fighting for the Turks,
    And bombarding Russian works,
But a hidden purpose lurks in our eye, Jerry Sly—
Yes, a hidden purpose lurks in our eye.

If the Turks were let alone, Jerry Sly, Jerry Sly;
If the Turks were let alone, Jerry Sly,
    Where were Franky Joseph's throne?
    Wouldn't Hungary have her own?
And would Poland longer groan in her chains, Jerry Sly?
And would Poland hopeless groan in her chains?

Wouldn't Italy be up, Jerry Sly, Jerry Sly?
Wouldn't Italy be up, Jerry Sly?
    Where would revolution stop?
    'Tis a hydra-headed crop;
Into England it might pop, as you know, Jerry Sly,
And the queen would have to hop, as you know.

For a week or something more, Jerry Sly, Jerry Sly;
For a week or something more, Jerry Sly,
    We heard the cannon roar
    All along Silistria's shore,
But no volley did we pour for the Turks, Jerry Sly?
But we hoped that all was o'er with the Turks.

Oh! we helped the Turks a deal, Jerry Sly, Jerry Sly;
Aberdeen declares a deal, Jerry Sly;
We held back their "headlong zeal,"
Gave the Cossacks time to heal
The bites of Turkish steel, as you know, Jerry Sly;
'Tis a dangerous thing is zeal, as you know.

The Crimea we will take, Jerry Sly, Jerry Sly,
When the Russ is not awake, Jerry Sly;
And the Baltic we will make
Just a little English lake,
Where the queen a cruise can take, with her spouse, Jerry Sly.
(Lord of heaven, some pity take on her spouse!)

Thus we're fighting for the Turks, Jerry Sly, Jerry Sly;
To the Turks we give our aid, Jerry Sly, Jerry Sly;
To the Turks such precious aid, Jerry Sly,
That their soldiers we delayed,
Beating back the Russian raid,
While long protocols we made—they're in print—Jerry Sly;
No one reads them, I'm afraid, though in print.

Then we sent them Lord Dundas, Jerry Sly, Jerry Sly;
Sent them Admiral Dundas, Jerry Sly,
Saying, "Let the Russians pass!"
(He's a hoary, driveling ass,
Who, unless the sea were glass, wouldn't budge, Jerry Sly.)
So Sinope came to pass, as we judge.

As Sebastopol was strong, Jerry Sly, Jerry Sly,
And we hate to fight the strong, Jerry Sly,
We did with coward wrong
To unarmed Odessa throng—
By the rules of war 'twas wrong, as is said, Jerry Sly—
But her courage made her strong: so we fled.

Thus we're fighting for the Turks, Jerry Sly;
We are fighting for the Turks,
And bombarding Russian works,
But a hidden purpose lurks in our eye, Jerry Sly—
A most sinister purpose lurks in our eye.

THE AUTHOR'S RITUAL.

Who'er would desire to write a book
In days of such severe morality,
Let him even upon this precept look:
That to tell the truth is a plump rascality.

The world so virtuous now has grown
  That cant is the only way of wooing it,
The dog don't object to steal the bone,
  But barks when he's righteously kicked for doing it.

If to please the crowd you only write,
  Declare that your readers are all seraphim;
That this is the only age of light,
  And that all before with guilt were very dim.
Declare that if ever the angels trod
  A sinless earth, they now are treading it;
That your fathers deserved the wrath of God,
  And you wonder he took so long in shedding it;

But that, now the world is filled with saints,
  Your strongest praise than their worth is fainter;
The brighter each portrait the artist paints,
  Why, the more the painted applaud the painter.
In fact, 'tis the readiest thing on earth
  To win your way by fulsome flattery;
But make of a foible of vice your mirth,
  And its friends indict you for tort and battery.

Declare that each woman is now as pure
  As the new-fallen snow on the Himalayas;
That never did queen with more regal mien
  Or dignified footstep skim a daïs;
Declare that the moon and each starry world
  Grows dim in the blaze of her eyes' full lustre—
That the tendril vine has more neatly curled
  Since it borrowed the grace of her ringlet's cluster.

Declare to the men they are brave and just,
  Fulfilling in peace each ordination—
That they never are plagued with wine or lust,
  Nor find in mammon the least temptation;
Declare that each man who pretends to faith
  Devoutly feels what his tongue professes;
That truth gives her sanction to all he saith,
  And that virtue his every action blesses.

In short, if you will but tell lies enough,
  Giving each grown babe his toy of coral,
You may sell a heap of the baldest stuff
  That ever a parson dubbed as "moral!"
To "hold up the mirror" is not your part—
  The likeness then would be far too real;
The world from its own foul face would start—
  You must give it a rainbow-hued ideal.

THE OLD BACHELOR'S NEW YEAR.

Oh, the spring hath less of brightness
Every year,
And the snow a ghastlier whiteness
Every year;
Nor do summer blossoms quicken,
Nor does autumn fruitage thicken
As it did—the seasons sicken
Every year.

It is growing cold and colder
Every year,
And I feel that I am older
Every year;
And my limbs are less elastic,
And my fancy not so plastic—
Yea, my habits grow monastic
Every year.

'Tis becoming bleak and bleaker
Every year,
And my hopes are waxing weaker
Every year;
Care I now for merry dancing,
Or for eyes with passion glancing?
Love is less and less entrancing
Every year.

Oh, the days that I have squandered
Every year,
And the friendships rudely sundered
Every year;
Of the ties that might have twined me,
Until time to death resigned me,
My infirmities remind me
Every year.

Sad and sad to look before us
Every year,
With a heavier shadow o'er us
Every year;
To behold each blossom faded,
And to know we might have made it
An immortal garland, braided
Round the year.

Many a spectral, beckoning finger,
  Year by year,
Chides me that so long I linger,
  Year by year;
Every early comrade sleeping
In the church-yard, whither, weeping,
I—alone unwept—am creeping
  Year by year.

IN MEMORIAM.

QUEEN VARIETY—A SKETCH FROM LIFE.

A summer twilight, soft, serene,
  When—led by one, her earliest vassal—
The poet first beheld the queen
  Of many hearts and Carbon Castle.

An oval face, the eyes as clear
  As star-gleams on a fountain dashing;
The brows where pleasant thoughts appear
  Forever varied, changing, flashing.

A wealth of beauty seldom seen,
  A regal grace of form and gesture;
And—as might well befit a queen—
  Some silken opulence of vesture.

A queen by right of power to reign,
  Her sceptre hid in flowers that wreathe it,
For crown a royalty of brain,
  With a true woman's heart beneath it.

Eyes black and luminous, searching out
  The very soul's recondite essence;
And ease which sets at ease all doubt,
  Even of the timid, in her presence.

Oh, armory of a woman's wit,
  With side-arm smiles from floor to rafter,
I've seen a thousand facts submit
  Before her fire of Minié laughter.

Sweet laughter, silvery as the strain
  Which the lark sings when heavenward going;
Prismatic bubbles of the brain
  In currents musical outflowing.

Ah me! the long, calm summer eve,
The dusky twilight closing round us;
The porch wherein her words did weave
New meshes to the net that bound us.

The very breezes seemed to move
On tiptoe, dallying with her graces;
The fountains in the dark alcove
Shot starward up with listening faces.

She sings—and not the oriole's throat
Pours flusher music summer mornings;
Each gesture of the hand or foot
Is instinct with most subtle warnings.

A garland from Titania's bower,
Where twice the same leaves never enter,
Save only one unvarying flower—
The rose of kindness in the centre.

A crown of jewels or a ring
In different lights each moment changing;
A fancy ever on the wing,
To novel scenes and topics ranging.

The fairy rooms, the glittering queen,
The many splendors scattered round us;
The rich good taste which ruled, I ween,
Where that sweet summer evening found us.

The ebony casket of cigars—
On each brown tube a memory lingers;
That night beneath the watching stars
No sweeter contrast to white fingers.

Peace to that casket I have said,
And peace be with the golden-throttled
Small flasks in which lay iced and hid
The sun-wines they are dust who bottled.

The echoes floating, fluttering yet,
From all dear nooks of memory starting;
The talisman—"We once have met
And parted, neither glad for parting:"

No cloud this halcyon memory screen,
Raze rather all that leads or follows;
And let this evening with our queen
Be still her faithful vassal's solace.

SECOND BOOK OF HORACE, SIXTEENTH ODE.

FREELY TRANSLATED BY CHARLES BROADBENT.

TO WIDESWARTH.

Wideswarth, the man who sails on the wide ocean
  When a dark tempest has obscured the moon,
And not a star shines through the fierce commotion
  Of warring clouds along the horizon strewn—
No light to guide his vessel—will he cease
To ask of heaven the one great boon of peace?

Thrace prays for peace when her wild lances shiver
  Amid the shock of battle, and for peace
The Mede, whose shoulders wear the graceful quiver,
  Prays to the gods—but it is not for these;
Not by rich gems the treasure can be bought,
Gold crowns and purple can affect it not.

'Tis not in ancient pride or regal treasure
  To win us rest; nor can the arm of law
Eject grim care from the abode of pleasure,
  Nor bid it from the inmost heart withdraw;
Around the gilded roof grief wings its flight,
Even like an owl amid the noonday light.

The man has peace who, happy on a little,
  Sits down contented to his frugal board;
Who knows and feels that Fortune's gifts are brittle,
  Nor like a miser seeks to swell his hoard;
Him neither care nor avarice will keep
From days of joy and nights of gentle sleep.

Why do we change our country for another,
  That glows perchance beneath a brighter sun?
Can we escape ourselves, or can we smother
  The griefs that with us o'er the wide earth run?
Swift as the stag, and with the whirlwind's force,
They climb the ship, and ride beside the horse.

A mind well based ne'er questions of the morrow—
  It feels the present, and enjoys the hour;
Nor asks the future for its share of sorrow—
  'Twill come one day, and we must bide its power.
Even then a smile will gild the gloomy strife,
And mingle sweetness in the cup of life.

Fate snatched away Achilles ere his glory
  In its meridian brilliancy had shone;
Tithonus wept that he grew old and hoary,
  And lived, though all that he hath loved were gone;
And Time with partial hand may give to me
Some joy or hope that it denied to thee.

A hundred flocks bleat round your happy dwelling,
  Sicilian heifers low, and horses neigh;
Rich purple robes, of costly odors smelling,
  Enwrap you round; while on my humble way
Fate hath bestowed a smaller 'state—some wit,
And a contempt for those who laugh at it.

A BLOOMER LYRIC,

"MOST MUSICAL, MOST MELANCHOLY."

Oh, ladies, list the ditty sung—
  A doleful ditty, very—
About a Bloomer fair and young—
  They called her Mrs. Perry;
Who, quite regardless of the law,
  Did leave her spouse—oh, heavens!
She wore the pants, and panted for
  The lawless love of Levins.
            Bow, wow, wow.

In Monson, Mass., the luckless spouse
  (Made lucky by the riddance)
Proprieted a virtuous house
  (That is to say, he did once);
But Levins Clough, with brass enough
  To make a copper kettle,
On Mrs. P. (ah! woe is me!)
  His lewd regard did settle.
            Bow, wow, wow.

And she did say unto herself,
  "Shall I, the slave of duty,
Be laid upon the matron shelf
  To waste away my beauty?
No, no. Henceforth I bear command,
  Though prim Miss Prudence quarrels;
I've worn my husband's breeches, and
  I'll make a breach of morals."
            Bow, wow, wow.

So, like a "high, strong-minded wife,"
  She told him her intention,
Prepared to face his jealous strife
  Against her vow's infraction;
But he (oh! what a brute is man!)
  Cried, "If we may be sundered—
I'm very poor—but yet I can
  Afford to pay a hundred."
    Bow, wow, wow.

So let us drink to Mr. P.
  Both in Champagne and Sherry—
May each be-Bloomered husband be
  As fortunate as Perry.
And may the naughty girls, who wear
  The manly pants and braces,
Ne'er be embraced by manly arms,
  Nor kissed by bearded faces.
    Bow, wow, wow.

And here's a glass to Mrs. P.—
  A full-fledged Bloomer, very—
Who found a way at least to make
  Her doleful husband merry.
And may all wives, who lead their lives
  At sixes and at sevens,
Exchange a husband's honest love
  For such a scamp as Levins.
    Bow, wow, wow.

NEW YORK CRYSTAL PALACE.

Ye wha direct the Exhibition,
An' manage a' things wi' precision,
Mock na a simple bard's petition,
    Wha's pouch is bare,
An' yet wad like to feast his vision
    On yon big fair.

'Tis true I'm but a poortith wight,
Come here to wrastle and to fight
For roof an' hearth, claes an' bite;
    My voice is sma',
But no afeard to crack the right
    Afore ye a'.

Though fifty cents be sma' to you,
A mere card-counter, like eneugh,
There's mony an honest lad wad rue
That sma' amount;
His bairns' bellies maun be fu',
An' trifles count.

If yours were like a kintra show,
To which but aince we speer to go,
Your bonnie charge, though far frae low,
I wad na shun;
I'd in, an' tak the foremost row,
An' see the fun.

But yours is nae sic feckless play
That ane can ken it in a day,
Unless, in a bewildered way,
He gapes an' glowers;
Sic wark demands an' wad repay
Saxscore o' hours.

An' how, I ask, can chiels afford,
Wha's gains are sma' an' labor hard,
A muckle sum that should be shared
Wi' his wee bodies?
I'm feared they'd lack for bed an' board,
An' shoes an' duddies.

Forbye, in an industrial tilt,
Though ither flags be bonnier gilt,
Wha's banner should gang first in till't
Unless o' those
Wha's joints hae crack'd, wha's sweat was spilt
Afore it rose?

What hae the rich, the dizzen'd crowd,
In a' the place to mak them proud?
They've neither welded, wove, nor plow'd,
Nor blear'd their een,
Whyles Labor may proclaim aloud,
"The show is mine!"

"Frae deep foundation e'en to dome,
The glitt'rin' aisles through which you roam,
The gallery that, light as foam,
O'er a' expands,
The palace an' its treasures come
Frae these rough hands."

Let Sedgwick now—a sonsy man—
Tell the directors o' his plan,
An' say, "Though wrangly we began,
'Tis time to truckle;
A thousand mickle soon outrun
The fivescore muckle."

Here folk frae ilka clime are met—
A wae-disposed, monarchic set—
A' peerin' roun', if they can get
(Lang may they need them!)
Some proofs to say that "Labor yet
Wins nocht frae Freedom."

Ye may despise us an' ye will,
But we're the els maun foot your bill;
The "Upper Ten" hae looked their fill,
An', should you flout us,
I'm feared ye'll hae an empty till
At least without us.

An' what for no should we na win,
Some points demand it out an' in?
The stummocks o' us workin' men
Are easy snarlin',
But ower the whirligig we grin
Like Sternie's starlin'.

Let Sedgwick tak anither thought:
Kickshaws to labor's wame are naught,
Nor can we pay the prices sought
By those bright lasses
Frae whom mysel', yestreen, I bought
Twa jelly glasses.

Dupont an' Davis—soldiers baith—
I swear till ye, upon my aith,
That, though ye aft hae grappled death
Wi' sabres carvin',
Ye wadna bide the risin' wrath
O' downright starvin'.

I'm done; nor care I now a flea
If high or low you gar it be;
But this I swear, nae doit frae me
Your nieves shall mortar,
Till into your big house the key
Is "Cash—one quarter."

THE EVERGLADES WITHDRAW.

SENATORS YULEE AND MALLORY TAKING LEAVE.

As they rose to take their leave
  Of the old familiar hall,
Their manly sides did heave
  In the bitterness of gall;
'Twas a sad and gloomy hour
  To men so framed as they,
For, besides their loss of place and power,
  They also lost their pay;
Yes, besides their loss of place and power,
  They also lost their pay.

As they view the frescoed hall,
  Still loth to quit their mates,
In the filtered beams that fall
  Through the blazoned shields of state.
Though no argument for love
  Of our common flag they sought,
Yet the sunlight streaming from above
  This Union lesson taught—
Yea, the blessed sunlight from above
  This Union lesson taught:

"As the sun, supreme and bright,
  Shining equally on all,
Poureth down a common light
  On this crystal-covered hall,
So our Union—orb of orbs—
  Sheds a glory fixed and true,
Though the shield of every state absorbs
  Some beams of different hue;
Though the shield of every state absorbs
  Some beams of varied hue.

"Would you tear the temple down,
  Change our blessing to a bane,
And pluck from nationhood the crown
  It cost so much to gain?
If no inner voice upbraids,
  If no patriot promptings warn,
Back to your swamps and everglades
  Where alligators swarm—
Those Indian-haunted swamps and glades
  Where alligators swarm.

"We may hearken to your call,
  And take pity on your fate,
When the monsters round you crawl,
  And the red men lie in wait;
Some relief we may afford—
  But tempt us not too far;
A thousand years have not restored
  The Pleiads' wandering star—
The six bright sisters have ignored
  That sad, repentant star.

"Now go, if go you must;
  We fling the portals wide;
Go, if you think your quarrel just,
  And dare its trial bide;
Our Union's dome beneath
  We miss no single star,
No weapons shall our hands unsheath
  Your homeward way to bar—
Twine for yourselves a separate wreath,
  And shine a single star.

"Of many flowers and vines
  In glittering contrast, now
The garland of the Union shines
  On freedom's radiant brow;
The bud you gave take down,
  But think of this and heed—
To-day 'tis portion of a crown,
  To-morrow but a weed—
To-day 'tis part of Freedom's crown;
  Removed—a worthless weed."

* * * * *

The two grew pale and thin,
  And they trembled in their shoes;
Yea, every inch of quivering skin
  Exuded icy dews;
But to treason they were pledged,
  Though they found the trial sore,
And, as nearer to the door they edged,
  They blubbered more and more;
To Disunion as they nearer edged,
  Her features shocked them more.

At last they fled away
  Into darkness—to their fate.
God speed them! we can only pray,
  And save them ere too late;

And God save all the weak
Who, from some fancied wrong,
Throw off—not knowing what they seek—
The buckler of the strong—
The Union's bond to sever seek,
The buckler of the strong.

TEN YEARS TOO LATE.

I own thy beauty once did thrill
My every vein with living fire,
My soul lay subject to thy will,
To kill with frowns—with smiles inspire;
But passion calms its headlong tide,
And youthful dreams will dimmer grow
When met with that unyielding pride—
Such as was yours ten years ago.

One heedless word can oft destroy
The hope to which a soul is clinging;
The tender flower of love and joy
Can brook no storm across it winging.
So, lady, let us both forget
The thought 'tis only pain to know,
And meet as though we ne'er had met
In that past life—"ten years ago."

BIRTH OF THE BATTLE YEAR.

OMENS OF EIGHTEEN SIXTY-ONE.

Gloomy and dark was the night, when a Fate
Clamored, and loudly, outside the gate:
"Open and fling the Dead Year out—
Welcome the New with a festal shout!
'Tis a ruddy child, with dimpled limbs,
And eyes that no care or sorrow dims;
Welcome it, then, with cheers and hymns—
Welcome the young New Year!"

Never a laugh through the castle rang,
But the bolts shot back with a heavy clang;
The flickering lamps gave a wan blue light
As the blast rushed in from the sleety night;

And around the couch of the dying year,
With faces reflecting both sorrow and fear,
Gathered the waiters from far and near—
Not a smile for the young New Year.

Beneath black rafters, curving down
O'er a floor of black and walls of brown,
Stretched on a pallet, with struggling breath,
The Old Year sought the escape of death;
While around him stood, in a mute, sad ring,
Many who only had felt his sting,
But who feared some more evil and hideous thing
In the reign of the young New Year.

"Fling wide the carved and ponderous door:
Lift him gently, and walk before,
Ye with the hoods and rods of white;
Carry him out into empty night;
For the clock betokens the midnight hour,
And his death-knell tolls in the ivied tower—
This moment, for weal or woe, to power
Ascends the young New Year.

"Dark Fate, with clouds and shadows capped,
In whose wide mantle, close enwrapped,
The young New Year is hither borne,
Hath the world cause to smile or mourn?
What say the omens of his reign?
What do the Destinies ordain—
Is it peace or battle, joy or pain?
Speak for the young New Year."

No word the dark, mute Fate let fall
As her shadow flitted across the wall;
But, bending over the vacant couch,
One moment she appeared to crouch;
Then, rising, towering higher and higher,
Seen by the light of the flickering fire,
Just on her exit the lamps expire—
Sad sign for the young New Year.

"Trim the lights afresh till they all burn bright;
Fill the wassail bowl for one festal night;
Burn larger logs till the flames reveal
Those shapes which the shadows now conceal;
Let the oldest flagons of wine be brought,
And the best old stories our fathers taught,
And the songs that were dearest in youth be sought
To welcome the young New Year."

So passed the night in a feverish dream,
In pleasures that had a hectic gleam;
For beneath the gayest smile, thus forced,
Cold tremors of terror thrilled and coursed;
And the groined roof, curving grimly down
O'er a floor of black and walls of brown,
Had a mystical threat—a prophetic frown—
As we toasted the young New Year.

When morning dawned and the shadows fled,
We drew the curtains, and round the bed
All gathered to see what the Fate had left
To replace the Old Year, of life bereft.
'Twas a sickly child, of a wan, pale face,
With many a mutter and strange grimace—
"'Tis a poor exchange we have had in place
Of the dead and gone Old Year."

But let's make the best of the evils known—
Let the boldest front to the foe be shown;
For still in the heart of the nation dwells
A pulse that true to the Union swells;
And perhaps the omens we now deplore,
Heralding carnage from shore to shore,
May be lessons merely, and nothing more,
Designed for the young New Year.

So bring the garlands and deck the couch,
Let the prophets of good their faith avouch;
Let every foreboding of evil fade,
And the birth of this ominous year be made
So joyous and festive, with song and wine,
That, even though coming with ill design,
The purpose of wrong it may yet resign—
Thus we drink to the young New Year.

THIRTY YEARS OLD.

'Twas twelve o'clock, and the house was hushed;
The fire was low—'twas wintry weather;
The mirror with lurid light was flushed,
And the very chairs seemed to creep together.
I sat and thought, in a dreamy way,
Of dear old friends and dear old places,
And round me gathered an odd array
Of old, fantastic, friendly faces.

Sitting alone in my easy-chair,
  Slippered and gowned for a night of leisure,
Suddenly came a step on the stair,
  Halting and slow as an old man's measure.
Twisting around with a nervous start
  As I heard the door-knob click and rattle,
You could hear the beatings of my heart
  As I braced myself for a burglar battle.

Nearer and nearer the footsteps grew;
  Holding my breath, I braced my sinews;
Slower it came as closer it drew—
  "'Tis death," I muttered, "if this continues.
Come!" I cried, with a nervous twinge;
  And opening stealthily, half way shrinking,
The door revolved on its silver hinge,
  And my heart the while kept sinking—sinking.

In then popped an old white head,
  Curiously wrinkled, curiously ruddy:
"Old Father Time I am called," he said;
  "May I pay you a visit in your study?"
I laughed: "Oh ho! no burglar this!
  Welcome, old Time, thou doubt-dissolver;
But it's well for you, by Jove it is,
  That I hadn't my hand on a Colt's revolver."

Bitterly smiled the wrinkled man—
  Bitterly smiled as in sad derision:
"Killing old Time is an easy plan,
  Which thousands appear to have made their mission.
But you," and here he grimly bowed,
  The grimmest of all grim smiles dispensing,
"Are neither so hot-brained, nor half so loud
  As you were when the race was first commencing.

"You've learned, I guess, that the world is not
  A bowl in which only sweet things mingle;
That pleasure and pain are the common lot,
  Which seldom or never approach us single;
You are taught that words do not always show
  The heart's sincere and true confession;
And you've learned to scan the straight-laced man,
  Who is loudest and longest in fair profession."

"So far, all's well; but more remains:
  You must now take care of the dollars dirty;
A man should have something to show for his pains
  By the time he turns the stile of thirty.

Get you a wife!" At that fearful thought,
Waking, from out my chair I started;
"Copy!" my printer's devil cried,
And my vision of Time was a thing departed.

SIMILES.

One asked me where the sunlight grew,
And where it never dies?
In silence then I pointed to
The heaven in Sylvia's eyes.

Another, where the moon doth go
When paled by morning's glare?
"Gaze—gaze on Sylvia's breast of snow,
You'll see the moonlight there."

A third said, where doth Virtue rest?
Then forth my words did start:
"In Sylvia's face you'll find express'd
The goodness of her heart."

In search of beauty, grace, and wit,
No longer vainly stray,
Seek Sylvia's shrine, and at her feet
Your humblest homage pay.

NEW VERSION OF JOHN BROWN,

AS CHORUSED WITH IMMENSE EFFECT BY THE THIRD RHODE ISLAND NEGRO MINSTRELS, ATTACHED TO THE TENTH ARMY CORPS, MARCH 30, 1863.

Words by Rev. M. A. French, LL.D.; Music by Smiff.

[Ye first verse recites ye entirely triumphal manner of General Foster's entry into Port Royal Harbor, thereunto adding ye attitude in which ye general returned to Norff Caroliny.]

John G. Foster, oh! he brought his body South,
John G. Foster, oh! he brought his body South,
But Johnny has gone homeward with his fingers in his mouth,
As we go marching on.

Sing [chorus led by y'at distinguished soldier-man, Brigadier General E. E. Potter]
Sing Glory, glory hallelujah, etc., etc.

[Verse Second, chanted after ye manner of a dirge by ye Brigadier General Ledley, with ye starred, red shoulder-straps, sets forth ye object which brought ye great General Foster South, and reflects unbecomingly on ye powers of ye second Big Ingin Potter as a pleader.]

John G. Foster, oh! for Charleston he was hot,
John G. Foster, oh! for Charleston he was hot,
He gave his case to Potter, but ye pleader went to pot,
And Hunter marched him on.

Sing [chorus led by ye man with starred, red shoulder-straps, and illustrated with recriminating variations by ye great soldier-man Potter]
Sing Glory, glory hallelujah, etc., etc.

[Verse Third pays ye homage of devout admiration to ye unsurpassed and magnificent qualities of ye members of ye great Conqueror Foster's staff—all ye members of ye staff, without exception, joining in ye chorus at ye top of their voices, but none others singing. Chorus led by Surgeon Snelling, ye medical director.]

John G. Foster, oh! had a brilliant staff,
John G. Foster, oh! had a brilliant staff,
But honest Uncle David, oh! he couldn't stand their chaff,
And so he marched them on.

Sing [chorus led with a will by Lieutenant Colonel Francis Darr, ye chief commissary, who has pledged himself to issue extra rations of ye beverage known as "B. Whisky" to every one outside ye staff itself who will join in ye above verse]
Sing Glory, glory hallelujah, etc., etc.

[Verse Fourth recites, with a vigor and terseness that is refreshing, ye action taken by ye real Big Ingin of ye department, otherwise known as ye "Uncle David," and which action was communicated to ye brilliant staff aforesaid, as his high appreciation of their many excellent qualities, by ye fierce little man y'clept Major E. Worthington Smiff, with two effs.]

"Git out of my department," was our Uncle David's cry,
"Git out of my department," was our angry uncle's cry,
"Away to John G. Foster by the first conveyance fly,
And say I'm marching on."

Sing [chorus led by ye gay and festive Fessenden, with accompaniments of high old equestrian feats by ye boy Skinner and ye Acting Assistant Adjutant General Sealy, Acting Deputy Commodore Kinzie playing a break-down on ye banjo, and dancing ye same, while ye agent of Adams's Express chimes in with ye appropriate melody of a Hebrew's labial and dental harp]
Sing Glory, glory hallelujah, etc., etc.

[Verse Fifth is of ye deeply and touchingly pathetic kind, all the chief mourners having wet red cotton kerchiefs applied to their streaming eyes—the youth Samuel Stockton giving an occasional mop with his own wipe to ye streaming visionary orbs of General Seymour, whose hands are occupied in playing ye Dead March of Saul on a flute specially muffled for ye occasion by Lieutenant Colonel J. F. Hall, P.M.G.—meaning Provider of Musical Gear for the Department. Several cullud pussuns enter while this chorus is going, squeeze the red cotton kerchiefs into buckets, which are then carried down to ye good ship "John Faron," and there presented to ye great soldier-man E. E. Potter, in a neat speech, delivered in Congo dialect by ye boy "Congress," who has been retained for this ceremony.]

For John G. Foster, boys, we drop our tender tears,
And for the staff of Foster, boys, we shed severial tears;
They've gone up in a big balloon, and won't come down for years,
As we go marching on.

Sing [chorus led by Major Smiff, in a pair of blue soldiers' pants, fitting miraculously round his flanks]
Sing Glory, glory hallelujah,
Glory, glory hallelujah,
Glory, glory hallelujah,
As we go marching on.

Headquarters, Hilton Head, S.C.

O'MAHONY OF THE COMERAGHS.[30]

AN IMITATION OF THE ANCIENT IRISH, FROM THE WORKS OF THE FOUR MASTERS.

Give me your hand, O'Mahony;
Come to my heart, O'Mahony;
Friend of my soul, O'Mahony—
Chief of the Comeraghs!
Great have your toils been, O'Mahony;
Long has your watch been, O'Mahony;
Soon we will rest, O'Mahony—
Rest on the Comeraghs.

Let the dogs bark, O'Mahony;
Snarl at your heels, O'Mahony;
Snarling and barking, O'Mahony—
Chief of the Comeraghs!
This they can prove, O'Mahony—
All they can prove, O'Mahony—
They are not fit peers for O'Mahony,
Chief of the Comeraghs!

Black are the mountains, O'Mahony,
Swift are the streams, O'Mahony,
Fruitful and green are the valleys,
Far hid in the hushed Comeraghs.
Gray are the rocks, O'Mahony,
Golden the furzes, O'Mahony,
And purple and drooping the heather bells,
Clothing the Comeraghs.

Wildly the eagles, O'Mahony,
Scream o'er the peaks, O'Mahony,
Where the soft clouds of the morning
Stoop to the Comeraghs;
There we will rest, O'Mahony—
Rest on some ledge, O'Mahony,
Looking far down, O'Mahony—
Down from the Comeraghs.

Thousands of smoke-wreaths, O'Mahony,
Curling up bluely, O'Mahony,
From the thatched roofs beneath us,
Couched in the Comeraghs,
These we will waken, O'Mahony—
Waken with bugles, O'Mahony,
When our old banner goes homeward,
And visits the Comeraghs.

High on that ledge, O'Mahony,
Soon the green banner, O'Mahony,
"Sun-burst and harp" far flashing,
We'll give to the Comeraghs;
While thick through the valleys, O'Mahony,
Swarm all the true men, O'Mahony,
Shouting and pushing to join us,
High up on the steep Comeraghs.

Oh, by the God of all battles!
Oh, by the great God of battles!
The spirits of Hugh and Tyrconnell
Will smile on the Comeraghs.
By the ghosts of Kildare and of Lucan,
By the blood of O'Niel and Lord Edward,
By Emmet and Tone, our lost leaders,
We'll meet on the Comeraghs!

And then, like a torrent, O'Mahony,
Bursting down headlong, O'Mahony,
With fair Tipperary before us,
Behind us the grim Comeraghs,

Our land shall be free, O'Mahony—
Free as the eagles, O'Mahony,
Swooping and screaming in circles
Round the peaks of the great Comeraghs.

A TOAST AND A CHEER.

Gather round me, friends and comrades,
Let us drink a wassail bowl
"To the gentle hearts that love us,
To the pure and good of soul."
Life is short, too quickly passing,
And each year seems but a day—
Then accept each flying moment,
And enjoy it while we may.

What is sorrow met with courage?
For it can not bring disgrace,
And misfortune soon will vanish
If you look it in the face.
The coward shrinks and shivers
When the clouds their shadows cast;
The brave man trusts in God alone,
And struggles to the last.

What matter if dull slanders' tooth
Hath fastened on thy name,
Or years of labor find thee still
Without a golden fame?
Time settles with us, one and all:
So pay no worldly toll,
But drink "to those who love us,"
To the pure and good of soul.

LABOR'S WAR SONG.

Up, brethren, up! The world is not
So bad as some would make it,
Although we till a stubborn lot,
The plow of toil can break it;
And wheat—a sea of amber-froth—
White apple bloom and blushing cherries,
Will soon replace the thistle growth
And bitter bramble-berries.

For life's a field—a goodly field,
Where skill and long endeavor
Can make the barren wilderness
Her Eden bower forever.

Wherever Reason bids you go,
Be prompt and firm to follow;
Never build a house on Age's snow—
Tradition is but hollow.
With eyes that never shun the light,
Even though it show your past mischances,
Ride down the phantom blood of night
With troops of gallant fancies.
For life's a fight—a stubborn fight,
Where hope and fresh endeavor
Can overcome the host of Care
Forever and forever.

Should sorrow hem you in upon
Some bleak and lonely mountain,
Ne'er sigh for the forsaken lawn
And willow-shaded fountain;
But on the lightning-shivered top,
Learn of the eagle self-reliance,
And let the whirlwinds, as they drop,
Bear down your bold defiance.
For life's a fight—a gallant fight,
Where heart and strong endeavor
Shall win the palm and wear the palm
Forever and forever.

Besieged in Want's despised retreat,
And with resource but scanty,
Fling over half you'd like to eat,
That men may think you've plenty;
'Twas thus the Goth was driven from Rome,
And 'tis a maxim broadly Roman,
Whate'er the tears that fall at home,
Laugh loud before your foeman.
For life's a siege—a long-drawn siege,
A fierce protracted trial,
Where fate forever gives the palm
To hope and self-denial.

Should those you befriended in distress
Forget you—'tis the fashion—
Ne'er let them know their worthlessness
Had power to move your passion;

Be cool, and smile; the war of life
  Again may place you far above them;
And, should you chance to meet in strife,
  Then prove how much you love them.
    For life's a fight—a varying fight,
      Defeat and victory blended,
    Though wrong may triumph for a while,
      Right wins ere all is ended.

Should she who shared your summer lot
  Now shun your cold caresses,
Oh, blame her not—oh, hurt her not,
  But loose her golden jesses;
She never loved: no power on earth
  Can change a woman's true affection,
Nor is the haggard falcon worth
  A moment's sad dejection.
    Forget her frailty in the fight
      Where brain and bold endeavor
    Still win at will a changeless crown
      Forever and forever.

Avoid the fruitless strife of creed—
  You can not turn or guide it;
Let heaven award the victor's meed,
  And priest with priest decide it;
Believe that life is fleeting breath,
  Be just to man and love your neighbor,
And take this ritual for your faith—
  "Truth, temperance, and labor;"
    And thus the clouds of wrong that veil
      The heaven of life will sever,
    And the palm be his who wears the mail
      Of faith and firm endeavor.

TRANSLATIONS FROM HORACE—NO. XI.

BOOK III., ODE XXI. VERY FREELY TRANSLATED BY CHARLES BROADBENT.

Thou precious cask, sealed up on the same morning
  Mine eyes first opened to the sun's bright ray,
My dusty cellar-bin so long adorning,
  Come forth, and shed your fragrance on my way.
Whether you hold within you food of quarrel,
  Or wit, or love, or gentle sleep, or play,
Come from your shelf, my old and trusty barrel,
  We'll tap your side on this auspicious day.

Descend! for Wideswarth comes, and would inspect thee;
  Pour forth a flood of rich and mellow wine;
His soul will not Maine-lawishly reject thee,
  Though it has drunk the music of the Nine.
Old Cato's iron virtue is recorded,
  When full of thee, more tenderly to shine,
And many a careworn spirit is rewarded
  By the soft stimulant it finds in thine.

You ease the cares, and fears, and secret sorrows,
  Even of the wise, with each inspiring drop;
The trembling soul from you fresh courage borrows,
  And weak men cry to wealthy tyrants "Stop!"
Inspired with thee, the coward fears no longer,
  For thou unto him art a sturdy prop;
And poor men bow not down unto the stranger,
  But call them truly either knave or fop.

Come, Father Bacchus, and thou, Cyprian goddess,
  If in good humor, come, and bring along
The Graces, each with an ungirdled bodice—
  Come to the wine-cup and the gladdening song.
Come; and with mirth, and reveling, and dancing,
  We'll drive away whatever doleful seems,
Until bright Phœbus, o'er the mountain glancing,
  Outshines our light in his more plenteous beams.

THE SOUVENIR.

Ah! lady, howsoe'er it fall
  In Time's protracted race,
No flowers are needed to recall
  Thy pure and gentle face.
Within my heart thy image lives
  Through all life's busy hours,
While hope a greater perfume gives
  Than e'er was breathed by flowers.

But thanks for the memorial sent,
  The leaf and pansy too,
So neatly and so sweetly blent
  Within the ribbon blue.
When fades from every leaf the tint,
  Yet prized by me the same;
My beating heart shall proudly hint
  From whence the leaflets came.

Fit emblems of our summer hours,
  Without a cloud o'ercast,
The ribbon with its votive flowers
  Shall well recall the past—
Recall me to the beach of sand
  Where still the breakers shine,
And the gentle lady from whose hand
  This pansy passed to mine.

TO A WEALTHY AMATEUR CRITIC.

NOT AT ALL SUPPOSED TO BE WRITTEN BY LORD BYRON.

They tell me 'tis decided you condemn;
  You may be wrong, or I, perhaps, too vain;
I have no power the critic-power to stem,
  Nor, though I had, should I incur the pain;
Far easier is it for me to contemn
  You and your censure, as you scorn my strain.
My verse, it seems, calls forth your moral fears,
And o'er each page you shed "Pecksniffian" tears.

I wrote—still scribble—and for this have lost
  Some idle hours and your esteemed esteem;
Nor do I yet regret what it hath cost,
  Nor your sharp stricture as conclusive deem;
No tender flower that withers in the frost,
  No milksop minstrel in a sickly dream,
I still can sleep, walk, dance, and drink and dine,
Read your critiques—and some are really fine.

Your pen is of your life a thing apart—
  It is my whole existence. You may gain
An hour's amusement from the scribbling art—
  I write for bread; and if this be a stain
Upon my muse's 'scutcheon, ask your heart
  What could you do should fortune not remain
Your friend as now? Is this conclusion right—
I eat and scribble; you would starve and write?

You will proceed in your unguerdoned way,
  Condemning fifty and perusing one;
For me, so long as publishers will pay,
  I own my course of rhyming but begun.
Scalp as you will—no leniency, I pray;
  I neither hate a critic nor a dun;
Both, to be sure, are necessary evils—
Bad at the best, but not entirely devils.

"My verses are unequal." Be it so.
The world itself is full of woe and weal:
My pen still follows where my feelings flow,
And, good or bad, I speak the thing I feel.
As the muse wills it, why the jade may go;
I own no snaffle, and I use no heel;
The spavined Pegasus just takes her leisure,
Nor e'er for business will forego her pleasure.

I have no more to say—yet scribble still,
Eking out lines as spinners do their flax;
I had not lived till now could critics kill
(What rhyme will serve? Oh tell me, John G. Saxe!
In words, I know, thou hast a pretty skill—
Arch wielder of the jingling lingual axe.
See! conjured thus by him, their master-spirit
Rhymes hap into my lines soon as his name they hear it.)

And so farewell, my critic. I have brought
A friend to help me in the dire distress
Of that last stanza, where I else was caught
In what the world calls "an infernal mess."
Pour out your vials; let each sentence, fraught
With scorn and hatred, down upon me press;
I wait with meekest patience your review,
But, for the present, wish you well. Adieu!

SYLVIA.

Oh fly, my heart, to Sylvia fly,
And tell her that I pine—I die—
That every breath is but a sigh
Of grief—of pain—for love's desires.
Oh! tell her that so fondly shrined
Within my heart her image kind,
To all beside my soul is blind,
And love consumes me with its fires.

Oh! tell dear Sylvia that my brain
Awakes to life and hope again,
And thoughts that long have dormant lain
Come rushing at a headlong pace.
Oh say, my heart, that she alone
Has taught thee secrets long unknown,
And all my soul to her has flown—
The queen of beauty, love, and grace.

Return, my heart, from Sylvia's arms,
And say responsive love alarms
Her breast—so fair from virgin charms,
And bids me to her bosom fly.
My passion knows no purer bliss—
No love—no other life but this;
One hour of heaven in Sylvia's kiss—
One warm embrace of love—then die!

OLDEN MEMORIES.

Once again, with memory toying,
Brings a vision of the past—
Every olden will employing,
Opening treasures rich and vast.
Comes the early passion, seeming
All a world of rapturous bliss,
Boyhood's youthful hopes and dreaming
Crowned and radiant with a kiss.

Sorrowing pass in endless number
Shadowy files of marching years,
Buried in perpetual slumber,
Dimmed and stained with bitter tears.
Falls, in gentle dalliance, longing
O'er the mirror of my brain
One fond shape, and round it thronging,
Love and hope awake again.

Ah! that phantom let me follow;
Nothing can its place supply;
All succeeding hopes are hollow—
Dust and ashes to the eye.
Gone the glorious inspiration,
Girdling life with passion's zone,
Leaving but the dull stagnation
Of the heart when all is known.

Panting, longing for the highest,
And condemned to sigh in vain,
Seeing hopes that seemed the nighest
Vanish like a ghostly train:
Little left to make exertion
Worth the labor of its cost—
All that is a weary version
Of the perished and the lost.

Oh! in many a night of sorrow,
  When the hours have no relief,
And the darkness seems to borrow
  Deeper shadows from our grief—
Then again, with memory toying,
  Comes the vision of the past,
And on these our thoughts employing,
  Daylight breaks on us at last.

THEATRICAL GINGERNUTS.

In the upper crust ring there's a gay little clique,
  Who greatly admire one another,
And who go to the theatre once in a week
  To splurge it and kick up a bother.
They hire a cheap box, and within it they crowd
  Till as full as a bandbox they've packed it,
And they laugh and tell stories so noisy and loud
  That the whole of the house is distracted.

"The Gingernut Club" they are happily called,
  And a gingerbread crew you will find them;
By frowns of impatience and raps unappalled,
  No restraints of decorum can bind them;
They grin and they smirk, do these small upper "crust,"
  On a mutual plan of admiring,
And you'd think, as you watched them in pain and disgust,
  'Twas the house, not the box, they were hiring.

THE MARCHIONESS.

A summer languor dreaming o'er her face,
  A look half smile—yet breathing half a sigh—
Her step an echo whispering every grace,
  The stately marchioness sweeps grandly by.

A form that no rude gesture ever mars,
  Its glowing beauty radiant in repose;
Warm as the sunbeam—tranquil as the stars—
  Chaste as the lily—sensuous as the rose.

A brow as clear as April morning air,
  A mild gray eye of rich and lustrous hue;
Soft waving tresses of dark auburn hair,
  And shell-shaped ears, small and vein-penciled blue.

Lips, rivaling Cupid's roseate bed of flowers,
Stand sentry at a gate of glistening pearl;
A voice like melodies of childhood's hours
Bridging the lost years of the budding girl.

A vesture regal as an Orient queen,
A single jewel flashing vainly bright,
Seeking to rival with its brilliant sheen
Her swan-like bosom, pure and ivory white.

Her motion was one grand harmonious swell
Of charmed music when the eye is fair;
And as she walked, a fragrant incense fell
From garment perfumes to anoint the air.

Ah! life, that lingered in that placid look
Like dreams of sunset on some autumn day—
Ah! grief, my very soul its God forsook,
And in her smile passed all content away.

Fair marchioness, to every memory dear,
A glance of Eden's symmetry was given
To thee, to show how angels—even here—
Are found and draped to fill the choirs of heaven.

COOL OF THE EVENING.

Lady, it but little matters—
Matters least of all to you—
Whether I am warm or callous,
False to love, or fond and true.

Be assured you need not fear me—
Ne'er to you a pledge I'll break;
For the plain and simple reason
That I have no pledge to make.

All the sighs to you I offer
Shall be passionate and sincere;
Only when you hear them, tell me,
For I too might like to hear.

Blame not that my eyes will kindle
Gazing on a beauteous form—
Heaven has saved you from the insult
Of such glances, keen and warm.

Madam, from your thoughts dismiss me,
  Cease to rail against my name;
Time has been when you grew careless,
  And 'twas my care saved your fame.

I am careful, when not eager,
  Where to love would be a task;
And chaste as Joseph when temptation
  Woos me in an ugly mask.

Therefore silence, and forget me,
  Or my memory, at last,
May present some startling pictures
  Sketched and painted in the past.

THE MYSTIC VOICE.

Earth is a realm of ceaseless change,
  Where forms are merged in fresher forms,
And still the beautiful and strange
  Are cradled in destructive storms;
For Nature's alchemies impart
  New life to all transmuted things,
And lend the flesh-decaying heart
  The external spirit's tireless wings.

The sordid shrine, whose vestal fire
  Burns dim within the grosser frame,
May perish, but the rays aspire,
  And reach once more from whence they came.
We pass, as through the entrancéd flood,
  From Egypt's toil to Canaan's bloom,
And with the sacrifice of blood
  We find new life beyond the tomb.

Still, through the vast and deepening void,
  Like sentient flames the spirits come—
Eternal, changeless, undestroyed,
  And speaking, though the grave be dumb.
Within the soul their vital spell
  Reveals the fount from whence it rose—
The beautiful—the terrible—
  The strange preamble to the close.

And thou whose soul with ardor filled
  Hast seen the fire and heard the voice,
For whom the future field is tilled,
  And waits the harvest, make thy choice.

It lies before thee; struggle, strive,
  Thou canst not beat conviction back;
Weak fugitive from higher life,
  Eternal wings pursue thy track.

Ah! traitor soul, for whom in vain
  The veil of heaven was drawn aside,
As if to give thy cleansed brain
  An ampler scope, a steadier guide—
Thou slave of sense, still madly hurled
  Across the unfruitful waste of years—
Thou stagnant ship, whose white sails, furled,
  Rot idly, dropping stagnant tears.

Awake! Beyond the impassive grave
  The spheres of being spread afar,
Circle on circle, wave on wave,
  An ocean, where each freighted star
Is as a bark that bears along,
  From suffering to the blissful shore,
The beautiful, the good, and strong,
  Their term of sad probation o'er.

Earth dies, and heaven with purer light
  Prepares to clothe our mystic orb;
Bright spirits move in viewless flight
  To cheer the dying, and absorb
The falsehoods which have mingled still
  Their pain in life's enchanted bowl;
Heaven's only keys are human will,
  A striving love, an earnest soul.

A DRINKING SONG.

Oh! here's to the wine—the ruby wine,
  That touches the lips with bloom,
Like a purple fire consuming care,
  And lighting our darkest gloom.
It gladdens the heart with rosy light—
  May its glory ne'er decline;
For our souls are glad and our hopes are bright
  While quaffing the purple wine.

Then here's to the wine—the flashing wine,
  As it beadeth the cup of joy,
And, king like, mounts upon Reason's throne,
  Making dull sense its toy.

Oh, it claspeth the hand of our fainting soul,
  With passion lights the eyes,
And radiant from out the burning bowl
  We see young Love arise.

Then here's to the wine—the deathless wine;
  No kingly jewels surpass
The liquid rubies which flash and shine
  In the depths of each brimming glass.
All praise we give to the nectar sweet,
  All praise to the bearing vine—
Praise to the board at which true friends meet,
  And praise to the purple wine.

THE RUBY RING.

Dear brother, when the listless pen
  Sways idly in my wearied fingers,
And round my throbbing heart and brain
  No ray of brighter fancy lingers,
I catch the sparkle of the stone
  That speaks of friendship undecaying,
And straight the clouds aside are thrown—
  A fresher light is round me playing.

They say that talismans of old
  Protected from all hidden dangers;
That spirits lay within the gold,
  At once protectors and avengers.
The ring you gave, like these, may prove
  The bane of grief, the source of pleasure;
For all is pleasing that can move
  Remembrance of an absent treasure.

Like friendship's fire, the brilliant toy,
  Deep set in memory's golden circle,
Throws back the ruddy beam of joy,
  And in the dullest night will sparkle.
The ring, like memory—endless both—
  Its warmth from out my heart is getting,
And, like myself, of foreign growth,
  Rejoices in a Yankee setting.

My muse—a woman, and you know
  The female heart inclines to jewels—
Whene'er she wants "full speed" to go,
  Her engine at the ruby fuels.

The pistons of alternate rhyme
  Move up and down with steady motion;
The train of thought, defying time,
  Speeds on through earth, and air, and ocean.

The Koh-i-noor in Britain's crown
  Is India's blood-mark set upon her;
The sapphire clasp of beauty's gown
  Perchance was purchased by dishonor.
The miser's gold is dim with tears,
  And rusted thick with cent. per centage;
My ring, then, clearly it appears,
  O'er these can claim immense advantage.

The lips, by Cyprian Venus planned,
  Convey love's telegraphic greeting,
But friendship meets us hand to hand,
  To feel how either's pulse is beating;
And on that hand this ring I hold,
  As prized as talisman by dervis,
And may that hand be foul and cold
  When 'tis not warmly at thy service.

TO NEA.

I never dreamed that you could love me,
  And now 'tis time we part;
You are too fair, and far too high above me—
  I may not reach thy heart.
On different paths our feet must press:
  You, bound for pleasure's blossomed altar;
While o'er the hills, with heavier stress,
  My fainting footsteps falter.

Alas! the hopes my soul that haunted
  In the now spectral past;
You the sole treasure that my spirit vaunted,
  My first love and my last;
This single passion filled my breast,
  Through all my manhood burning clearer;
And Fame I measured by the test—
  To thee it brings me nearer.

But gone—all gone the glorious vision;
  Shadows across it fall;
And time has taught me, with its chill precision,
  The lesson taught to all:

That love, like other mortal things,
  Grows weary of protracted waiting,
And that it rends its shining wings
  Against the rough world grating.

I've learned the world more fully now,
  But still, till memory perish,
Your image, with its radiant brow,
  My faithful heart shall cherish;
And wheresoe'er your fate be cast,
  In shade or sunshine, gloom or lustre,
Borne from the friendships of the past,
  My thoughts shall round thee cluster.

With all a lover's eager care
  I watch thy happy lot,
Praying for thee a fortune fair—
  Myself perhaps forgot.
And still I feel through all my strife
  Thy holy influence gliding—
Thou art the loadstar of my life,
  My soul from earth dividing.

THE FERRY-BOATS OF GOTHAM.

The ferry-boats of Gotham,
  How gloriously they glide,
With lamps of red and lamps of blue,
  Across the starless tide;
Through long defiles of blazing light
  On each street-studded shore;
No sound to break the hush of night
  Except the paddles' roar.

Around the Island City lie,
  Encircling block and mart,
Vast ships that rear against the sky
  A forest-growth of art;
And girdled thus with winged might—
  Though now the wings are furled—
Manhattan is, what Venice was,
  The Sea-Queen of the world.

Oh, ferry-boats, the argosies
  That tyrants launched of yore,.
To bring them gold, and gems, and spice
  From India's plundered shore,

Ne'er knew a freight so rich as this,
  That humbly, day by day,
To Brooklyn homes and social ease
  From business ye convey.

Let Russia launch her birds of prey
  Against the Crescent Moon,
And butcher in Sinope's Bay
  The convoy of Batoon;
Let France and England, holding back,
  Deny the aid they swore,
Until the sea that once was Black,
  Grow red with Turkish gore.

But ye, undaunted ferry-boats,
  Your pathless course pursue,
Nor any nobler navy floats,
  Nor manned by hearts more true;
Your mission is to spread content,
  Love, joy, and wealth to bear—
Odd's life! I haven't got a cent
  To pay my blessed fare.

THE FIRST OF MAY.

The first of May, the first of May,
What lying poet called it gay?
There is the very devil to pay,
And no pitch hot, on the first of May.

The house I took a twelvemonth since,
And furnished fit to lodge a prince—
That cheerful house I quit to-day,
Because it is the first of May.

My carpets all are torn to shreds,
We have not where to lay our heads;
The beds are all unscrewed, and we
Are "screwed" as tight as men can be.

Our new piano, new no more,
In fragments lies upon the floor;
Our China service, once so neat,
Now helps to pave the laughing street.

"Alas!" I cry in utter grief,
"Would heaven I were an Arab chief!
He roams about unrented places,
And camps in every green oasis."

The wagoners alone can say
The festival is truly gay;
The scallawags get a fortnight's pay
For working on the first of May.

A LOST LOVE.

The glory of the dream is past,
The sweet illusion melts in air,
And, calmly facing a despair,
I whisper, 'tis the last—the last—
The last and most divinely fair,
The brightest, sunniest, and the last.

All forms of life, with rapid eye,
To seize, to ponder, and survey;
To watch the scales turn either way,
And every truth to test and try—
To try, and yet how far we stray
When judging that for which we sigh!

Your friendship in its gilded bark
Glides on as calmly as before;
But my impetuous fancy bore
A helmless boat beyond the mark,
And on a far surf-whitened shore
The wreck beats, drifting through the dark.

Henceforth we meet with less to dread,
And less to hope on either side;
You balanced on a holy pride,
And I on that which serves instead—
A stubborn jealousy to hide
The wound which most of all hath bled.

THE REJECTED.

He bowed his head as if the chords
Of life had snapped in twain;
I could not catch his hurried words,
But they sounded full of pain;
His eyes were lit with a feverish fire,
His cheek had a hectic stain,
And as he stooped to kiss my hand,
His tears fell down like rain.

We met once more in after years,
  When I—another's bride—
Had learned to measure by my tears
  The costliness of pride.
Amid the gay, unheeding crowd,
  Chance threw us side by side;
He seemed the wreck of a noble heart
  Whose hope had early died.

The unforgotten look returned—
  The sad, impassioned look;
It seemed to pierce my very soul,
  And read it as a book.
He bowed his head and strove to smile;
  Alas! I could not brook
To know how worthless all I gained,
  And see what I forsook.

THREE OF US AT THE FOUNTAIN.

BY WIDESWARTH.

Come, Broadbent, Creyton, sit ye by my side,
  And view yon column with its foamy crest
Upspringing from the frog pond's glassy tide,
  To fall again in snow upon its breast.
Oh, it is very beautiful; and mark
  The golden glow it borrows from the west,
As the red sunlight dwindles to a spark,
  And fevered day sinks languidly to rest.
Yet that hoarse measure sadly fills my ear—
  My soul with dark emotions is oppressed;
A voice comes mingling with the murmur here—
  A stern and solemn voice that may not jest—
Wideswarth, it says, 'tis thus you vainly climb,
To fall as flat as this upon the tide of rhyme.

THE FOUNTAIN ON BOSTON COMMON.

TO CHARLES BROADBENT AND PROFESSOR WIDESWARTH, BY PAUL CREYTON.

The heart of childhood is a virgin soil
  All bright with birds, and brooks, and sunny showers—
  A paradise, whose vernal vines and flowers
The hounds of youthful folly spurn and spoil,
And manhood tears it with the plow of toil,

And builds thereon a city—towers of pride,
And temples for its idols, side by side,
And streets jarred with the crash of life's turmoil;
But noble souls like yours, oh honored friends,
One pure bright fountain in the midst will leave,
All green-begirt, like this, which now, at eve,
A liquid silver willow heavenward tends,
Its murmurous branches in the moonlight blends,
And to the peaceful scene a sweet enchantment lends.

THE FOUNTAIN.

TO WIDESWARTH AND CREYTON, BY CHARLES BROADBENT.

Green wooded fountain, with how glad a rush
Thou leapest up from the surrounding clay,
Cleaving toward heaven thy rainbow-colored way,
And gleaming brightly in the crimson flush
Spread o'er the west! Anon the starry hush
Of night will lull thee, and thy drifted spray
No more shall fall, like an alighting fay,
On the dry leaves now reveling in thy gush!
Say, friends, if Love's rich fountain e'er shall fail
To fling its freshening waters from the heart,
In sorrow's night shall its loud tide depart,
And its bright plumage cease to fan the gale,
Shall we, who shared its noontide, ever know
That Love, like it, has but a summer flow?

THE OPIUM DREAM.

BY AN EATER OF THE DRUG.

The shadows gather deeper round,
They come with a tumultuous sound
Of muttering thunder, and they swim
Above me, o'er me, faint and dim.
A thousand forms of speechless dread
Flap on with slow wings o'er my head,
And slowly stooping—while their eyes
Dilate to an unnatural size—
Let fall a ghastly funeral gleam
Upon their own self-conjured dream.

They come! They sail from darkness out,
A hideous and fantastic rout—

Red eyes in every formless head,
Red clots upon the ghastly dead,
Red robes on every sweltering corse,
Red squadrons, rider, rein, and horse—
They leap from the walls and fill the air,
Their flying garments fan my hair—
God! what an icy touch was there!

Old wrinkled women, in russet clad,
Advancing silently and sad—
Old wrinkled women, whose gleaming eyes
Hint of immortal agonies,
Peeping from under each shadowy hood
Like phosphor sparks in a rotten wood.
Stealthy and silent the beldames all
Creep up the perpendicular wall,
And, turning, drop in my lidless eyes
Their own unspeakable agonies.

Oh, tide of doubt and utter woe,
Horrible tide, that lies below
The unsounded sea of waking thought—
Dim tide with every monster fraught—
While others, nor more pure nor strong,
Hear in their sleep the seraph's song,
And mount, as ne'er awake they rose,
Superior to our common woes—
What weird, magnetic spell is thine,
That drags me to your hateful brine
Whene'er my wearied Reason lowers
Her strained hands from the burning oars?

VENICE'S NEW CHANCE.

The hands that moved on Freedom's clock
  Already strike the appointed hour;
The tocsin sounds, the people flock,
  Majestic in their banded power.
Italia wakes! From town to town
  The leaders cry "To arms! obey us!"
The Austrian sword, the papal crown,
  Reel on the verge of chaos.

Up! all who bear the Latin heart;
  Up! all who love the vengeful joy;
Let your fierce wrath like lightning dart
  Upon the tyrants, and destroy!

Up! from the Tiber to the Arve;
  Let Insurrection's tocsin toll,
While weaponed arms united carve
  A path for the free soul.

Let Austria's cut-throat legions learn
  To feel and fear the Roman rage;
Let the fierce pontiff's eyes discern
  The dawn of the millennial age.
Tell fratricidal France her hordes
  No more shall bid Italia weep;
Reap a full harvest with your swords,
  And garner what you reap!

Up, Latins! by the foulest wrongs
  That ever suffering manhood bore;
By ruffian steel and priestly thongs
  Imbued in patriot gore;
By every scaffold through the land;
  By dungeons, vault, and leprous spy—
Up! up! and with an armed hand
  Strike down this living lie.

No more be scourged by priestly cords,
  No more be ruled by foreign steel,
No more be robbed by foreign lords—
  Arise! the tyrants reel.
Expect no mercy, breathe no sigh
  In this last desperate throe for life;
Let "Death or Victory!" be the cry,
  And war unto the knife.

TO LAURA—SINGING.

A breathless hush is in the hall,
  A silence deep as death;
The sculptured cherubs on the wall
  Appear to hold their breath,
While floating forth in silvery strain
  Thy voice rings clear and high,
Now filled with passion's rapturous pain,
  Now lost in sorrow's sigh.

Ah! Lady Laura, such a tone
  As thine is seldom heard;
So lightly breathed, so quickly flown,
  And yet how deep it stirred

Those chords of feeling that have lain
Unmoved and silent long,
Now roused again in heart and brain
By thy awakening song.

Thy thoughts into the music flow,
And mingle with its tide,
And thou dost share the poet's woe,
Or feel the poet's pride.
Thy genius, like the crystal spring,
Reflects each passing form,
If rosy boughs above it swing,
Or drifts the wintry storm.

I've heard, and yet again would hear
The music of thy tongue:
Entranced in pleasure, eye and ear,
My soul upon thee hung.
Thy voice, like the old Hebrew's rod
Stretched o'er the prisoning sea,
Rolls back the dark and shadowy flood,
Making our spirits free.

OH, WANTON WIND.

Oh, wanton wind, world-kissing kind,
Thy zephyrs twined my Laura's tresses;
Bathed lip and hand with fragrance bland,
And even fanned those deep recesses
Where love is seen—warm couched, serene—
A rose-leaf dropped on summer billows.
Oh, heedless wind, to beauty blind,
Where couldst thou find more tempting pillows?

The lily bell, whose anthers tell
The time so well, by you set ringing;
The rival rose, wherein repose
Queen Mab, and those unto her clinging—
The violet sweet, the daisy neat—
Should I repeat each fragrant blossom—
Oh, careless wind, could all combined
So please thy mind as Laura's bosom?

Insensate still! hence—hence and fill
The idle sail of yon bright vessel;
And yet—ah stay! ere hence you stray,
Leave me, I pray, your right to nestle;

Give me to seek her damask cheek,
  And, whispering, speak what thou ne'er dreamest;
For me to lie one moment nigh
  Her heart, and die, were bliss supremest.

ADVERTISEMENT EXTRAORDINARY.[31]

Lost, a politician's wallet,
Portmonnaie, or what-you-call-it,
  And the happy man who saw
What the fate that did befall it
  May on RUFUS ANDREWS draw
For a place—a sinecure—
Worth two thousand dollars sure;
Yea, to this snug sum each year
He can "read his title clear."

'Twas a pocket-book mysterious,
Filled with papers jocund, serious,
Business, social, patriotic,
Journalistic and erotic;
Plans of caucus and Convention
Swelled its bulk beyond dimension;
Every kind of scrip and docket
Found its place in THURLOW's pocket;
But the book is lost, and we
Search for its recovery.

It contained a note from GREELEY,
Asking THURLOW "if he really
Had decided as to who
Should be suddenly put through
For BILL SEWARD's vacant shoe?
GREELEY was prepared to take it
If all right 'my lord' could make it;
And he then no more would tramp
In the wake of any scamp;
But he wanted 'Yes' or 'No,'
That he might be governed so."

Then there came a note from RAYMOND,
With a sort of oblique aim and
Purpose cautiously suppressed:
He in Paris wished to rest,
And for consul would be glad
If LORD THURLOW's aid he had:

"The prospects of the times were bad—
Very dismal, very sad;
But whate'er the *Times* could do
Of service—zealous, constant, true—
LORD THURLOW might make up his mind
He ever in its page should find,
If he to SEWARD a word would slip
For RAYMOND's Paris consulship."

And next there came—that we should pen it—
A sharp, clear note from J. G. BENNETT:
"French mission wanted—circulation
Larger than any in the nation—
Why is the weak, dull DAYTON sent
To where wit rates at cent. per cent.,
With PENNINGTON for his secretary,
Who, when they speak French, answers 'Nary?'
The administration then may sway
The *Herald's* influence day by day,
And THURLOW, without cost of dollar,
Become 'a gentleman and scholar.'"

This note from CUMMINGS—short and sweet—
"The *World*, my lord, is at your feet;
Its empty columns gape to find
The astute impress of your mind;
But don't let CAMERON dispose
Of all the jobs in army clothes,
Rations and weapons, transportation—
The royal profits of the nation—
Without remembering mine and me,
Stanchest of all your friends, A. C."

Dozens of other papers were
Confided to the lost book's care,
All equally of weight with those
The drift of which we here disclose.
Now who, by any "crook" or "hook,"
Can find for us this wondrous book,
And gain at WEED an "inside" look?
Who can reveal to after ages
The curious secrets of its pages,
And let us know how THURLOW noted
The schemes which round his path have floated?

MY DOVE IN HER NEST.

"Nay, your wine will make me heady;
We have ta'en enough already;
Let us go while we are steady;
Do not stir—I know my way."
So I lit my chamber candle,
Sought my room, and turned the handle—
Lady togs, from ruff to sandal,
Loose across the lounger lay.

"Heavens!" I cried, alarmed and shaken,
"Surely I have been mistaken;
If the sleeping beauty waken,
What excuse for me remains?"
Fear the dangerous joy enhances,
Love with eager step advances—
Oh, the dreams, the languors, trances,
Throbbing in my dove's young veins.

Blissful watch above her keeping,
Angels guard their sister sleeping—
Would they wake her should a peeping,
Bearded mortal ope the door?
Cautiously a pace advancing,
Round the rose-silk draperies glancing—
Oh! the sight divine, entrancing,
Haunts my dreams for evermore.

Flushed as May's young wealth of roses,
Laura on the couch reposes,
And the billowy snow discloses
Outlines worth a sculptor's note:
Tresses loose—a golden wonder—
Crimson lips that smile asunder,
And one small hand creeping under
The crisp lace which fringed her throat.

Now a kiss were easy stealing,
But I dared not trust the feeling,
For my very soul seemed reeling
In the fullness of her view;
So I bowed my head and blessed her,
Prayed the angel host to rest her,
Softly said, "Sweet dreams, fair sister!"
And from that small heaven withdrew.

A BRACE OF SONNETS,

DEDICATED TO PROFESSOR WIDESWARTH BY CHARLES BROADBENT.

I.

Oh, Wideswarth! Feebly in these latter days
We seek to build the imperial sonnet's throne,
Monarch of verse and poesie: the tone
Of modern converse ill can reach the lays
Which bound old Petrarch with immortal bays,
And gave him o'er this rhythm to rule alone.
Milton, who drank his spirit, and made known
To our rough tongue the harmony that plays
And lightens o'er the undivided thought
Of this intensest poetry, hath shown
How near the rude Norse utterance may be brought
To the soft music in Italia wrought.
And thou—alas! to mockery sometimes prone—
A portion of the melody hast caught.

II.

And I have listened gladly to thy strain,
And thrilled in spirit to the solemn swell
Of music poured from out the rosy shell
Which some pale muse had touched—nor touched in vain—
With her white feet when wandering on in pain
Of meditation through the sea-worn cell;
Her white brows knit, and crowned with asphodel
Gathered by moonlight on the breezy plain
Which skirts Parnassus; and I wondered how
Thy soul could deem so lightly of the spell
With which Apollo had adorned thy brow
(Still niggard to my prayer and earnest vow)
As to enweave the silken-threaded muse
With darning-cotton, such as housewives use.

THE TROPIC BIRD.

Not of our forests art thou! Here the cold
Of winter soon would mar
Thy glittering plumage—from afar,
From lands of gold,

And from the streams that roll along beneath
The quivering lotus bowers,
Where spreads the palm, and amaranthine flowers
In blushing wreath
Aye greet the kisses of the Eastern dawn,
Comest thou to us, bright bird.
I envy not his heart who, all unstirred,
Can look upon
Thy glittering wing, nor give his fancy rein
To tropic shore and glowing sky,
Streams, temples, woods, and with a sigh
Receive it back again.
For me, I look on thee, and in a dream,
Before the gazing eye,
The gorgeous pageant of the East rolls by
On Ganges' stream.
Gem-studded galleys, and the crimson slaves
(Their tunics woven o'er
With sapphire studs and braids of yellow ore),
The cedar waves
Her emerald boughs above them; and on high,
Throned on the ivory poop,
The swarthy sultan, with a hoop
That well might buy
Our barren kingdoms on his ample brow;
And those young Georgian girls—
The raven tresses looped with sparkling pearls—
Before him bow,
All duteous to his nod. The silver oars
Flash as they hurry on
The peopled argosies! 'Tis gone!
The purple shores
Are silent, save the speechless melody
Poured from the myrtle bowers.
What is't to me that here the hours
Of daylight flee?

A VALENTINE.

TO DOLLY B——, TEN YEARS OLD.

On this pleasant day, dear Dolly,
When, from young Love's lips,
Touched by sweet Saint Valentine,
The bond of silence slips;

Now, when 'tis allowed us
  All our hearts to bare
At your modest maiden shrine,
  Thus I kneel and swear:
    "Hear and heed me, Dolly,
      I pledge my love to-day,
    And when you come to womanhood,
      Oh, then the debt repay."

The bright glad hours of girlhood,
  The frolic soul that trips
On silvery feet o'er rosy paths—
  The pure and laughing lips;
The golden curls, the mantling blush,
  The blue and sinless eyes—
Oh, never may the future bid
  A cloud o'er these arise.
    "But hear and heed me, Dolly,
      I pledge my heart to-day,
    And when you come to womanhood,
      Oh, then the debt repay."

Each year, while ripening beauty
  Gives roundness to your form;
When the heart now full of gayety
  Grows softer and more warm;
When your blush hath deeper meaning,
  And your eyes are darker hued,
Again, before your altar-shrine,
  This pledge shall be renewed:
    "So hear and heed me, Dolly,
      My heart is thine to-day,
    And when you come to womanhood,
      Oh, then the debt repay."

MY SOUL IS SAD.

NEW VERSION.

My soul is sad! Oh, quickly bring
  The cup I yet can love to drain,
And let its fragrant sweetness fling
  Delicious languor round my brain.
If in this heart one joke remain,
  The cup shall charm it into line;
If there be any balm for pain,
  It is—it is in glorious wine.

But bid the cup at first be mild,
  Nor let its strength come on too soon;
I tell thee, waiter, I have smiled
  At least a dozen times since noon.
And now I ask of thee a boon
  (Here—take this quarter for your trouble)—
Do you observe a double moon,
  Or is it I that now "see double?"

MORE LIGHT.

More light—more light—more light!
This is the cry of unhappy humanity,
This is the prayer of poor blinded humanity,
Groping in passion, in pain, and inanity
Round the bleak walls of the prison of vanity—
Every where seeking a ray of divinity,
Every where finding the terrible trinity!
Darkness, and dolor, and doubt inexpressible—
Numbness, and dumbness, and pain inexpressible—
Doubts irrepressible, woes unendurable,
Tears that fall laughingly, smiles that are sorrowful;
Longings and gleams of superior existences,
Voices that whisper from infinite distances—
Mystical distances—soul-haunted distances—
Beauty that flings back the folds of a cerement,
Skeletons veiled in the garments of merriment,
All that is exquisite, all that is wonderful,
Earth a vast theatre, over and under full—
Full to the brim of discordant existences,
Matter and spirit, and powers and resistances—
Every where opposites: anguish and levity,
Mortal reality, hoped immortality,
Art for long years, and man's life but a brevity.
  Oh, in this shadowed and whispering night,
  This mystical stage with its curtain of night,
  Grant us Thy wisdom—Thy comfort—Thy light—
    Grant us more light, or we perish.

PHILIP AND I.

You, asking me how Philip fared,
  Received reply that he and I,
  Some years ago, had said good-by,
Since which I neither knew nor cared.

It was a peevish answer, spoken
  In bitter sorrow and regret
  That such a brilliant, brightly set
As was our friendship, should be broken.

Shattered with purpose fell and strong,
  Without the warning of a word—
  An arrow whistling through a bird,
Even while her throat was full of song.

Happy her fate! The spirit winging
  Ere sense of treachery or pain
  Can reach conception in the brain,
She dies within the act of singing.

So the shrill shaft which sudden cast
  Our dream of friendship to the ground,
  Of its dread coming gave no sound,
But smote and shattered—and was past.

One moment in amaze I stood,
  Thinking—it can but be in jest!
  Another, and within my breast
The laboring heart gave sobs of blood.

Less happy than the bird, I live
  To know the treachery, bear the pain,
  And feel that on this earth again
Such friendship I no more can give.

So to your quest how Philip fared,
  I made reply that he and I,
  Some years ago, had said good-by,
Since which I neither knew nor cared.

FORENSIC ELOQUENCE—A PORTRAIT.

"What is the secret of your friend Brady's success?"—*Query in a private letter.*

Not with fast-flashing volleys of vain speech
  Fired off at random, and revealing naught
  But verbiage used to hide the want of thought—
Mere summer-thunder—the kind schoolmen teach—
  And never to a definite purpose wrought;

But with most apt precision, and a tongue
  Linked in such harmony with the weighing brain
  That every phrase is balanced there again,
Dropping like gold on truth's own touchstone rung—
  Results arrived at by a perfect chain:

Quick sympathy with every trait and touch
  Reflected in the natures round him brought,
  And an assimilating power of thought
So like our own, we let it pass for such,
  Priding ourselves as teachers when but taught.

One other power—an undecaying flame
  Of human charity—soft, religious warmth;
  Never was wreck but tells him of some storm;
And, pitying what his judgment yet must blame,
  He sees God's image in the meanest form.

These are the weapons wielded by my friend—
  These, and an orderly, analytic mind,
  Grouping strong facts beneath the heads assigned,
And making all to one conclusion tend:
  Ears to the deaf, and eyesight to the blind.

A VISIT.

Ah me! how time doth gallop now
  With headlong stride and pace;
But yesterday thy youthful brow,
  And gentle girlish face,
Were set in memory like a gem
Worn in some queenly diadem.

How changed to me the picture seems
  In tinting, shape, and air;
The child I thought of in my dreams
  Now smiles a woman fair;
And while her graceful form I see,
The past seems but an hour to me.

A light heart glows within thee still,
  Though not exempt from pain;
And Nature, in her task to fill,
  Let all thy youth remain,
And gave thee, with a woman's form,
A charm to keep all friendship warm.

Since last in by-gone years we met,
  How many hopes are fled!
What joys we think of with regret,
  To all save memory dead;
But with our being still will dwell
The magic of their holy spell.

Thus may the future yet reveal
  New joys to equal those,
And o'er our spirits too may steal
  The bliss of calm repose,
Coming like gentle summer showers
To give new life to drooping flowers.

THE TROOPER TO HIS MARE.

Old girl, that hast borne me far and fast
  On pawing hoofs that were never loth,
Our gallop to-day may be the last
  For thee or for me—or perchance for both.
As I tighten your girth, do you nothing daunt—
  Do you catch the hint of our forming line?
And now the artillery move to the front,
  Have you never a qualm, Bay Bess of mine?

It is dainty to see you sidle and start
  As you move to the battle's cloudy marge,
And to feel the swells of your wakening heart
  When our cavalry bugles sound a charge.
At the scream of the shell and the roll of the drum
  You feign to be frightened with skittish glance,
But up the green slopes where the bullets hum,
  Coquettishly, darling, I've known you dance.

Your skin is satin, your nostrils red,
  Your eyes are a bird's or a loving girl's;
And from delicate fetlock to dainty head
  A throbbing vein-cordage around you curls.
Oh, joy of my soul! if you they slay,
  For triumph or rout I little care;
For there is not in all the wide valley to-day
  Such a dear little bridle-wise, thorough-bred mare.

BREVET RANK.[32]

TO THE SENATORS OF THE UNITED STATES.

To Sheridan's heroes and Sherman's men,
And the bull-dogs of Grant who drove Lee from his den,
Give brevet promotions of honor; and then
Find some foul detective, some leprous spy,
His labors a loathing, his life but a lie,

Some wretch who hath planned half the crimes he exposed,
Chief plotter himself of the plots he disclosed,
And place on his shoulders—not cowhide thongs,
But the brevet which rightly to honor belongs;
And when this you have done, will your brevets then
On Sheridan's heroes and Sherman's men,
And the bull-dogs of Grant who drove Lee from his den,
Sit proudly as trophies they won in the fray,
Or shrivel to shameful mementoes away?

Oh, think of it, senators! Thousands have died,
Pouring out their young lives in an eager tide,
While to win this prize of honor they vied;
And this prize—past price—can you now degrade
To a badge of the mouchard's odious trade?
If the spy hath done well, pay him store of gold—
By thousands, or fifties of thousands told;
Or should you lack means his reward to defray,
Take all that we have—our last dollar of pay,
But leave us the honor our swords have won
As a glory to boast, not a shame to shun;
Nor bid Sheridan's heroes and Sherman's men,
And the bull-dogs of Grant who drove Lee from his den,
On their straps, as a blistering symbol to bear,
What this human sleuth-hound is free to share.

GENERAL ORDERS OF THE CITIZEN.

GENERAL ORDER NO. I.

A paragraph to make one laugh
Should be of ten lines just a half;
A trivial theme—a brilliant stream
Of verbiage, metaphor, and dream—
Such as this paragraph, I deem.

A stirring song is never long,
But must be fiery, terse, and strong,
With much of thought, not fully wrought,
But in quick glimpses shown and caught:
Such are the rules Bob Burns has taught.

A good critique should ever seek
To check the proud and help the weak;
Not swayed by fame, nor prone to blame—
Calm, energetic—never tame—
And free from mercenary shame.

K

A tale or sketch should never fetch
Its hero from thy hand, Jack Ketch;
Though for a time the tide of crime
Roll down white-crested and sublime,
It leaves a track of venomed slime.

In short, be brief. Each added leaf
Is so much to your reader's grief:
The point is gone; the lightning shone
And dies while yet we labor on;
True wit ne'er knows a second dawn.

Observe these rules, and mock the schools
Of composition taught by fools.
Briefness and wit together fit,
And fly, like Parthians, when they hit—
The urchins are too wise to sit.
By order of the Editor commanding.
JOHN JONES, Lieut. Col. and A.A.G.

TRUTH IN PARENTHESIS, OR THE FORTUNE-HUNTER.

I love—oh, more than words can tell
(Your ninety thousand golden shiners);
You draw me by a nameless spell
(As California draws the miners);
You are so rich in beauty's dower
(And rich in several ways beside it),
Had I your hand within my power
(Across a banker's draft to guide it),
No care my future life could dim
(My tailor, too—what joy to him!).

Oh, should you change your name for mine
(I've given my name—on bills—to twenty),
Existence were a dream divine
(At least so long as cash was plenty);
Our home should be a sylvan grot
(Bath, billiard, smoking-room, and larder),
And there, forgetting and forgot
(My present need, I'd live the harder),
Our days should pass in fresh delights
(Lethargic days, but roaring nights).

Oh say, my young, my fawn-like girl
(She's old enough to be my mother),
Let "Yes" o erleap those gates of pearl
(My laughter it is hard to smother);

Let lips that Love hath formed for joy
  (For joy if they her purse resign me)
Long hesitate ere they destroy
  (And to a debtor's jail consign me)
The heart that beats but to adore
(Yourself the less, your fortune more).

Consent—consent, my priceless love
  (Her price precise is ninety thousand);
I swear by all around, above
  (Her purse-strings now, I feel, are loosened),
I have not loved you for your wealth
  (Nor loved at all, as I'm a sinner);
Oh bliss! you yield; one kiss by stealth!
  (I'm sick—that kiss has spoiled my dinner);
Now early name the blissful day
(My duns grow clamorous for their pay).

THIRD ODE, FOURTH BOOK OF HORACE.

Him on whose humble birth a gentle light,
  O Muse! you shed, no wrestling-prize may win,
No war-steed bear him in the triumph bright,
  Nor shall his voice be heard above the din
Of armèd hosts; for him no laurel springs
From threats hurled back on subjugated kings.

But where through Tibur's vale sweet waters flow,
  Amid dense bowers of thickly shadowing leaves,
There shall his brow beneath dark ivy glow
  As his wild harp the Æolian measure weaves;
For queenly Rome hath deigned to hear his song,
Nor envy dares to do him farther wrong.

Oh, gentle Muse, whose fingers modulate
  The dulcet music of the golden shell—
Thou whom from dumb fishes even canst create
  Such notes as from the dying cygnet swell,
It is your gift that I can touch the lyre,
While those who pass me hearken and admire.

'Tis by thy gift—oh bounteous beyond measure—
  That I to strangers as a bard am known;
Yea, that I live, and that my songs give pleasure
  (If please they do), the praise is thine alone,
For thou hast given his all of poet-fire
To thy poor stringer of the Roman lyre.

IGDRASIL.

The tree of life, that shone so fair
  In spring's alternate shine and shower,
What bitter fruit its branches bear—
  How soon 'tis stripped of leaf and flower,
As if athwart the sheltering glade
  Had swept the pestilent simoom;
Nor ever more beneath its shade
  Shall violet ope or primrose bloom.

No more beneath its spreading leaves
  Shall weary lambs at noontide throng,
While overhead the linnet weaves
  The silken tenor of his song.
No more the pale and sorrowing moon
  Her dewy tears above it weep;
No more at night's unbroken noon
  Shall Muse beneath its branches sleep.

For blight hath fallen on bud and leaf,
  And turned its fruitful sap to gall,
And, mildewed in the showers of grief,
  It totters to an early fall.
The bough the redbreast used to love
  Now nightly hears the owlet hoot—
The locust gnaws the leaves above,
  The cankerworm is at the root.

Then shall it fall, and leave behind
  No record of the brighter past,
Uprooted by the idle wind,
  And whirled away upon the blast.
Forfend it, Heaven! a soil too warm
  Hath nursed this plague; transplant it now
Where drifting rain and eddying storm
  May purge the root and cleanse the bough.

And Hope—who long had listened mute—
  Now raised her azure eyes and smiled;
She whispered low of future fruit,
  And pointed to the distant wild.
Oh, bear it thither; trust in God;
  Have faith in my prophetic words—
Again 'twill spread its arms abroad,
  And shelter its deserted birds.

THE FENIAN SCARE.

Half in terror, half in wonder,
  Johnny Bull, with open mouth,
Just begins to feel the blunder
  Of his favor to the South;
And he sees, wherever turning
  His distraught and haggard view,
Minatory meteors burning
  In our banner's field of blue;
And within the panorama
  Which foretells his flag's eclipse,
He beholds the Alabama
  And her kindred pirate-ships;
And he sees the Fenians reaching
  To assault him in his lair—
And, his own bad conscience preaching,
  This explains "the Fenian scare."

AN ANTI-MAINE-LAW LYRIC.

Air: "The Old Oaken Bucket."

How dear to the heart is the bottle of brandy,
  When fond recollection presents it to view,
As it stood in the cupboard, so neat and so handy,
  With its neck tapered off, and its belly of blue!
The old cottage walls are now crumbling to pieces,
  As I, who am old, must soon crumble myself,
But ah! every woe and embitterment ceases
  When I think on the bottle that stood on the shelf—
The big-bellied bottle—the taper-necked bottle—
  The bottle of brandy that stood on the shelf.

The loosely-corked bottle, I held it a treasure,
  For often, when weary I came from the field,
I found it the source of an exquisite pleasure—
  Such pleasure as brandy and weariness yield.
In a moment I seized it, and, hastily bringing
  Some spice from the closet, I mixed me a bowl,
And soon was my weariness changed into singing,
  And the dust of my labor was washed from my soul
By the big-bellied bottle—the taper-necked bottle—
  The bottle of brandy that stood on the shelf.

How sweet from the thin crystal brim to receive it,
  As I turned up my finger and moistened my lips;
Not a fountain of diamonds could tempt me to leave it,
  Nor all the cold water that lies under ships;
And still, though in Maine is my present location,
  And although 'tis a good one for gathering pelf,
As fancy reverts to the ruby temptation,
  I sigh for the bottle that stood on the shelf—
For the big-bellied bottle—the loosely-corked bottle—
  The gurgling blue bottle that stood on the shelf.

PARTANT POUR LA SYRIE.

FROM THE FRENCH.

Dunois, the young and gallant,
  For Syria sailing soon,
Prayed to the Virgin Mary
  That she would grant his boon:
"Grant, Mary, thou who savest,
  Immortal Queen!" he cried,
"That I may be the bravest,
  And win the loveliest bride."

Upon her shrine engraven
  His prayer forever shone,
And, with his lord to battle,
  Dunois rushed bravely on;
And, to that good oath steady,
  This charging cry he gave:
"Love to the fairest lady,
  And honor to the brave!"

His lord cried, "All the triumph
  Is thine, Dunois, I swear;
And as you have given me conquest,
  Thy fortune is my care.
My daughter Isabella,
  Thou shalt wed her to-night—
She is the fairest maiden,
  And you the bravest knight."

At the altar of the Virgin
  Their nuptial troth they plight—
Oh, blessed is the union
  Where hands and hearts unite.

And all who thronged the chapel
  This benediction gave—
"Love to the fairest lady,
  And honor to the brave!"

NINTH ODE OF HORACE, THIRD BOOK.

FREELY TRANSLATED BY CHARLES BROADBENT.

A DUET BETWEEN HORACE AND LYDIA.

HORACE.

Whilst thou wert mine, and round your bosom tender
  No youth more loved his happy arms might fold,
I envied not the Persian monarch's splendor,
  More proud of thee than he of all his gold.

LYDIA.

Whilst thou with warmer fire adored no other,
  Nor Lydia bowed to Chloe's hated name,
I envied not Rome's Ilia, our great mother,
  Proud of thy love as she of her son's fame.*

HORACE.

The Cretan Chloe now commands my duty,
  Skillful in song, and mistress of the lyre,
For whom, if Fate but spared her shining beauty,
  I would not dread this moment to expire.

LYDIA.

Calais, of Thurian Orynthus descended,
  Inflames my passion with love's fiery breath;
Were his life spared when my brief days were ended,
  Twice, and that gladly, would I suffer death.

HORACE.

What if our love returned, and, reunited,
  Our spirits beat in harmony and hope?
If Chloe of the golden locks be slighted,
  Would Lydia's arms to me, repentant, ope?

LYDIA.

Though he yon star's rich lustre is excelling,
  You, light as cork, and passionate as the storm,
With you, my love, should be my happy dwelling,
  And in your grave would I resign my form.

* Romulus, son to Ilia.

A COLLEGE SONG.

Well, the world goes round forever,
  Whether we are sad or gay,
Floats the cloud and rolls the river,
  Though we pine our lives away;
  Night usurps the throne of day,
And, when morning's lances quiver
  O'er the mountains, flies away,
But returns at sunset ever—
  Earth alternates night and day,
    Grave and gay.

If the world so little care us,
  Why should we regard the world?
Still her flowery meadows bear us,
  And the star-tent is unfurled;
  Even the stars from heaven are hurled;
And the grasp of death will tear us
  From the tree round which we curled—
From the tree of life will tear us,
  Round which our affections curled—
    From the world.

Comrades, soon the world will leave us
  Stranded on the shores of time;
Years of all our joys bereave us,
  Age is like the serpent-slime,
  Staining roses in their prime;
Every day will deeper grieve us,
  Every parting hour will chime
A knell for the sweet hopes that leave us
  Buried in the by-gone time—
    Hear it chime.

Comrades, seize the passing moment
  Lent us by eternity;
Use it wisely, for 'tis so lent,
  As a drop from out the sea,
  Rolling backward instantly;
Age advances, gray and low bent
  As the waves of pleasure flee;
Drives us to our latest moment,
  To the dread eternity—
  To that vast and trackless sea,
Over which the clouds are low bent,
  And uncounted shadows flee.

FOURTH ODE, FIRST BOOK OF HORACE.

Once more, thank heaven, the western breeze is sounding,
And Winter yields to Spring's delightful sway;
The skiffs, long moored in ice, are bounding
O'er the bright waters of the rippling bay;
The flocks we stall-fed seek the tender clover,
The plowman quits his fire and yokes his team,
The snowy robes that lately covered over
The swelling uplands melt into the stream.

Now, by sweet moonlight, Venus and the Graces
O'er the green sod the flying dancers urge;
The Cyclops toil in their appointed places,
And fiery Vulcan labors at his forge;
Now let the myrtle wreath be placed upon us,
And all the flowers that earliest brave the cold;
Now let us offer sacrifice to Faunus
In shady groves, the firstling of our fold.

Pale Death, with equal step, is seen approaching
The peasant's hut and palace-home sublime,
And the dark flood of age so fast encroaching,
Forbids us fix our hope on distant time;
Darkness and death, oblivion of the spirit,
Soon from our brow shall tear the shining crown;
The grave is all from Nature we inherit,
And Pluto there in silence binds us down.

In that cold mansion, farewell the dominion
Of jovial cheer, the wine-cup, and the song;
Love in its gloom ne'er bathes his rosy pinion,
Nor grants his pleasures to the ghostly throng.
Nothing can please that erstwhile did excite you,
Nor from your face remove the heavy frown;
Not even can Laura's tender glance delight you,
She now the toast and beauty of the town.

AN EXILE'S GRAVE.

He sleeps, and o'er his humble grave
No gilded trophy meets the view,
And yet the man beneath was true,
Just, resolute, and brave.

He paid his folly's farthest debt—
Inurn it with his mortal part!
His qualities of mind and heart
Will long survive him yet.

Oh, friends, it is a bitter thing
To die alone in a wide land,
Without a friend, without a hand,
Or hope, or help to bring;

To know our bones may never rest
In the green valleys of our youth—
To feel that many a foul untruth
Our memory may molest.

He bared against a vengeful foe
The steel to freedom consecrate,
And died, the victim of a hate
That spares nor high nor low.

For there are ways of killing men
Beside the sword, the axe, the rope—
Great hearts will break when lost to hope,
And yet no blood be seen.

In simplest guise, and borne by some
Who knew his worth—his will to bless—
He presses, as our noblest press,
The couch of martyrdom.

Peace to his soul! Let him who ne'er
Hath felt the long-protracted pains,
The life in death of prison-chains,
Speak lowly and beware.

Let him who ne'er was gagged, and torn
From home and kindred far away—
Who hath not steeped from day to day
His bread in tears of scorn,

Let him be mute, or meekly pray,
Thus kneeling on the grassy sod—
"Thy sore temptations, known to God,
Have washed thy sins away."

WE MIGHT HAVE BEEN.

There is a whisper ringing clear
In every sleepless listener's ear—

A whisper of but scanty cheer,
And heard more clearly year by year—
"You might have been—you might have been."

Breathing throughout the hush of night,
It shuns companionship and light;
A knell, a blessing, and a blight,
We profit if we hear aright,
"You might have been—you might have been."

As memory bids the past arise,
The soaring hopes that swept the skies
(Each in its narrow grave now lies),
We hear, and not with tearless eyes,
"You might have been—you might have been."

We might have played a nobler game,
Essayed and reached a worthier aim,
Had less of grief and more of fame,
Nor heard, as from a tongue of flame,
"You might have been—you might have been."

FOURTH BOOK OF HORACE, THIRTEENTH ODE.

FREELY TRANSLATED BY CHARLES BROADBENT.

The gods have heard my prayer, girl,
The gods have heard my prayer;
For thou art old, yet still dost wish
To be reputed fair.
You drink the rosy wine, girl,
And coo like any dove,
With your half-tipsy, husky voice,
The tender hymn of love.

The butterfly of love, girl,
Still shuns the withered tree;
His home is in the summer bower,
And such is not for thee.
Your foul and straggling teeth, girl,
The wrinkles on your brow,
The elf-locks of your whitening hair
Can little please him now.

Nor purple robes restore, girl,
Nor gems bring back the age
Which winged Time in passing wrote
On History's open page.

Oh! where is beauty gone, girl?
  The grace? the bloom?—what part
Hast thou of her remaining now
  Who once o'erswayed my heart?

Next to Cynara wert thou
  In wit, and form, and face,
But the gods removed Cynara
  Ere time destroyed her grace.
But the gods preserved Vestina
  To rival the raven's years,
And that glowing youth should mock the torch
  Now quenched in time and tears.

WIDOWOLOGY PHILOSOPHIZED.

I.

Oh! none of your boarding-school misses,
  Your sweet, timid creatures for me,
Who rave about Cupid and blisses,
  Yet know not what either may be.
I don't feel at all sentimental,
  Nor care I for Byron a rap—
But give me a jolly and gentle
  Young widow, in weeds and a cap.

II.

To her I would offer my duty,
  For, in truth, all belief it exceeds—
How vastly the blossom of beauty
  Is heightened by peeping from "weeds."
She is armed cap-a-pie for the struggle,
  To her cap I a captive belong;
And the wink of her magical ogle
  Is a challenge to courtship and song.

III.

The tremors of girlhood are over,
  Love's blossom has ripened to fruit;
And her "first love" asleep under clover,
  Is the soil where my passion takes root.
'Tis pleasant to know "the departed
  Was tenderly cared to the last,"
And that she will not die broken-hearted
  If I should pop off just as fast.

IV.

Her temper is never so restive—
  Her duty she knows—and a shape
Is never so sweetly suggestive
  As when it is muffled in crape.
The maid wears one ring when she marries,
  In proof she all others discards,
While the widow-wife wiselier carries
  A pair of these marital guards.

V.

So none of your boarding-school misses,
  Your sweet, timid creatures for me,
Who rave about Cupid and blisses,
  Yet know not what either may be.
I don't feel at all sentimental,
  Nor care I for Byron a rap—
But give me a jolly and gentle
  Young widow, in weeds and a cap.

UNCLE THAD STEVENS.

Gnarled and tough from seventy winters,
  A gritty, grisly, bitter "Rad"—
Though our Union fall to splinters,
  Here's to Pennsylvania Thad!

Brown his wig, but green his vigor,
  Angry often, never sad—
Full of wit and prone to rigor,
  Here's to Pennsylvania Thad!

Though lame his leg, his mind is rapid,
  And all the House is hushed and glad
When, to squelch some talker vapid,
  Rises Pennsylvania Thad.

He's in candor a believer;
  All may know the thought he had;
For no mealy-mouthed deceiver
  Is our wrinkled Uncle Thad.

Into epithets he rushes:
  All are "traitors" or are "mad"—
All who dare to cross the wishes
  Of our Pennsylvania Thad.

Thad, we like you; you are able;
  And the biggest brick that we have had
In our loud congressional Babel
  Is our Pennsylvania Thad.

Spite of age, he still is human,
  And while to man he is not bad,
Oh dear! a good man to a woman—
  The kindliest man is Uncle Thad.

Naked truth for him hath charms;
  And for the negroes, like a "Rad,"
And for their right to "be in arms,"
  Nobly fought our Uncle Thad.

Go it, my old shoulder-hitter!
  For, though we think your logic bad,
You're just as brilliant as you're bitter—
  Here's to Pennsylvania Thad!

THE HILL OF KILLENARDEN.

Though time effaces memory,
  And griefs the bosom harden,
I'll ne'er forget, where'er I be,
  That day at Killenarden;
For there, while fancy reveled wide,
  The summer's day flew o'er me;
The friends I loved were at my side,
  And Irish fields before me.

The road was steep; the pelting showers
  Had cooled the sod beneath us;
And there were lots of mountain flowers,
  A garland to enwreath us.
Far, far below the landscape shone
  With wheat and new-mown meadows,
And as o'erhead the clouds flew on,
  Beneath swept on their shadows.

Oh, friends, beyond the Atlantic's foam
  There may be nobler mountains,
And in our new far Western home
  Green fields and brighter fountains;
But as for me, let time destroy
  All dreams, but this one pardon,
And barren memory long enjoy
  That day on Killenarden.

THE LIFE CHASE.

They started when the morning blushed
Above the wave,
Earth, in its dewy freshness, hushed
As is the grave;
They started whence a torrent rushed
Down from the hill,
And many a flower their footprints crushed,
On hurrying still.

A rosy child—the quarry—tripped
Adown the vale;
Each dew-drop from the rose he sipped,
And lily pale;
Oft in the crystal stream he dipped,
Nor thought of fear,
But, merry-eyed and cherry-lipped,
Made music there.

He recked not that he was pursued—
So youth is blind,
But mocked the dull decrepitude
That lagged behind;
He sought the covert of a wood,
And loudly laughed,
"Old huntsman of the fearful mood,
I scorn thy shaft."

Nor frowned nor smiled the huntsman old,
But tottered on;
His eyes were keen, his hands were cold,
His visage wan;
A drapery of darkness rolled
Around his form,
And still he chased through wood and wold,
Through shine and storm.

When evening o'er the mountains came,
The child grew weak;
Gone the rich vigor of his frame,
And pale his cheek;
But the huntsman's eyes are still aflame,
And deep his breath—
Life is that huntsman's dying game,
That huntsman, Death.

THE DIFFERENCE.[33]

When the news of Jim Lane's suicide
Was bruited through the city,
Some few—a very few men sighed
"Dear me! oh, what a pity!"

But when the news "Lane has not died"
Fell sadly on the city,
Then all the town, like one man, cried
"Dear Savior! what a pity!"

LECOMPTON'S BLACK BRIGADE.[34]

A SONG OF THE CHARLESTON CONVENTION.

Single-handed, and surrounded by Lecompton's black brigade,
With the treasury of a nation drained to pay for hireling aid;
All the weapons of corruption—the bribe, the threat, the lie—
All the forces of his rivals leagued to make this one man die,
Yet smilingly he met them, his heart and forehead bare,
And they quailed beneath the lightnings of his blue eye's sudden glare;
For all behind him thronging the mighty people came,
With looks of fiery eagerness and words of leaping flame—
"A DOUGLAS and a DOUGLAS!"
Hark to the people's cry,
Shaking the earth beneath their feet,
And thundering through the sky.

Crooked and weak, but envious as the witches of Macbeth,
Came old and gray BUCHANAN a-hungering for his death;
And full of mortal strategy, with green and rheumy eyes,
JOHN SLIDELL—he of Houmas—each poisoned arrow tries.
With cold and stony visage, lo! BRECKINRIDGE is there,
While old JOE LANE keeps flourishing his rusty sword in air;
But still the "LITTLE GIANT" holds unmoved his fearless way,
While the great waves of the people behind him rock and sway—
"A DOUGLAS and a DOUGLAS!
No hand but his can guide,
In such a strait, our ship of state
Across the stormy tide."

A poisonous reptile, many-scaled and with most subtle fang,
Crawled forward CALEB CUSHING, while behind his rattles rang;
And, mounted on a charger of hot and glossy black,
The Alabamian YANCEY dashes in with fell attack:
Lo! BAYARD is aroused, and quits his favorite cards and dice,
While JEFF DAVIS plots with BIGLER full many a foul device;
But, smiling still, against them all their One Foe holds his own,
While louder still and louder the cry behind has grown—

"A DOUGLAS and a DOUGLAS,
Who every base trick spurns;
The people's will is sovereign still,
And that to DOUGLAS turns."

Half horse, half alligator, here from Mississippi's banks
The blatant BARRY caracols and spurs along the ranks;
From Arkansaw comes BURROWS, with his "toothpick" in its sheath,
While that jaundiced Georgian, JACKSON, shows his grim and ugly teeth;
And BARKSDALE barks his bitterest bark, and curls his stunted tail,
And snarls like forty thousand curs beneath a storm of hail;
But smiling now—almost a laugh—the DOUGLAS marches on,
While many million voices rise in chorus like to one—

"A DOUGLAS and a DOUGLAS!"
Louder the war-song grows:
"God speed the man who fights so well
Against a thousand foes."

Long and fierce was the encounter beneath the burning sky,
Fierce were the threatening gestures—the words rang shrill and high;
In a struggle most protracted, after seven and fifty shocks,
Like those old gigantic combats in which Titans fought with rocks
(And with "rocks," but of a different kind, no doubt BUCHANAN fought),
This first pitched battle of the war unto its end was brought;
And smiling still, with stainless plume and eye as clear as day,
The "LITTLE GIANT" held his own through all that murderous fray:

"And a DOUGLAS and a DOUGLAS!"
Still louder grows the roar
Which swells and floats from myriad throats
Like waves on some wild shore.

Oh! a cheer for Colonel FLOURNOY, who to help our chief did press,
May memory perish if his name we cease to love and bless!
And a cheer for all the good and true who faced the music's note,
Who seized old HYDRA* in his den, and shook him by the throat.

* *i. e.*, The too domineering spirit of the Slave Power, which expected the Northern delegations to accept whatever candidate and platform the South demanded.

Though our country stand forever, from her record ne'er will fade
The glory of that combat with Lecompton's black brigade;
And when June comes with her roses, at Baltimore we'll crown
The "LITTLE GIANT," who has met and struck corruption down.

So a DOUGLAS and a DOUGLAS!
While hearts have smiles and tears,
Your name will glow, your praise shall flow,
Through all the coming years.

THE LYRIC OF TWEDDLE HALL.[35]

RESPECTFULLY INSCRIBED TO THE CENTRAL RAILROAD AND THE STATE CENTRAL COMMITTEE.

Who killed the Democracy?
"It was I," said Pete Cagger,
"With my poisonous dagger—
It was I killed Democracy."

And who helped him to do it?
"It was I," said D'ri. Ogden,
"'Twas an act by a hog done,
And I helped him to do it."

And who held the blood-basin?
"It was I," said Sam Tilden;
"When the red blood was spilled in,
It was I held the basin."

And who'll have to pay for it?
"Alas!" cried the "Central,"
"I feel in my ventral
And heart that I'll pay for it."

And who'll keep the soul quieted?
"I'll gladly," sighed Cassidy,
"Pay the priest for a mass a day
To keep its soul quieted."

And who'll have revenge for it?
"We, we," yelled the young men—
"Bold, honest, and strong men,
We'll have deep revenge for it."

And who'll write its epitaph?
"Woe's me," sang O'Reilly,
"It was butchered most vilely,
But I'll write its epitaph."

When and where shall we bury it?
  "We'll do that next November,
  With our watchword 'Remember!'—
Oh, most nobly we'll bury it."

What may mean this "Remember?"
  "Cagger's yoke to shake off, man,
  As we should have done Hoffman
When he ran last November."

Can't the thing be "made nice," boys?
  "No; we'll fight as we've chosen
  Till a hot place is frozen—
Then we'll fight on the ice, boys."

Dare you beat the state ticket?
  "To disgrace we're not wedded,
  And we'll go 'double-headed,'
Just to beat that state ticket."

What! let Radicals win, boys?
  "Ay, we'll vote for the devil
  Till we get this thing level—
We'd let Beelzebub win, boys."

Are you all of this thinking?
  "All! all!" cried the masses:
  "Too long we've been asses,
But we now do tall thinking."

Will you hold to this pledge, boys?
  "Ay, so help us our Savior!
  All our future behavior
Shall be true to this pledge, boys."

What! no bargain or compromise?
  "Everlastingly damn any
  Man who, with Tammany,
Talks of a compromise."

Then you hoist the black banner?
  "Ay, it's war to the knife—
  It is now life for life,
And we hoist the black banner."

Against odds you'll be fighting?
  "'Gainst 'the deck and the devil,'
  Till we get this thing level,
We'll do nothing but fighting."

Don't you fear old Pete Cagger?
  "Pooh! the red-faced, wee fellow,
  With his wig of bright yellow—
We'll just p-p-p-p-puff at Pete Cagger."

"GIVE ME GUANO OR GIVE ME DEATH!"[36]

Jerry Black to Johnson.

Alack! alack! poor Jerry Black,
  Do you call yourself a man, oh,
Yet on the President go back
  For a dunghill of guano?
Your bust let Cloacina hold,
  While Clio will record your
Foul name, as one who Freedom sold
  For so much penguin's ordure.

TO UNCLE SAM.[37]

A CRY FROM THE AMERICAN SOLDIERS IN MOUNTJOY PRISON, NEAR DUBLIN.

Air: "*The Wearing of the Green.*"

Oh, Uncle Sam, and did you hear
  The news that's going round?
Protection in your starry flag
  No longer can be found;
For Seward he is England's tool,
  A truckler cold and mean,
And he outlaws every citizen
  Whoever wore the green.

Oh, as citizens—Americans—
  We gloried in the name,
And on many a field our blood we shed
  To guard your flag of fame;
But to-day we lie in bonds, as if
  Mere felons we had been:
The only charge that England brings,
  "These boys were for the green."

We are citizens twice over,
  By the law and by the sword,
By adoption and by service—
  But our claims are now ignored.

Say, Uncle Sam, is this your wish,
  And do you really mean
That you've outlawed all your faithful sons
  Whose birth was of the green?

We have had no trial—every prayer
  For justice is refused;
Never heard of our accusers,
  Nor of what we are accused.
But England, grinning, holds us here
  In bondage close and keen,
While Seward smiles, and says no word
  To save the boys in green.

Say, Uncle Sam, did England earn
  Our Seward's wish to please,
When her pirates drove your peaceful flag
  Of commerce from the seas?
And it was from her great arsenals
  The South was armed, I ween,
While we were fighting on your side—
  We boys who wear the green.

Oh, if we are not citizens,
  Then—for your own fair fame—
Disclaim us quickly, openly,
  And save your flag from shame.
But if citizens you think us yet
  (And made so twice we've been),
Bid Seward write: "Release at once
  Our boys who wear the green."

THE PRESIDENT TO CONGRESS.[38]

Air: "Yankee Doodle Dandy."

General Orders, No. 1.

Headquarters in the White House, January 31, 1867.

I.

Andy Johnson is my name,
  Tennessee my nation,
"Swinging round" it is my game,
  And President my station.
Yankee Doo may squirm and screech,
  Yankee Doodle Dandy,
But Yankee Doodle won't impeach
  His "great plebeian," Andy.

II.

Uncle Thad is drunk or mad
  When he the scheme proposes,
For heaven's own plan made me the man
  To be your "second Moses!"
Let Ashley rave and Phillips preach,
  Yankee Doodle Dandy,
But Wall Street can not yet impeach
  The "second Moses," Andy.

III.

It seems that I'm the "anvil" now,
  And Congress is "the hammer;"
The sparks of fight fly far and bright,
  And deafening is the clamor;
But no "dead duck" by hunter struck
  Yankee Doodle Dandy,
So far can reach as to impeach
  The "circle-swinging" Andy."

IV.

I had better, p'r'aps, have shut my mouth
  Than Congress so have pelted;
Perhaps too quickly for the South
  My bowels may have melted;
But 'twas a generous fault, you'll own,
  Yankee Doodle Dandy,
And not enough to cost his throne
  To your repentant Andy.

V.

You've stripped me of my dearest power—
  To use it none were braver;
Even Mrs. Cobb can't get a job
  Of pardoning now to save her;
I'm only President in name,
  Yankee Doodle Dandy,
Then why impeach, and blast the fame
  Of the once "most pop'lar" Andy?

VI.

I can't appoint the man I want
  To aid my re-election;
My spoils are lost, and, tempest-tossed,
  My friends are in dejection.
I nominated men of fame,
  Yankee Doodle Dandy,
But the Senate won't confirm a name
  That so much as smells of Andy.

VII.

And once—'twas in the Cleveland scrape,
  When the boys required a preacher—
My private Miles, wid his "winnin' smiles,"
  Seduced even Father Beecher!
But worse to keep than to seduce,
  Yankee Doodle Dandy,
For Beech., as never did my "goose,"
  Took wings and fled from Andy.

VIII.

Along the railroads, near and far,
  With patriot resolution,
I left "the flag with every star,"
  Likewise "the Constitution."
I did the level best I could,
  Yankee Doodle Dandy,
But "by fantastics misunderstood"
  Is the epitaph of Andy.

IX.

Impeach me if you think 'twill pay—
  But it won't pay, I'll be bound, sirs;
For, driving things this reckless way,
  You'll drive 'em in the ground, sirs.
The people may have thought me wrong,
  Yankee Doodle Dandy,
But a punishment too long and strong
  Will win them back to Andy.

By order of the Commander-in-Chief,
MILES O'REILLY,
Asst. Adjt. Gen. and Chief of Sinners.

A true copy:
WRIGHT RIVES, Colonel and A. D. C., U. S. A.

ST. TAMMANY'S TERROR.

Ah! I sicken contemplating
  Next election day—
Sicken with a sad forewarning
That, when comes that fatal morning,
  Fifty thousand freemen waiting,
    All will block my way;
  Yes, my heart sinks contemplating
    Next election day.

Ah! my heart grows full of terror—
Terror of the fray—
And my mind is busy shaping
Some small loop-hole for escaping—
'Scaping from the fatal error
Of provoking such a day;
Yes, my blood congeals with terror,
Thinking of that fray.

Ah! my heart is sore with sighing
"Were I safe away!"
But my wish must fall unheeded,
Now the sacrifice is needed—
I must do my public dying
On election day;
And my heart is full of sighing
"Were I safe away!"

Ah! my heart is pained with thinking—
Thinking of lost sway—
Thinking of a city plundered,
Party bonds and friendship sundered,
All the honest voters shrinking
From my side away;
Yes, my heart is pained with thinking
Of next election day.

"MANHOOD AGAINST THE MACHINES."[39]

Air: "The Wearing of the Green."

Oh, brothers dear, and did you hear
The woful news to-day?
The "Lunch Club" of the City Hall
Aspire to boundless sway.
So Connolly, he must die the death,
And Hardy not be seen,
Nor Walsh, nor any other boy
That ever wore the green;
For Sweeny of the black mustache,
And Hoffman of the brown,
And Tweed with no mustache at all,
Now claim to own the town.

These princes of Mustachiodom—
Their spirits black and brown—
Now claim that they, and they alone,
Are masters of the town;

So Waterbury he must fall
  Beneath their guillotine,
In favor of A. Oakey Hall,
  Who cursed the Irish green.
      And the children of the Rhineland
        Were cursed by him, I ween,
      But now we all must vote for Hall,
        Both German boys and green.

But before we own the "Lunch Club"
  Has arrived at boundless sway,
We'll have a rising of the pikes
  On next election day.
Our beltane fires we'll kindle,
  As in Ireland they were seen,
When Ireland's sons, in 'ninety-eight,
  Were rising for the green.
      And the heroes of the black mustache,
        The no mustache, and brown,
      Will find, before the fight is o'er,
        They do not own the town.

Oh, against the grim Excise Law,
  And to crush the Tammany "Ring,"
And against an Albany Police
  Our flag abroad we'll fling;
For the people's rights we stand arrayed—
  An army grand, I ween,
As Sarsfield led at Fontenoy
  Beneath the Irish green.
      And we mean to win the battle;
        For among us here are seen
      The Germans and the native-born,
        And the boys who wear the green.

We have chieftains tried and gallant
  As ever faced a foe—
The "Big Judge" and the "Long Judge"
  Arm-in-arm we see them go;
Smith Ely, too, and Billy Walsh,
  Are brigadiers, I ween,
While the color-bearer of our line
  Is Miles, who wears the green.
      So Sweeny, Twéed, and Hoffman now
        May fairly set it down,
      The "Lunch Club" reign is over,
        And we boys have won the town.

SOON WE'LL HAVE THE UNION BACK.

CAMPAIGN SONG: M'CLELLAN AGAINST LINCOLN.

Air: "The Hunters of Kentucky."

Good people all, both great and small,
  I sing a tale of pity,
My hand I fling across the string,
  And waken up the ditty;
A ruined land that once was grand
  Is not a joking matter,
Though Abe, we know, the more our woe,
  The more his jokes he'll chatter;
    Oh, M'Clellan,
      Georgie B. M'Clellan,
    Shall we have the Union back?
      Tell us "Mac"—M'Clellan.

All evils sure we could endure,
  Thrice all the ills we suffer,
Could we but glance on any chance
  Our Union to recover;
There gleams one way a flash of day,
  But one bright bow of promise—
Good Lord, alack! just give us "Mac,"
  An' take Abe Lincoln from us!
    Oh, M'Clellan,
      Georgie B. M'Clellan,
    The one to bring the Union back
      Is only "Mac"—M'Clellan.

Then not a rag of our old flag
  Should ever part asunder;
"Fair terms of peace if you will cease—
  If not, we'll give you thunder!"
A million swords to back our words
  Beneath M'Clellan gleaming,
And soon, you know, Jeff D. and Co.,
  For France they would be steaming.
    Oh, M'Clellan,
      Georgie B. M'Clellan,
    Soon we'll have our prisoners back
      Under Mac—M'Clellan.

The people all, both great and small,
  Except the sons of "shoddy,"
Are on the track for Little Mac—
  They're with him soul and body;

For well they know the nation's woe
  Can never be abated,
Till in command of all the land
  Our chief we have instated.
    Oh, M'Clellan,
      Georgie B. M'Clellan,
    The Union will come leaping back
      Under Mac—M'Clellan.

EPIGRAM BY THE COLLECTOR.

Around my neck he placed his wing,
And cooed and billed as doves may sing—
    This treacherous and dull bird;
While yet his beak, with bloody art,
He strove to fasten in my heart—
    This vulture—Judas Hulburd.

JOHN MORRISSEY MY JO, JOHN.[40]

AN EARNEST CRY AND PRAYER THAT HE MAY NOT BE CORRUPTED BY HIS ASSOCIATIONS IN CONGRESS.

John Morrissey my jo, John,
  When first I kenned ye weel,
Your airms were like twa iron flails,
  Your hands like slugs o' steel;
But now ye've gaithered pelf, John,
  An' to Congress ye maun go,
Where they fight less fairly than yourself,
  John Morrissey my jo.

John Morrissey my jo, John,
  Wi' braid and monly breast,
Ye hae faced fu' mony a mon, John,
  To try which mon was best;
There were tough knocks fairly dealt, John,
  But to Congress now ye go,
Where they gouge an' strike below the belt,
  John Morrissey my jo.

John Morrissey my jo, John,
  We hae played an' drank thegither,
An' fu' mony a "tiger" fight, John,
  We hae had wi' ane anither;

Oh, at cheatin' still ye mocked, John,
  But to Congress now ye go,
Where the dice are cogged and the cairds are stocked,
  John Morrissey my jo.

John Morrissey my jo, John,
  Wi' grief our hearts are stirred,
For still to friend an' foe, John,
  Your bond was aye your word;
But I fear ye'll learn to lie, John,
  When to Congress now ye go,
For twad tak a saint to resist the taint,
  John Morrissey my jo.

John Morrissey my jo, John,
  On your good pluck ye relied,
An' against no pitted foe, John,
  The "hocussing game" ye tried;
But ye'll find it "hocus" all, John,
  When to Congress now ye go,
An' we fear frae your high stand ye'll fall,
  John Morrissey my jo.

John Morrissey my jo, John,
  These politicians deal
From a faro-box false-bottomed
  Wi' springs o' patent "steal."
Will your scruples never melt, John,
  When to Congress now ye go?
Can ye deal the same square game ye dealt,
  John Morrissey my jo?

John Morrissey my jo, John,
  It ne'er was kenned your plan
To kick a fallen foe, John,
  Or spurn a helpless man;
But ye'll find a different rule, John,
  When to Congress now ye go,
For they kick the South, having gagged its mouth,
  John Morrissey my jo.

John Morrissey my jo, John,
  My heart in terror beats,
For you've got into unco' company—
  A gang o' patent cheats.
Ye hae fought an' gambled fair, John,
  But to Congress now ye go,
An' I fear they may corrupt you there,
  John Morrissey my jo.

FERNANDO'S CARD.[41]

TO THE VOTERS OF THE NINTH CONGRESSIONAL DISTRICT.

The royal prince who reigns in hell
  Has been maligned in various matters,
And now would have the people tell
  How silly they regard such clatters.
He asks your votes; 'tis not for pelf,
  But to rebuke all saints and sages
Who say the archangels and himself
  Have not been cronies through all ages.

FOURTH CONGRESSIONAL DISTRICT.[42]

Our theatres with "Box and Cox"
  Were crammed from pit to rafter,
But now the farce of "Cox and Fox"
  Fills the whole town with laughter.

A BUMPER TO GRANT.

FIRST GUN OF THE LYRICAL CAMPAIGN.

Air: "Benny Havens, oh!"

Come, fill your glasses, fellows,
  And stand up in a row,
On a presidential drinking
  We are going for to go;
Let us have no more sobriety—
  At least no more to-night—
While for President Ulysses Grant
  We take our foremost flight.
    Oh, for President Ulysses
      Let every glass be bright—
    May he rule the country he has saved,
      And God defend the right.

His hand is soft to meet a friend,
  And mailed to meet a foe—
He's the Mississippi River horse,
  Resistless as its flow;
He's the conqueror of leaguered towns,
  And victor in the field—
No foe has ever grappled Grant
  That was not forced to yield.

So to President Ulysses
  Brim every glass to-night,
May he rule the country he has saved,
  And God defend the right.

In the world to-day no prouder name
  Is borne on any breeze,
And with Grant to steer the ship of state,
  Our flag shall rule the seas;
No "dominion" shall be north of us,
  And south of us no foe—
Our stars and stripes in the Canadas,
  And likewise Mexico.
    For with President Ulysses
      There'll be few who care to fight—
    May he rule the country he has saved,
      And God defend the right.

No more shall Irish officers
  In English dungeons pine,
No more shall Seward's endless notes
  In endless terror whine;
We'll assert our place of nationhood,
  And take our proper rank,
With iron-clads to guard our shores,
  And bullion in the bank:
    All this when Grant is President,
      To whom our faith we plight—
    May he rule the country he has saved,
      And God defend the right.

Oh, the Queen of the Antilles
  Must be wooed and must be won,
With her groves of palm and orange
  Flashing brightly in the sun;
And our brethren of the beaten states,
  Who suffer wrong to-day,
Will find a generous hand held out
  When Grant has come to sway;
    For generous is Ulysses
      To the men who felt his might—
    May he rule the country he has saved,
      And God defend the right.

We are sick of old Thad Stevens,
  We are sick of Butler too;
Sick of Kelly, Ashley, Sumner,
  And that God-forsaken crew.

Let the men who faced the music
  When the storm ran high and hard,
All join to make Ulysses Grant
  Our captain of the guard.
    For with candidate Ulysses
      We can make the bulliest fight
    To rule the country he has saved,
      And God defend the right.

Then old John Bull at Liverpool
  Will some day wake and groan,
Finding Farragut at anchor
  And his ports wide open thrown:
"Settle up your Anglo-rebel bills,
  And quickly, if you please,
For General Grant is President,
  And I command the seas."
    To this we pledge Ulysses,
      And to him we drink to-night—
    May he rule the country he has saved,
      And God defend the right.

So, boys, a final bumper,
  While we all in chorus chant—
"For next President we nominate
  Our own Ulysses Grant."
And if asked what state he hails from,
  This our sole reply shall be,
"From near Appomattox Court-house,
  With its famous apple-tree."
    For 'twas there, to our Ulysses,
      That Lee gave up the fight—
    Now, boys, "To Grant for President,
      And God defend the right."

A STORM BREWING.

"You are growing masculine, my dear,"
  Said a husband to his wife;
"You are disimproving with every year
  Since you became my wife."

"A bitter thing of yourself you have said,"
  Was the lady's answer true;
"For an angel you thought me when I was wed—
  What has changed me to be a shrew?

"And if I have now a harder heart,
'Tis in order my griefs to bear;
For when husbands forget what is manhood's part,
Then the wives for themselves must care."

A PRESIDENTIAL WARNING.

Air: "Ould Ireland, you're my darling."

Musha, Andie dear,
I mightily fear
That your chance is ashleep—can you wake it?
For the Faynian vote
Seward gripped by the throat,
An' clane out of its boots did shake it.
The gallant O'Nale
He did impale
The wrong side of the Canada bordhers;
An' the Faynians wor shtopped,
An' their rations wor lopped,
Undher Grant's imperative ordhers.
Faix! Seward and Shpeed—
Who detest you indeed—
May well choke with malicious laughter;
For, while this is the deed
Of Bill Seward an' Shpeed,
It is Johnson the Faynians are afther.

Sind Seward away,
Clane across the say,
To them English he loves so dearly;
An' that you are for Pat—
If you'll only do that—
The Faynians will recognize clearly.
But in case you don't,
Or you can't or won't—
Though they like you, an' like your notions—
The Faynians, I fear,
May start off right here,
To the Radicals payin' devotions.
An' then Seward an' Shpeed—
Who detest you indeed—
May well choke with malicious laughter;
For, while this is the deed
Of Bill Seward an' Shpeed,
It is Andie the Faynians are afther.

I am for you, my boy,
My jewel an' joy,
Till a sartain warm raygion is frozen;
And if my friendship firm
Could prolong your term,
Faix! the chair you now fill you might doze in;
But these Faynians grand
Are a hot-headed band,
An' they think they wor thrated unfairly;
An' if somethin' ain't done
To cut short their fun,
Och, their votes will be cast mighty quarely.
An' then Seward an' Shpeed—
Who detest you indeed—
Their midriffs may shplit wid laughter;
For, while this is the deed
Of Bill Seward an' Shpeed,
It is Johnson the Faynians are afther.

CHURCH, CAGGER, AND PIPER.[43]

Poor dead "Regularity,"
Claiming our charity,
Lies in a plight most horrid—
Mangled all sadly,
Lifeless, and badly
Gashed in the breast and the forehead.

Who used the dagger?
With insolent swagger,
"'Twas I," says PETE CAGGER,
Of the murder a bragger—
"'Twas I used the dagger."

And who'll have to pay for it?
Who'll rue the day for it?
Who'll have to do all the weeping?
"We, we," said the REGENCY;
"We a grim legion see
On to avenge her sweeping."

And think you that CAGGER,
Who now has the swagger
Of a bravo who slays for his stipend,
Will still be a bragger
Of using the dagger
When the time to avenge her has ripened?

"No," said DEAN of the Central,
Slow patting his ventral,
As if in each entrail
An agony rose which half rent it;
"He who killed 'Regularity,'
PETE CAGGER the carroty,
That man without charity,
You'll find him the first to repent it.

"In each Presidential
Convention, essential
We found the strong aid she supplied us;
Oh, deed of dark horror!
At Charleston, but for her
The South would our seats have denied us.

"It was CHURCH held the basin,
That grim anti-mason,
He caught her, and gagged her, and bound her;
But 'twas PETER who killed her,
'Twas his dagger spilled her
Most innocent life-blood around her.

"Assisted by PIPER,
That venomous viper,
In secret the plan was agreed on;
But now in blank terror
They see their mad error,
And fear is the food they must feed on."

These men without charity
Killed "Regularity;"
Yonder small carroty
Man used the dagger:
"Down with Old Tammany!
Butcher her—damn any
Man who can't sham any
Love for PETE CAGGER."

PETE is not mendable—
Salable, vendible,
Prone to assumption,
Wanting in gumption,
Playing Old Nick with the Central;
CORNING must stop him,
RICHMOND close crop him,
Snub and subdue him,
Wholly undo him,

Or TAMMANY HALL will yet give to the Central
A punch in that region which doctors call ventral—
A twinge in each kidney, and membrane, and entrail—
Just to make it remember
That, after November,
The war-path before us,
The Wigwam's flag o'er us,
Knives and tomahawks ready,
Our warriors all steady,
We can whip such Old Fogydom till it begs charity,
And surrenders each wretch who assailed "Regularity."

LINES TO A CONGRESSMAN.[44]

Air: "Jeannette and Jeannot."

You are voting the wrong way,
Oh my Congressman of note;
You spoke against it t'other day,
But now it has your vote.
You're on this and t'other tack,
Alternating like my rhymes,
And in vain we try your course to track
Through the columns of the Times.

When you wear a Johnson coat,
In the Philadelphia style,
Then you're sure to cast a Radical vote,
Howe'er the House may smile;
Let whatever happen hap,
Disregarding all advice,
Oh, you turn your coat and turn your cap
As jugglers change their dice.

Now if I were in your seat,
I would make an open rule,
One day with the Johnson men to meet,
And the next with the Stevens school;
Consistency 'twould give,
And we should not think you mad
If each odd day "Conservative,"
Each even day a "Rad."

Take an almanac for guide,
And your prospects will improve;
Heed not although Le Blonde deride,
And the House with laughter move.

With this odd and even rule
  We may guess at your "posish,"
While now you're neither hot nor cool,
  Neither cabbage, meat, nor fish.

VOICE OF THE ARMY.

A CAMPAIGN SONG FOR M'CLELLAN AGAINST LINCOLN.

Air: "Scots wha hae wi' Wallace bled."

Comrades of the tented field,
Who the flag would never yield,
Making of your breasts a shield
        Where the pennon flew—
Men who have with steady breath
Rushed on lines of blazing death,
Thus a wounded brother saith—
        "To yourselves be true!"

Faithful to the nation's chief,
Work he bliss or work he grief,
Till the hour of just relief,
        When our votes we fling;
If he err, not ours to heed;
If he err, 'tis ours to bleed—
This the soldier's simple creed,
        And to this we cling.

But, at length, the hour is here,
When with soldier conscience clear,
We in judgment may appear
        On his hateful thrall;
Past respect for his high place
Bids us only veil the face—
Shrinking back from the disgrace,
        Sad and silent all.

Turn, oh comrades of the tent—
Of the flag with bullets rent—
Of the field with blood besprent,
        Turn to brighter skies.
See, with soldier brow and hand,
Sympathizing, calm, and grand,
Chosen chief of all the land,
        Our own M'Clellan rise.

Let no ribald king or clown
Lie away our chief's renown—
Strike the coward scoffers down;
Teach them what they are.
Bats and owlets dread the dawn,
Cowards, plunderers—all the spawn
Far from our dread work withdrawn—
Strive his way to bar.

Vain their efforts, brother tried—
Sharer of our woe and pride,
"Little Mac," our friend and guide,
Our watchword and our star.
Hail him, drums, with glad alarms—
Hail him with your fiery charms—
All the din of battling arms—
Ye his music are.

SOLEMN POLITICAL DEATH-BED.

LAST WORDS OF FERNANDO WOOD TO HIS BROTHER HENRY WOOD, OF WOOD'S NEGRO MINSTRELS.

Bring the fiddle, bones, and banjo—play a dirge, my brother Hen,
For I feel that I'm a goner, down among the deadest men;
In the Limbo, drear and dismal, where lost politicians roast,
They are stoking up the furnace for the brownest kind of toast;
And I feel it in my bones, Hen,
And hence are all my moans, Hen,
That the toasting-prongs are ready,
And the white heat sure and steady,
The hungry imps all grinning,
And the cooks prepared for skinning,
While I feel myself the victim doomed to feed this hungry host.

Well, I played my last card boldly, but the Wigwam trumped my trick,
And when I heard the ticket named, that moment I grew sick.
On that instant flashed before me all my dark and hideous past,
And I heard them in the Limbo cry, "We'll get our own at last."
You may think it was some "Birds," Hen,
Who chirped those fatal words, Hen,
But no; I felt them wreathe me
From the deep, fierce pit beneath me,
Like serpents coiled and hissing,
Their forked fangs never missing,
And I know 'twas Limbo shouted, "Oh, we'll get our own at last."

Since the game at length is over, and my bully hand played out,
Of the past and its achievements I begin to feel a doubt;
Perhaps it had been better had I played a squarer game—
Been less false and heartless to my friends, less selfish in my aim;
But it's now too late to think, Hen,
I can only cower and shrink, Hen,
For they're piling up the fagots,
And I see some fiery maggots
Wriggling upward to receive me
When the last puffs, panting, leave me—
Through all my limbs political I feel the creeping flame.

No use to sigh or struggle, 'twas a bold, bad game I played—
No private ties, no public ties to break was I afraid;
Still my loaded dice threw sixes, and my dupes paid out their gold,
And my coat-sleeve had an open mouth the ace and king to hold.
Oh, the tricks were easy won, Hen,
And my dupes so nicely done, Hen,
That I stood knee-deep in clover,
While long years and years rolled over,
Cheating all the fools around me,
Breaking all the bonds that bound me,
Impassive as a granite rock—as bloodless and as cold.

But after all, perhaps there are some surer cards to play;
It is not wise *all* friends we have to use and fling away;
There may be policy in faith and folly in deceit—
I think, had I a partner now, I'd try hard *not* to cheat.
But the knowledge comes too late, Hen,
Comes while the yawning gate, Hen,
Revolves on fiery hinges,
And the red heat redly tinges
The fiery hands extended
To tell me life is ended—
They have found an "altered invoice," which they tangle round my feet.

Well, I *had* some friends at one time—the Irish, warm and true,
And the Germans, who, for many a year, my standard would pursue;
Lord! in our secret lodges, our encampments, and grim schools,
How we of the Know-Nothings used to mock these generous fools!
'Twas a desperate game to play, Hen,
But it won for many a day, Hen;
Too monstrous for believing,
'Twas the easiest thing deceiving;
Secret oaths in secret muttered,
False professions loudly uttered—
These were the stock in trade with which I duped the generous fools.

No matter. Let your tears, Hen, for other griefs be kept;
At Lorenzo Shepard's funeral a thousand good men wept;
Against my schemes of rapine he taxed his glorious mind,
Till his great soul shattered the weak case in which it moved enshrined;
But not a tear for me, Hen,
This weakness must not be, Hen;
If I lived for self, and perish
With none my name to cherish—
False, hating men and hated,
To long oblivion fated—
The King of Terrors nears me, and to death I stand resigned.

When I'm dead and in my coffin, under fifty thousand nails—
When the News, released from mortgage, my cruel yoke assails—
When even Plumb and Brisley, Tom Hen Ferris and Ben Ray,
Regard me as a played-out dog who has no future day—
Oh, then I ask of you, Hen,
To this last office true, Hen,
With Mer. Brewer to deposit
The papers in that closet;
Round my coffin-edge and borders
Hang my full Know Nothing orders—
Cold as clay must be the nearest I can come to Henry Clay.

So bring the bones and banjo—play a requiem, Brother Hen,
For I feel that I'm a goner, down among the deadest men;
In the Limbo, drear and dismal, where lost politicians roast,
They are stoking up the furnace for the brownest kind of toast;
And I feel it in my bones, Hen,
And hence come all my moans, Hen,
That the toasting-prongs are ready,
And the white heat sure and steady,
The hungry imps all grinning,
And the cooks prepared for skinning,
While I feel myself the victim doomed to feed this hungry host.

TWEEDLEDUM AND TWEEDLEDEE.[45]

That eternal cocklorum old jamboree
Betwixt H. Greeleygrum and T. Weedledee
Has burst out again worse than ever, you see,
And they're deep in a high old sparring spree,
And cross-buttocking other to such a degree
That it forms a sight for all Christians to see.

But the public, I notice—that's you and me—
Have to bear all the blows of the sparring spree
Betwixt H. Greeleygrum and T. Weedledee.

T. Weedledee blows on a mighty horn,
And blows with a vengeance, as sure as you're born;
And crows like a rooster who finds in the morn
Six new pullet wives and a bushel of corn
Lying loose near his dunghill; and crows to warn
All the rest of creation, with loftiest scorn,
That they neither must tread on his pullets or corn.

While H. Greeleygrum, from his sanctum's height,
Puts on his whole armor to face the fight,
And cries to Sid. Gay, "Where my coat of white
Gleams in the battle, be sure all your might
Is directed to doing some grievous despite
To that elderly rooster who still will write
His letters and paragraphs, keen and bright,
Against me and mine, and against truth and right,
Above the initials, so hateful to me,
Which mark out the old man known as T. Weedledee."

THE HEALTH BILL.[46]

A TALK BETWEEN TWO REPUBS AT ALBANY.

"Shall we pass this great bill for the public health?"
  "Why, that is no longer the question;
But shall endless sources of power and wealth,
And unlimited chances of public stealth—
On the cholera-plea and the public health—
  Be secured for our party's digestion?"

"And if to our party this power is to glide,
  And these chances of wealth be won for us?"
"Why, the next question, then, we have got to decide
Is this: Shall we make it 'an equal divide'
Betwixt the Weed-Seward and the Radical side,
  Or give all to Lord Thurlow or Horace?"

"The Senate think Weed should be given the whole,
  And the Board of Police therefore packed on;
But the bully Assembly's as black as a coal,
And the Radical rascals say 'Thurlow's control
Is already too great for the good of his soul,
  And they're down like Old Scratch on Tom Acton."

"So between them the Health Bill is dragged either way,
And all kinds of fools' errands is sent on?"
"Why, yes; but you'll find they'll agree some fine day
Not to lose such rich chances for pickings and pay;
And the Health Bill—at least so I heard Lyman say—
Will be given to Lord Horace through Fenton."

THE TRIBUNE'S PRESIDENTIAL PHILOSOPHY.

Soon forget the bread that's eaten,
And let policy be shown;
Don't take Seward, or we're beaten—
Take some ninny quite unknown.
Take some fossilized curmudgeon,
One with no obstreperous brains,
And we'll hook the popular gudgeon,
Ay, and cook it for our pains.

Let us get our Bates all ready,
And go cruising near the Banks;
Years of service, stanch and steady,
We'll repay with—many thanks.
Gratitude with us is gammon,
But we'll win the spoils we wish,
Chase-ing that Ohio Salmon,
Or enjoying New York Fish.

Give us some old dancing dervis,
Just a puppet for our wire;
Seward has done too much service—
Has more brains than we desire.
Give us some old dumb curmudgeon,
One who neither writes nor prates,
And we'll hook the public gudgeon,
If some Weed don't snarl our Bates.

"MR. JOHNSON'S POLICY OF RECONSTRUCTION."

Greeley.

SOME COMMENT FROM THE BOYS IN BLUE.

"His policy," do you say?
By heaven, who says so lies in his throat!
'Twas our policy, boys, from our muster-day,
Through skirmish and bivouac, march and fray—
"His policy," do you say?

"His policy"—do but note!
'Tis a pitiful falsehood for you to say.
Did he bid all the stars in our banner float?
Was it he shouted Union from every throat
Through the long war's weary day?

"His policy"—how does it hap?
Has the old word "Union" no meaning, pray?
What meant the "U. S." upon every cap—
Upon every button, belt, and strap?
'Twas our policy all the way.

"His policy?" That may do
For a silly and empty political brag;
But 'twas held by every Boy in Blue
When he lifted his right hand, stanch and true,
And swore to sustain the flag.

We are with him none the less—
He works for the same great end we sought:
We feel for the South in its deep distress,
And to get the old Union restored we press—
'Twas for this we enlisted and fought.

Be it his or whose it may,
'Tis the policy, boys, that we avow;
There were noble hearts in the ranks of gray,
As they proved on many a bloody day,
And we would not oppress them now.

"Let us all forgive and forget:"
It was thus Grant spoke to General Lee,
When, with wounds still raw and bayonets wet,
The chiefs of the two great armies met
Beneath the old apple-tree.

RING RHYMES.[47]

Ho, brothers! drawn from many lands,
Who drive the plane or swing the hammer—
Beneath whose swift and knotted hands
Our shops and ship-yards clamor.
Ho! all who live by thinking brow,
By touch of art or strain of sinew—
Rise, brothers! rise and swear a vow
That the foul Ring-rule, rampant now,
No longer shall in power continue.

Choked sewers of filth and streets of mire—
  These to King Pest a premium proffer;
And the young, and the old, and the weak expire,
  That the Ring may fill its coffer.
And who are these men who can thus afford
  To plunder and spurn our princely village?
See this beetle-browed, skulking, and ruffian horde,
Who, when true men sprang to the musket and sword,
  Remained home here to organize pillage.

They have seized all posts of power and pride,
  They mock as vain our passionate struggle,
Conscious how well is fortified
  Their rule of theft and juggle.
They think us weak, for they know how long
  We have borne their sway of shame and plunder—
Up, brothers, now against the wrong;
Up, in one effort fierce and strong,
  And rend their villainous Ring asunder.

Up, for our city's tarnished fame—
  Let justice urge and manhood quicken;
Up, ere we grow quite dead to shame,
  With moral palsy stricken;
Up, and hunt down this brood of Theft,
  As bloodhounds bay the wolf's hot haunches;
Up, ere of all we prize bereft;
Up, and—if nothing else be left—
  Let's swing the rogues on gallows-branches.

"OUR BIG THING ON ICE."

Air: "Tim Donnelly, the Giant."

Success to you, big Mike Connolly,
  So burly an' so defiant,
You're twice bigger than ould Tim Donnelly,
  That was our great "Irish giant."
Your heart is big, an' your brain is big—
  Out o' jail you're our "biggest big thing,"
And 'tis Big Judge Mike, wid his big shtick,
  That'll break the Tammany "Ring."
      So long life to you, Big Mike Connolly,
        So jovial an' so defiant,
      You're twice bigger than ould Tim Donnelly,
        That was our great "Irish giant."

It was our Big Mike, wid his big shtick,
  That gave the "Excise" its bolus,
An' he's taught Tom Acton many a trick
  In spite of all his poliss.
It's him that shmites for the poor man's rights,
  It's to him that wid hope they cling,
An' it's his big fist into smithers will twist
  The "Lunch Club" an' its "ring."
    Och, bully for you, Judge Connolly,
      So plucky an' so defiant,
    You're twice bigger than ould Tim Donnelly,
      That was our great "Irish giant."

John A. Kennedy calls you "blatherin' Mike,"
  An' the Tammany leaders curse you,
But the more at you, Mike, such haythins sthrike,
  The more in our hearts we'll nurse you.
Och, you'll fill the place wid most mortial grace,
  An' you'll do the hangin' highly;
But I want you to shwear (for I'm undher a scare)
  That you'll never hang Miles O'Reilly.
    Now, good luck to you, Big Mike Connolly,
      It's well you may be defiant,
    For you've twice the shtuff of Tim Donnelly,
      That was our great "Irish giant."

And here's a glass to you, Billy Walsh,
  My king of the bould Fourth Warders;
It's you that can shtump, an' it's you that'll jump
  Like a li'n over Tammany's bordhers.
You're of dacint shtock—you have brains an' pluck—
  You have faith—you have youth an' honor—
An' I wouldn't, 'tis thrue, whin he meets wid you,
  For a five-dollar bill be Bill Connor.
    So I dhrink to you, Billy, in good poteen,
      My king of the bould Fourth Warders,
    For it's you that can shtump, an' it's you that'll jump
      Like a li'n over Tammany's bordhers.

Come round me, ma bouchals, come all of you near me,
  For, faix! I'm the boy that can faithfully sing
All the blessin's—stand back there, and let the boys hear me—
  All the blessin's we get by supportin' the "Ring."
Sure we see our "ring-masthers," wid gorgeous inspection,
  From the hoighths of gilt coaches our labors survey;
An' we get a month's work—comin' on near election—
  A-clanin' the sewers for two dollars a day.

Look at Brennan. Time was he was "Mat" when we met him,
An' so civil he always 'ud bow whin we'd pass;
An', och! many's the good game o' "muggins" we bet him,
Whin he sould us bad rum at three coppers a glass.
But since by our votes to the "Ring" he was lifted,
On the Bloomin'dale Road he's a palace, they say;
And the flapjacks he ates must wid goold-dust be sifted,
An' poor divils like us must keep out of his way.

An' there's Charley Cornell—God be wid the time, Charley,
Whin dressed in your butcher-sleeves, blood to the edge,
Yourself and bould Terry—now Aldherman Farley—
Sat down wid us boys to a game of "ould sledge."
But it's now you're worth millions—an' how did you get it?
Didn't our votes first give you a sate in the "Ring?"
But we're honest and poor—and you sthrive to forget it,
An' the door in our faces, if callin', you'd fling.

An' there's Pether B. Shweeny—they say he is wiser,
An' cuter, an' darker than most in the "Ring;"
To the whole of them chickens he plays the adviser,
And shows how to cover their eggs wid their wing.
By me sowl, little Pether, the day will come hoppin'
That for all your "ring shwindles" you'll get what's your due;
An' aich three in the Park will be gayly out croppin'
Wid a rope and a noose for such spalpeens as you.

Look at Tweed—holy Father! Bill Tweedie—look at him;
Did you ever see feedin' like that in your life?
Like a Suffolkshire pig when you stuff him and fat him—
An' I guess—like the pig—he's just fit for the knife.
Musha Tweedie, ahagur! 'tis you have soft weather,
It was we tuned your pipes and we taught you to sing;
Do you mind o' the time we wor "bunkers" together,
Before you grew rich, fat, and proud in the "Ring?"

An' there's Boole! Oh, be jabers! the scoundhrelly Blue-nose
Has brought all his brothers to share in the swag;
He has houses, seven-thirties, and greenbacks, and few knows
The size of the "stale" he has tied in his bag.
"An' the moment," he says, "that they shtop him from thievin',
He'll to Canady carry his bones and his purse."
May the divil go wid him our counthry when leavin'—
On the black British spy be the Irishman's curse.

Och, boys! shall the rule of these villains continue—
Shall we still be the slaves o' the rogues we despise?
These trauneens who use neither brain-work nor sinew,
And forget us the moment we help them to rise?

By the Church of Ardagh and the great Cross of Cashel,
To the dioul both themselves and their tickets we'll fling,
Let us thry a new game—just for fun, boys—and smash all
The schaimes, an' the heads, an' machines o' the "Ring."

Air: "The Shan Van Voght."

Och, Fernandy Wood, the bould,
It is he has got a hould
On the votes an' the affections of the Mozart choir;
An' they'll sing, as he expects,
All the chimes that he directs,
An' they'll only call their sowls their own at his desire.

Now Fernandy Wood, he made
Wid Cornell an' Tweed a thrade,
Sellin' out his Mozart chickens, feathers, bones, an' hide,
On a promise that they should
Make himself, Fernandy Wood,
Their mayor in next December, let whatever else betide.

An' for this Fernandy shwore
To do up a little chore
In the sindin' of Cornell to the Sinate o' the shtate,
Where Charley, shpry an' firm,
Might extind his little term,
An' fix up some other matthers on the lobby-shlate.

An' for this bould Charley then
Shwore to carry "Brother Ben"
To the Sinate by the power o' cash the Wigwam wields;
While Weed might oust Laimbeer,
Placin' Stewart there this year,
An' put Thomas Murphy snugly in the place o' Tom C. Fields.

An' sure Brennan was to take,
As his private "little rake,"
The Law Department, placin' John E. Devlin on the shelf;
And this—to Weed's abhorrence—
He might give to A. R. Lawrence,
As the nominee of George Law and his very noble-self.

'Twas the purtiest little plot
Out of—somewhere that is hot—
But Fernandy, as he oulder grows, is proner still to gabble;
An' so it cum—by-an'-by—
That this saycret threaty shly
Was developed in the Herald to "the outside haythin rabble."

Whereupon blue murdher rose
'Twixt Fernandy's friends and foes,
An', faix: Weed was in a corner, an' Cornell was much the same;
For the Tribune axed the blood
Both of Weed and Benjie Wood,
An' the Herald vowed to fight to death agin the schaime.

Upon this Fernandy fine
Sinds for Daniel M. O'Brine,
To whom he had pledged the Mozarts in Cornell's disthrick;
An' says he, "My bully Dan,
Such an' such things are my plan,
So in favor of Cornell, Dan, you must back out quick."

"Divil resayve the fut I'll back
From the sinatorial thrack,"
Shpakes out the brave O'Brien, more courageous nor a brick;
"You have pledged my elevation
By the Mozart nomination,
An' 'tis I will be next senator from my disthrick."

Then Fernandy, mad wid rage,
Findin' flatthery wouldn't assuage,
Shwore a pistil-ball should whistle through O'Brien his heart,
If to tell he ever dared
The bad bargain thus declared,
An' by which Fernandy hoped again as mayor to shtart.

"Now, by this an' by that," says Dan,
"You're mistaken in your man,
If you hope to frighten any boy who is called O'Brien;"
An' wid that right off he goes,
Writes an' signs a full expose,
An' wid this has put a tombstone on Cornell's design.

So Fernandy's cake is dough,
An' the bould Bill Tweed's also,
An' the ould man's busy writin' dodgin' letthers o' denial;
An' the sea for Thomas Murphy
Now looks tempest-black an' surfy,
An' Stewart in his cockle-boat doesn't dare to make a thrial.

And the galliant "Brother Ben,"
Down among the deadest men,
Is decayin' like a stale jack-pike the honest fish-wife shpurns;
While o'er him, high in air,
As the emblems o' despair,
Gleam the banner and bright sabre of the brave young Col. Burns.

As to Brennan—faix, 'tis he
Is the cowed-est man you'd see,
While of Lawrence an' his ruined hopes he still is fiercely stormin';
An' for corporation counsel,
I'll bet tulips agin grounsel
That the next to fill the place will be our own bould Dick O'Gorman.

Oh, brothers—one an' all—
Let us organize this fall,
An' charge agin the Ring-chiefs in resistless line;
An' for leaders let us take—
Plucky, honest, wide-awake—
Just such candidates for every place as Daniel M. O'Brien.

Air: "Tune the old cow died of."

Musha, boys, did yez hear the news?
Sure Ben Wood is tuk bad wid "the blues,"
An' Fernandy's turned all soorts o' hues
That a shkin from the rainbow could borrow,
Since he heerd that the bargain or thrade
Wid Cornell an' the "ould man" he made
Has gone up in a big balloon
Twist higher nor is the moon,
An' himself an' poor Ben must sup sorrow.

For Ben sees, howsumdever he turns,
The victhory lanin' to Burns,
While all kinds o' hard kickin's an' shpurns
Are haped on Fernandy's alliance;
An' Karl Sprackensie Bryant O'Dutch
Isn't popilar—not overmuch—
An' Mat Brennan's attimpts to conthrol
How the people shall vote at the poll
Are met wid most haynious defiance.

An' Cornell! Sure the scoundhrel O'Brine
Has just wheeled all the boys into line,
An' bad luck to the hope or the sign
Of poor Charley's election this minnit;
For the Tribune's had somethin' to say
In gettin' Dane out o' the way;
An' no dodges or "Albany thricks"
That the "ould man's" so famious to fix
Can now sind poor Cornell to the Sinate.

As to Fields—well, the thing was too plain
That it lay between him an' M'Lane,
An' so poor Tommy Murphy in vain

Spinds the profits he made upon shoddy;
For the boys go M'Lane—nothin' shorter—
Neglectin' "the snorer and snorter,"
Tom Fields, who, in somnolent riot,
So oft broke the dignified quiet
Of our state sinatorial body.

An' to me, who am fond o' the "Ring,"
An' to Brennan an' Shweeny, who cling,
An' believe public theft is the thing
That our boys should admire an' remember—
Faix! I'm sick at the heart whin I look
At the figures that's writ in the book;
For to me it 'ud seem, darlin's dear,
That the "Ring" chance looks mortially queer,
An' will die the first week in December.

An', boys, should that sad hour approach,
Tuck me dacintly into a coach,
An' sind me, without reproach,
Away to the Jarseys hidin';
An' sind Brennan, an' Shweeny, an' Bradley along,
An' let A. Oakey Hall swell the mournin' throng,
For the town will be then far too hot and too sthrong
For such jockeys as them to abide in.

Air (with a recitative chorus): "Ould Ireland, you're my jewel, sure."

Och, boys, hurra! now comes the day
The "Ring's" rank rule for smitin';
We'll make smithereens o' their foul "machines,"
An' sind their schaimes a-kitin';
An' this shall be the song for me,
Corruption's bulwark stormin'—
"Hurra! hurra! we win the day,
Wid Hecker and Richard O'Gorman;"
May the Ould Boy cling to yer thievin' "Ring,"
An' the plunder yez pocketed handy;
But ye've dhrained the cup, an' the game is all up
For that everlastin' (judgment-by-default-allowin' John E. Develin and his congaynial partner in all soorts o' villainies, that pucker-faced, stiff-dickied ould rapparee an' scallywag in gineral)—
Sure av coorse I mane Fernandy.

The "Ring" goes down—we'll clear the town
Of all the brood o' Brennans;
An', faix! Charley Cornell, an' Tweed as well,
Shall fly before our pennons.

Their day is past, an' we'll see the last
  O' their crew to Jarsey swarmin',
Afeard to be caught, an' be hung as they ought,
  By Hecker an' Richard O'Gorman.
"God grant it soon" is the only chune
  That honest men can be singin',
"That from every three in the Park we may see
  Some plundher-fed 'Ring'-rogue (an', by me sowl! whin I say thim words, Terry Farley, it isn't a hundhred miles away from your mother's son that my mind's eye is wandherin', an' it's thinkin' I am what a purty corpse you'd make)—
  Some plundher-fed villain swingin'."

Ay, an' then there's Boole—that Blue-nose tool—
  An' his pack o' rapayshis brothers,
Who have gorged their fill at the public till
  Until aich o' thim nearly smothers.
Och, we'll sind them back on the Canada thrack,
  The Faynians behind thim swarmin';
All such scamps we'll put down, an' dhrive out o' the town,
  Undher Hecker an' Richard O'Gorman.
Wirra, boys! it will be a nate sight to see
  How the flight o' those Booles will quicken
Whin behind thim, hot sweep, two or three inches deep,
  A few Faynians their bayonets (an' sure the world knows there's no nater nor purtier weapon than a bagnet, an' it's only a pity the bright point of it should ever be soiled in the corrupt bodies of such varmints)—
  A few Faynians their bayonets are stickin'.

Then rents will come down, an' throughout the town
  There will be a proud day of enjoyment;
For wages will rise, an' the loaf grow in size,
  An' no lack there will be of employment.
As our taxes decrease, all the blessin's of peace
  Our hearts an' our hopes will be warmin';
An' we'll have a good time, in our city sublime,
  Undher Hecker an' Richard O'Gorman.
"To the dioul we fling all the rogues of the 'Ring,'"
  Is the cry both of palace an' shanty,
An' next month we'll inurn, takin' aich in his turn,
  John E. Develin (that corporation counsel ours, who seems to think he is paid for no other living thing than to find out how we can be chayted an' plundhered, an' then employ his friend Fields to do the job, an' divide fair wid all consarned afther that)—
  John E. Develin an' Sheik Fernandy.

GRAND DEMOCRATIC CHOWDER.

In our city aquarium's shining bound,
  Fish of all species enjoy free quarter,
Poking with cold snouts round and round
  The crystal walls of their limpid fortress.
Fish with the biggest eyes are here;
  With fins—the pectoral, anal, dorsal;
Scales that like proof of mail appear,
  And wide mouths gaping for every morsel.

Over the pebbles and shining sand,
  Down on the bottom they grope and wander;
Next their little air-bladders expand,
  And up they shoot as of sunlight fonder.
In through the stems of the cool green reeds,
  Under the lilies and pendent mosses,
Still the sub-aqueous play proceeds,
  While porgies and pikes have their joys and crosses.

In our city aquarium all the choir
  Of fish have particular flies to follow;
Hackles and cocktails many desire,
  While palmers, well oiled, nearly all will swallow.
Lady-bird flies are a tempting bait;
  With duns, blue, or brown, your sport will be meager;
But with spinners or governors all are elate,
  And for shiners—the yellow, you'll find them eager.

But the day of our sport was a cloudy day,
  And the fly we used of a new description;
Senator-fly it is called, they say,
  And its use shall be told without color or fiction.
Never had anglers such royal sport
  As we all can have when it comes in season,
For the fishes their destiny seem to court,
  And rise at this fly as if reft of reason.

FOURTH SENATORIAL DISTRICT.

Dropping a senator-fly called Fourth,
  Tied to a string, just above the surface,
Lo! from the east, south, west, and north,
  Numberless fishes rise up, all nervous.

Mather, of Albany, first is found
  Poking his hungry nose above water;
He carries an old hotel-key round,
  And his carpet bag shows him a scaly squatter.

Jacob L. Smith, like a pike, we see
  Feeding all round on emigrant minnows;
William M. Tweed, and a rockfish he,
  Floats on his supervisorial sinews.
Moneghan Pete works his gudgeon fins,
  Watching the fly, in hopes to earn it;
While Alderman Stephens to work begins,
  Looking the stoutest of all red gurnet.

Bob Livingston Linn would be glad to win,
  And swims on his belly, a marshal flounder;
Richard T. Compton, we count him in
  As a fine iced cod, "many years a rounder."
Hughey Boy Smith is a trout of mark,
  Prompt to assume the stage of action;
While Winne Dick is a lawyer shark,
  Who to win would enlist in whatever faction.

Bold Johnny Shea is a fine fat carp,
  Red in the gills, and stout, and posted;
Kivlin Tom is a pickerel sharp
  Who will one day or other get hooked and roasted.
John Y. Savage is long and grim,
  Best of sub-aqueous swordfish fighters—
And such were the fish who appeared to swim
  'Neath the eye and the fly of the present writer's.

Round and round in a whirl they go,
  Working their gills in a fishy smother,
Making their glutinous eyeballs glow,
  And biting like devils at each and other.
Sides are peeled and the flesh is bare,
  Fins are lopped from our liquid cattle;
Scales and skin from each other they tear,
  And rage is the rule of the fishy battle.

FIFTH SENATORIAL DISTRICT.

Dropping a fly of another kind—
  Senator Fifth—above the water,
Wagging their tails and going it blind,
  Infinite victims rise up for slaughter.

Smith Ely rises—a senator eel,
  Tough as his leather this deep-sea conger;
And Fields, though his chance has improved a deal,
  We're afraid has to wait a little longer.

Chubb Theodore Tomlinson don't look bad,
  And with sardine sauce might be made taste pleasant;
Sam Webster we think quite a promising shad,
  But shadowed (though under the gas) at present.
Jim Reilly could hardly be taxed to rise
  For so small a bait, and he well may brag it;
But Winthrop Chanler, if only wise,
  Can hook all the rest with a Chanler's maggot.

Round and round they wriggle and dart,
  Bending the reeds and scattering the water,
Spry in their spines and terribly smart,
  Every one eager the other to slaughter.
With mouths wide open and goggling eyes,
  Fins in bedlamite motion working,
All for the Fifth Senatorial rise,
  While their tails and their heads have a crazy jerking.

SIXTH SENATORIAL DISTRICT.

Soon with a new senatorial fly
  Called the Sixth on our line suspended,
With much "speculation" in his eye,
  A sleek mud-turtle at once ascended;
Schell by name, with a shell on his back,
  Snapping—voracious beyond all telling;
At valuing forts or flies not slack,
  But afraid of snells since his fatal Snelling.

Wheeler John like a weakfish rose,
  Irresolute whether to pass or besiege it;
Dunham J. Crain poked a tautog nose,
  But hadn't the spring in his tail to reach it.
Philip W. Engs made a bully leap—
  A sort of big drum not easily beaten;
While the catfish Baldwin, though lying deep,
  Has a faith that this fly will by him be eaten.

John T. Hoffman, whose birth we ascribe
  To the big-headed species of sculpin finners,
And Livingston Bob of the Sheepshead tribe—
  These both on our fly hope to make their dinners.

So round and round in an endless coil,
  Biting and fighting, they dart and splutter;
Their chance of success is not worth the toil,
  But their play may give somebody bread and butter.

SEVENTH SENATORIAL DISTRICT.

Last of our flies for the present week,
  Seventh Senatorial we now exhibit—
A fly which all Mackerells eagerly seek,
  While the squidfish Connolly jumps to crib it.
That Dick feels sure you can see at a glance—
  He dallies and dandles, appearing listless;
While the luminous sunfish Johnny Vance
  Is advancing claims which appear resistless.

That perch of a Peck, if we take his word,
  Guarantees to return us double measure;
And the herring P. G. Moloney is heard
  Proclaiming the fly to be his at pleasure.
The mullet M'Spedon to win is bound—
  A fish full of humor, provoking laughter;
While the tipsy-fish Rutherford squirms around,
  But a cocktail fly is the one he's after.

Like a jolly fat halibut, Bartlett Smith
  Plashes around with uneasy jerkings;
Harry Genet shows his bottom and pith
  By biting the tail of Hosea Bream Perkins.
Noah A. Childs, an audacious dace,
  Has the thick, hard scales of the old-school hunkers;
And Masterson Pete, in his fireman face,
  Shows a clear descent from the line of bunkers.

Round and round in a whirl they go,
  Working their gills in a fishy smother,
Making their glutinous eyeballs glow,
  And biting like devils at each and other.
Sides are peeled till the bones lie bare,
  Fins are lopped from our liquid cattle;
Scales and skin from each other they tear,
  And rage is the rule of the fishy battle.

ST. TAMMANY AND THE NABOBS.

Oh, there was a delusion, in the good days of old,
That party was an army with soldiers enrolled;

There were privates with muskets, and sergeants on pay,
And captings with epaulettes both gallant and gay,
Singing tooral-liooral, etc.

In the good times we speak of promotion was won
By a record of friendship and services done;
Men marched in the ranks ere they rode in the van,
And the purse was no object—we looked at the man,
Singing tooral, etc.

Oh, shoulder to shoulder right onward we press'd,
All passions but envy had room in each breast;
Heart beating to heart, every thought seemed to blend,
And each looked to the banner which all would defend,
Singing tooral, etc.

Yes, triumph and sorrow, joy, anger, and pride,
We shared with the brothers who marched by our side;
When the bugle was heard, every soldier took arms,
And the world had no prize to give treachery charms,
Singing tooral, etc.

But a new light has dawned on political war,
And 'tis now "Will it pay?" ere you say who you're for;
'Tis no longer "What, he! my old friend wants my aid;
He shall have it." Ah no; the game's otherwise played,
Singing tooral, etc.

This course was all wrong, as some big nabobs say,
Who have kindly agreed o'er our lives to bear sway;
The man counts for naught till we see how he stands
In the matter of rent-roll, stock-jobbing, and lands,
Singing tooral, etc.

These nabobs have shirt-fronts with diamonds a-gleam,
And their Verzenay bubbles, an amber-hued stream;
Grand junction, commercial politicians they are,
And in "selling for cash" each man shines like a star,
Singing tooral, etc.

They sit in gay rooms under glass chandeliers,
And each bulbous-nosed squatter at Tammany sneers;
Oh, they look with big eyes on political jobs,
And then rattle the tin in their corpulent fobs,
Singing tooral, etc.

Big chunks of a golden humanity these,
Fat ingots with heads swelled as big as a cheese;
They twiddle their thumbs as they dream of their checks,
And 'tis they hold the people ker-chuck by the necks,
Singing tooral, etc.

Greedy handlers of bullion, bold signers of bills,
Immense in the matter of cleaning out tills;
The masses are asses—so Nature ordains,
For we all know that cash is the measure of brains,
Singing tooral, etc.

The only grand key to which Fortune accords
The power of revolving in popular wards,
Is a key made of gold by some nabob applied,
Which will give access free to the jam-pots inside,
Singing tooral, etc.

Oh, no more we'll look down to the leaders of wards,
But we'll all raise our eyes to these "national" lords;
They wear leather medals to which we bow low,
And at Charleston they'll make a splendiferous show,
Singing tooral, etc.

No man in this city could righteously dare
Over grandees like these to aspire to be mayor;
So they sail up North River the land to inspect,
And a mayor they'll "import"—whom, of course, we'll elect,
Singing tooral, etc.

All the papers will spend full two thirds or a half
Of their space to extol this auriferous calf;
Times, Herald, and Tribune will bless the bright day,
And the Leader will kneel, singing hal-le-lu-jay,
And tooral, etc.

So, in view of this new rule, all rising young men
Who have done party service—don't do it again;
For, until things are changed, this no longer can be
To party promotion the ladder and key,
Singing tooral, etc.

But change a bad check for good value, and run,
Or find a rich wife who will pay for your fun;
Either get rich or seem rich, for both will avail,
And you may join the nabobs—if not put in jail,
Singing tooral, etc.

So down with all weakness of friendly regard;
To cheat—for the first time—we know may be hard;
But whoever to cheat perseveringly tries,
Oh, he'll find cheating come just as easy as lies,
Singing tooral, etc.

So hurra for the nabobs, and long may they reign;
We kiss their kind whip, and we cuddle the chain;

We'll pull down the Wigwam, and choke the big spring,
While the praise of "commercial transactions" we sing,
Singing tooral, etc.

But perhaps, ere the Wigwam a ruin is found,
Ere we take our farewell of the old hunting ground,
Just to hear the last echo 'twill fling from its roof,
Of this rhymed invocation 'tis well to make proof,
Singing tooral, etc.

THE APOTHEOSIS OF JAY COOKE.

Hurra! hurra! I heard them say,
Hurra for the Cooke who is christened Jay—
A greater old joker than Rabelais.
May his name be great, and his purse expand,
And his fame and his shadow fill the land;
For 'tis he has proved, in a manner as yet
Defying all skill but his alone,
That of all great blessings, a national debt
Is the jolliest blessing that ever was known.

Our Jay like a jay-bird well may crow,
For a thousand millions of dollars or so,
To this side or that, like a ball, he can throw;
And it is by the skill of this mighty Cooke
That our last seven-thirties all "got took;"
And of all the nations that ever were known,
The richest and greatest is now our own;
And of all the cooks in the moneyed line,
"Doing things up brown" with a crisp that is fine,
There is never a chef, we swear by the book,
That can equal our own immortal Cooke.

His discovery acts like a Brandreth's pill
For the cure of all forms of national ill;
And the louder he cries as we nearer sink
To the verge of bankruptcy's dreadful brink—
"Oh, go it, ye cripples! your cares forget;
Plunge deeper in blessings—that is, in debt;
To pay what you owe, and to pay as you go—
These are old fogy notions our age below;
But believe with me, and never forget,
That the way to be blessed is to rush into debt.
At the cautions of fogy financiers scoff,
Never bother your head about paying it off;

But keep borrowing still, with a greedy clutch,
For of blessings you never can have too much;
And of all the blessings the world knows yet,
The greatest, I swear, is a national debt."

Oh, crown him with greenbacks, and let his heir
A chaplet of ten-cent currency wear;
And down from his shoulders, broad and tall,
Let a mantle of bonds (seven-thirties) fall;
And place in his hands a baton, rolled
With the thinnest film or foil of gold;
And—with this for his sceptre, a sorcerer's rod—
Let his feet with brazen shoes be shod—
Shoes like to Mercury's, wing combined,
  To show the flight that our wealth is taking;
And brazen, to typify the mind
  That a "blessing" of our great curse is making.

NEW YORK IN A NUTSHELL.

THE NUT CRACKED AND NUT-RITIOUSLY DIGESTED.

Ye curious Yankees, who, alas!
  Desire to visit Gotham,
Attend unto the dangers as
  We presently shall show them;
And ere with bodies safe and sound
  You launch upon the Sound, sirs,
Get up upon our Pegasus,
  And peg with us around, sirs.

The city stands upon an isle
  Or sand-bank called Manhattan;
It is a place given wholly up
  To brandy, silk, and Satan.
Its people love the broad Broadway,
  The "narrow path" they scoff at;
Their worship now is the cholera ghoul,
  And Schultz is their chief prophet.

The city's statutes are as dead
  As statues made of plaster;
Its streets are blocked—in Astor Place
  Can neither horse nor ass stir.
In Pearl Street there are pearl-ous vaults,
  Down which we turn pearl-divers;
And Bleecker is a bleaker street
  For passengers and drivers.

In Amity no friendship is,
  In Bond Street no security,
In Grand Street nothing great or grand,
  In Water Street no purity;
In Broome there's not a broom at work,
  Dry Dock is quite a puddle;
In Carroll Street no carol sounds,
  And Congress is a muddle.

The street called Gay is very sad;
  Both Ann and Catharine plague you;
The very name of Hague Street gives
  A Cockney bard the h'-ague.
In Dey Street we are like to die,
  Gramercy Place is pert, sirs,
And Chestnut Street and Cherry make
  A dessert we desert, sirs.

There's Bayard Street—but not, like him,
  Sans peur et sans reproche, sirs;
And in Attorney Street you find
  A tourney-coach to coach, sirs.
In Rose I never saw a rose
  Except a colored woman,
And Clement Street and Mersey are
  Most thoroughly inhuman.

In Greene Street not a blade of grass,
  In Fountain not a pailful;
The streets, with bales and boxes piled,
  Become each day more baleful;
A walk through Varick Street would give
  A varic-ose complaint, sirs,
And White Street is as black a place
  As ever mud did paint, sirs.

Our streets are piled with piles of brick,
  And "bricks" go staggering by them;
The rotten shingles covering pits
  With cautious feet we try them.
Our rich men's faces tell their wealth—
  Ten thousand for each wrinkle,
And on a ten times wizened face
  Each lady's glance will twinkle.

These ladies all are thin and tall,
  Large-eyed and pale—refined, too;
Superbly dressed—and for the rest,
  Ask them, if you've a mind to.

Some people say they have a way
  False calves and busts of padding,
And their teeth are sought and complexions bought
  When they take their daily gadding.

Oh, Muse of mine! thy classic foot
  Once wore a golden sandal,
But thou hast fallen on punning ways,
  And *c!* it is a s(c)andal.
Thy thoughts are turned to quiddities,
  The tortured language teasing,
For he who once but lived to please,
  Has now to live by pleasing.

POLITICAL OPIUM DREAM.

WRITTEN, AFTER SWALLOWING THREE DOVER'S POWDERS, BY THE POICK OF THE "PEWTER MUG."

In weary, nervous plight, one night
I sighed and panted for the light,
While buzzing in my ear a clear
Shrill whisper breathed these words of fear:
    Fernando Wood had forty-one thousand,
    Vowed and swore he had forty-one thousand,
    Swore that he owned full forty-one thousand—
        Forty-one thousand votes.

I groaned and could not sleep; a deep
And dread unquiet made me keep
Still asking, soon or late, their fate;
Then came the dream I now relate.
    A vision it was of the forty-one thousand,
    All that is left of the forty-one thousand,
    The wretched remains of the forty-one thousand—
        Forty-one thousand votes.

Suppose some giant "bore" of yore
Had found a gimlet more and more
Gigantic than himself, and he
Nine miles in height—circumference three.

Suppose the tool so found around
He turned and twisted in the ground,
Working to let some daylight through
On Kaffir Land or Timbuctoo.

Such was the tortuous pit, unlit
By any cheery ray of day,

Down which a winding, slippery stair
Curled, black and dismal as despair.

Still from the dripping walls there falls
An ooze of death; each step appalls
As giddily I wound around
This monstrous corkscrew under ground.

Each step new echoes woke, which broke
Like booming guns from battle smoke,
And, stifling for fresh air, the stair
Seemed leading down to—you know where.

Before me strode a guide, with wide
Funereal drapery loosely tied
Round head and waist; a bull's-eye lamp
Shot sickly rays through dark and damp.

At length we reached a hall, where all
A thousand galleries met, and yet
In each five yards of corridor
Stood in the dripping walls a door.

At one my grim guide paused, and caused
A door, which opened with a spring,
Back on its rusty hinge to swing—
And I beheld a hideous thing.
    Alack and alack for the forty-one thousand,
    Hither had come the forty-one thousand,
    All that was left of the forty-one thousand—
        Forty-one thousand votes.

There is a low vault, bare and square
(Blue burned the lamp in the stagnant air):
I saw green lizards sprawl and fall
On drizzly floor from slimy wall,

While ranged around the room, in gloom
More deep than any earthly tomb,
A score of coffins stood on end—
"Political corpses," said my friend.
    Corpses they were of the forty-one thousand,
    Wretchedest wreck of the forty-one thousand,
    All that were left of the forty-one thousand—
        Forty-one thousand votes.

Each bore a brazen plate, to state
The name, style, station, natal date
Of the "clean beat" who groaned within
This mortal sentry-box of sin.

Advancing to the first accused,
My guide tapped lightly; the lid burst
Wide open, and, as back it flew,
The ghastly tenant stood in view.
   Done to death were the forty-one thousand,
   Boxed in wood were the forty-one thousand,
   All that was left of the forty-one thousand—
         Forty-one thousand votes.

Protruding from the clothes—there flows
A shroud round each, from head to toes—
I saw and recognized a nose
Such as the people's chairman blows.

And, tapping round from shell to shell,
Each lid wide open slowly fell,
Revealing in this charnel hive
The following "beats" entombed alive.
   Buried alive of the forty-one thousand,
   Princes and sheiks of the forty-one thousand,
   Diddled remains of the forty-one thousand—
         Forty-one thousand votes.

Here galorious Dick had a hue of blue,
Mottled and streakėd in the parts in view;
And brother Ben made a grand display
Of "proud flesh" turning to decay.

Dick Schell looked bad in his white pine shell,
And the weary Drake had an ancient smell;
Cold sweat from wretched Ben Fairchild flows,
And Bill M'Intyre made us hold our nose;
   For "gamy" were they of the forty-one thousand—
         Forty-one thousand votes.

The features of monkey Gid were hid
By the shroud which he drew when his coffin-lid
Flew back, and General Hiram he
Was as "hi" as a corpse on the gallows-tree.

Myriads of malt-worms, fed and bred
In Seventh Ward bully Riley's head;
And charming Brownell looked almost as grisly
As the skin-peeled corpse of poor Billy Brisly.
   These were the whole of the forty-one thousand,
   All that is left of the forty-one thousand,
   Nary a more of the forty-one thousand—
         Forty-one thousand voters.

"Where is the chief?" I said; "for dead
I know he must be." Every head
In all that ghastly crew was raised,
And fury from their eyeballs blazed.

Each from beneath his shroud, with proud
And angry gesture, drew to view
Some limb or portion of the chief,
Now made "political hung beef."

Ben Fairchild had the hand which planned
So many "city diddlings" grand;
Gid Tucker had his rights—the lights,
Bile-duct, and spleen, to chew o' nights.

Legs, head, and breast went round; each found
His only solace under ground;
While Brandy Sour was glad to risk it
Upon the baser parts and brisket
Of him who owned the forty-one thousand,
Boasted and swore he had forty-one thousand,
Swaggered and lied about forty-one thousand—
Forty-one thousand votes.

I sickened, and my brain, with pain
And nausea, felt a nervous strain.
"Avaunt!" I cried; and, with a clang,
Back every coffin-cover rang.

A SONG FOR WHITE MEN.

Old Abe is good to crack a joke,
Heigh-ho, heigh-ho!
His fun in stories he can poke,
Heigh-ho, says I;
But there's never a joke that he can crack
Will help him to beat our Little Mac,
For we all go Mac blind—
Johnny, fill up the bowl.

The "nigs" for Abe the best may do,
Heigh-ho, heigh-ho!
He is patron saint of all their crew,
Heigh-ho, says I;
But we, unfortunates, who are white,
Yet for the nigger have to fight—
Oh, we all go Mac blind—
Johnny, fill up the bowl.

"We've broken the Rebellion's back,"
Heigh-ho, heigh-ho!
Bill Seward swears he heard it crack,
Heigh-ho, says I;
He swore 'twas broken three years ago,
But we see the tide of slaughter flow,
And we all go Mac blind—
Johnny, fill up the bowl.

No end of the war can ever come,
Heigh-ho, heigh-ho!
We shall hear the roll of the murd'rous drum,
Heigh-ho, says I,
Until at the head of affairs we place
The chosen chief of the martial race,
And we all go Mac blind—
Johnny, fill up the bowl.

Four millions of dollars every day,
Heigh-ho, heigh-ho!
For this nigger war we are forced to pay,
Heigh-ho, says I;
And there's never a hope, in Lincoln's track,
Of winning our good old Union back,
So we all go Mac blind—
Johnny, fill up the bowl.

For liberty of speech and press,
Heigh-ho, heigh-ho!
For outraged rights we seek redress,
Heigh-ho, says I;
The lettre de cachet and Bastile
Are things to make every freeman feel
We should all go Mac blind—
Johnny, fill up the bowl.

To Sherman, Farragut, and Grant,
Heigh-ho, heigh-ho!
Who our flag o'er conquered cities plant,
Heigh-ho, says I,
We fill the bumper and pledge the toast,
And to give them the aid they need the most,
We all go Mac blind—
Johnny, fill up the bowl.

With Mac at the head of our weaponed clans,
Heigh-ho, heigh-ho!
No "political dodges" would mar their plans,
Heigh-ho, says I;

And therefore Farragut, Sherman, Grant,
Declare "that Mac is the chief they want,"
And we all go Mac blind—
Johnny, fill up the bowl.

To all our heroes in the field,
Heigh-ho, heigh-ho!
Knowing how to die, but not to yield,
Heigh-ho, says I,
We fill the bumper and pledge the toast,
And to give them the aid they need the most,
We all go Mac blind—
Johnny, fill up the bowl.

WAR DEMOCRATIC VIEW OF M'CLELLAN'S NOMINATION.

"He will immediately take steps to bring about a cessation of hostilities."
Chicago Platform.

Private O'Reilly, solus:

Air: "Ould Ireland, you're my darling."

May I niver taste bite nor sup to-night,
But I joy to hear the story,
For the rebels'll catch in M'Clellan their match,
An' we'll soon have "payce" wid glory.
Such "steps" he will take as'll make 'em awake
To a sinse of their situation,
An' wid thrayson dead on a bloody bed,
Of the war we shall have "a cessation."

Chorus of soldiers:

Air: "Yankee Doodle."

That's the kind of talk for us,
That's the peace we covet—
Treason dead on a bloody bed,
And our starry flag above it.

Private O'Reilly, as before:

Little Mac's the man wid a wholesome plan
For an airly "payce" attainin';
Wid threble might to purshue the fight,
Decisive thriumphs gainin'.
We do hate an' abhor every form o' war—
We but fight for conciliation,
An' with thrayson dead on a bloody bed,
Of the war we shall have "a cessation."

Chorus of soldiers, as before:

That's the kind of talk for us,
  That's the peace we covet—
Treason dead on a bloody bed,
  And the stars and stripes above it.

Private O'Reilly, as before:

Och! the hour is nigh to see them fly
  In wild confusion scatthered,
From their broken lines an' their murdherin' mines,
  An' their earthworks torn an' tatthered.
Wid a fiery brand in wan stout hand,
  An' an olive-branch in the other,
They will all come back undher "Little Mac,"
  An' we'll have an end o' the bother.

Chorus of soldiers, as before:

That comes home to the Southern heart,
  That's the way to strike it—
The brand in hand if you still withstand,
  The olive-branch if you like it.

HURRA FOR ANDY JOHNSON.

Air: "Ould Ireland, you're my jewel, sure."

Och, Andy, you're my jewel, shure,
  For you our hearts are sighin';
'Tis your thrue aim that bags the game,
  An' sets the feathers flyin'.
Full many a duck your shot has sthruck,
  As you make your sportin' journey,
But—ourselves between—shure there never was seen
  Such a clip as you gave John Forney.
Och, Andy dear, some people here,
  They say that your thrade was a tailor's,
An' 'twas this, no less, makes you give, I guess,
  Such fits to them Jacobin railers.

Go on, my boy! our counthry's joy
  Is at stake upon your succeedin';
Let the Jacobins rave till aich whey-faced knave
  Is choked up wid the venom he's breedin'.
You are on the right thrack to win for us back—
  For shure love is a powerful magnet—
The union of hand and of heart in the land,
  Which these rogues would thransfix wid a bagnet.

Och, Andy, dear, your friends are here,
Down far in the sowls o' the people;
An' if we had our say, all who'd bar your way—
Faix! they'd swing from ould Thrinity's stheeple.

To bring back the states within our gates
As sisthers, we thought was our sole end.;
The Union, 'twas for that we bled in the war—
Not to make o' the South a new Poland.
But now these rogues who do the collogues
In the Sinate—from which the Lord save us!—
Shure they cry, it is said, that the Union is dead,
Just as loud as did ever Jeff Davis.
But, Andy, dear, while you are here,
Our Union no power can sever;
An', despite all their clack, we shall soon have it back,
An' the ould flag shall float forever.

THE ALDERMAN'S GHOST.

BEING A SPIRITUAL MANIFESTATION FROM A MEMBER OF THE DEFUNCT CORPORATION OF NEW YORK KNOWN IN LOCAL HISTORY, AS "THE FORTY THIEVES."

Hurra for Judge Edmonds! I have had
A mystical manifestation;
I saw last night—don't think me mad—
A ghost from the Corporation.
It came to my room—'tis truth I tell—
And rapped upon the table;
Alive, it loved the table well,
And dead, as well as it's able.

Said I, while I felt each sinew heave,
And the dew on my forehead gather,
Is that the spirit of Mother Eve,
Or the ghost of a city father?
The table stood up like a fighting-cock,
And danced with a glee satanic;
It rapped with force of a thunder-shock,
"The spirit is aldermanic."

How did you die? Come tell me smack—
Was it eating turtle-soup, or
An overdose of the canvas-back?
"I died of Peter Cooper;

An overdose of the canvass too"
  (The spirit a pun was sharp at);
The table here delirious grew,
  And rolled over and over the carpet.

How fare you now in the spirit-land?
  Are you melancholic or merry?
Have you got any good fat jobs on hand—
  A railroad or a ferry?
"I find the spirits are regular bricks,
  Nor the place of fat jobs barren;
I'll sell the monopoly of the Styx,
  And oust the ferryman, Charon."

Have you got a lobby ring up in the skies,
  Or are your briberies mental?
Is there any mayor in his strength to rise
  With a veto transcendental?
"I taste, as ever I did, the sweets
  Of jobs the most nefarious;
And I mean to appoint to cleanse the streets
  A mystical Arcularius."

God help the spirits, then, I cried—
  Is there no one to guard or care 'em?
If one were to think of suicide,
  Such a thought as this would scare him;
For, bad as it is on earth below—
  And it makes our heart-strings quiver—
Just think of an aldermanic woe
  Inflicted up there forever.

NEBRASKA AND KANSAS.

Air: "Eliza, my darling, you know—you know."

The Arabs are happy—no doubt, no doubt—
  The Arabs are happy—and why?
It ain't that they scamper about, about,
  Just as free as the clouds in the sky.
'Tis because they ain't worried, and scurried, and hurried
  With cries of "Nebraska" and "Kansas;"
They lie under palm-trees, enjoying the balm breeze,
  And sing the "sweet moon" in sweet stanzas.

Icelanders are happy—no doubt, no doubt—
  Icelanders are happy—and why?
It ain't that for train-oil they shout, they shout,
  And snug in their snow hovels lie.

'Tis because that "Nebraska" (to rhyme that's a task, ah!
  But else I must tear up my stanzas)
Has never perplexed them, and wofully vexed them,
  Nor care they a seal-skin for "Kansas."

The Fejees are happy—no doubt, no doubt—
  The Fejees are happy—and why?
'Taint because our friend Kimball, with tabret and cymbal,
  Exalted their mermaid on high;
'Tis because (every man says) "Nebraska" and "Kansas"
  Don't frighten them out of their lives;
They have dwellings of coral, and (wise men and moral)
  They sport with their salmon-tailed wives.

But we are unhappy—no doubt, no doubt—
  But we are most wretched—and why?
'Tis because we are deafened, and crippled, and spavined
  With buncombe, and bosh, and "my eye."
We offer a passage, a horse, and an ass each,
  To these Quixotes and sleek Sancho Panzas
Who share our communion, yet tilt at the Union,
  If they'll put for "Nebraska" and "Kansas."

BOB SMITH, OF FULTON STREET.

A BALLAD OF RECONSTRUCTION AND REHABILITATION.

Hail, Bobbie Smith, mine ancient friend,
  My harp hath sung your matchless garments
Long years before I southward went
  To fight them cussed secession varmints.
You're on the square, my bully Bob,
  Your honest faith no traffic smothers,
And, when I want a clothing job,
  I'll deal with you before all others.

I like you, Bob. Your clothes I find
  Just like your friendship—warm and lasting;
No mean thought ever crossed your mind,
  Its shadow on your actions casting.
One price you ask—small profit sought—
  And men must give the price or leave it;
I write of you my honest thought,
  And those who read had best believe it.

Go in, my Bob, and make and sell
  Your clothes till covering all creation;
The friends who know you love you well,
  And you have friends throughout the nation.

Deal with our erring brethren South
Kindly and well—for still they're cranky;
And put this saying in their mouth—
"At least there is one honest Yankee."

THE CRY IS MAC, MY DARLIN'.

Air: "Oh, my Nora Creina, dear."

Mac, my darlin', proud I am
To hear that you've been nominated;
Last we met at Antietam,
Where you the rebel might abated;
In the Seven Days' fight I stood
Beside you on the hills an' meadows,
And while our brave boys poured their blood,
We know your heart was throbbin' wid us.
Oh, my captain, dear an' thrue,
The coward tongues that would ignore you
Are base as false—thank Heaven they're few!—
Your soldiers thrust you an' adore you.

Abe may crack his jolly jokes
O'er bloody fields of sthricken battle,
While yet the ebbin' life-tide shmokes
From men that die like butchered cattle;
He, ere yet the guns grow cold,
To pimps an' pets may crack his stories—
Your name is of the grander mould,
And linked wid all our brightest glories.
Oh, my general, loved an' thrue,
The lyin' tongues that would defame you
Are base as false—thank Heaven they're few!—
For as our chosen chief we claim you.

They say—these dogs of currish heart,
Who never heard a Minié whistle—
You'd let the Union drift apart
Like down-flakes from a shaken thistle;
They say, oh captain—but the words
Stick in our throats—we can't adjust 'em—
But lift to heaven our dinted swords,
An' answer only this, "We thrust him."
Yes, oh friend of rights an' laws,
Despite the sneers of fool or craven,
Where hearts beat highest for the cause,
You have your home, your shrine, and haven.

Wid patient toil an' pityin' breast
  You sought your soldiers' blood to threasure,
Nor ever tried the cruel test
  How much we could endure to measure.
They feared you, for they saw our love;
  To win success they would not let you;
But while the white stars shine above,
  The boys you led will ne'er forget you.
    Yes, our captain, prized an' thrue,
      Desert you we would perish rather;
    Thank Heaven the hearts are not a few
      That call you brother, friend, and father.

"THERE'S NO SUCH WORD AS FAIL, BOYS."

BY ONE OF THE RANK AND FILE.

Air: "The low-backed car."

M'Dowell's day is over—
  A true and gallant man,
With a heart as big as a bullock's heart,
  But wanting a head to plan.
Now brighter hours are dawning,
  And brighter hopes we hail,
For with young M'Clellan to lead our lines,
  There's no such word as fail—
    There's no such word as fail, boys—
    There's no such word as fail;
For with young M'Clellan to lead our lines,
    There's no such word as fail.

No fault against M'Dowell,
  No blame have we to urge,
He wasn't a red-tape martinet,
  That soldiers' pest and scourge.
Warm-hearted was M'Dowell,
  His courage proof of mail,
But he did belong to that luckless class
  Who do know how to fail—
    Who do know how to fail, boys,
    As witness all our men,
But with young M'Clellan to lead our lines,
    We'll try the game again.

Virginia's western counties
  Resound M'Clellan's name,
Philippi, Grafton, Romney, are
  The first-fruits of his fame.

And soon the lurid halo
  Of the rebel flag shall pale,
For M'Clellan belongs to the chosen class
  Who don't know how to fail—
    Who don't know how to fail, boys,
    Who won't know how to fail—
Who couldn't be taught, at whatever price,
    The will or the way to fail.

So burnish up your weapons, boys,
  And keep your powder dry,
Bull Run will have done us a deal of good
  When next the game we try.
One fair, square chance but give us, boys,
  And you'll see the rebels quail,
For our leader is now of the chosen class
  Who don't know how to fail—
    Who don't know how to fail, boys,
    Who won't know how to fail,
And who can not be taught, at whatever price,
    The will or the way to fail.

LIVE-OAK GEORGE.

Here's to the man who of birth never boasts,
Who has girdled with commerce our seas and our coasts,
On whose flag the old sun never ceases to shine,
From the east to the west, from the pole to the line.
    Live-oak George,
    Live-oak George,
  He'll make the politicians
  All their spoils disgorge.

He ne'er to the mean arts of toadying flew,
He kept himself clear of the caucusing crew—
Relied on his worth and the will he had shown,
That Americans still should America own.
    Live-oak George,
    Live-oak George,
  He soon will make the Galphin crew
  Their spoils disgorge.

When poor, and a boy, he came into our town,
The Albany Regency trampled us down;
But the old fogy tyrants have now to give way
To the king of the steam-boats—the man of the day.

Live-oak George,
Live-oak George,
'Tis he will make the harpy crew
Their gains disgorge.

He sought for no place and he courted no clique—
If him they desired, it was their place to seek—
It was stanch Pennsylvania the first that did draw
Her sword from the scabbard for honest George Law.
Live-oak George,
Live-oak George,
'Tis he will make old parties
All their gains disgorge.

But others have followed, and others will come,
Like soldiers to roll-call of fife and of drum;
For the man that among us most voters can draw,
Oh! who should he be but our Live-oak George Law?
Live-oak George,
Live-oak George,
He'll make some foreign monarchs
All their pride disgorge.

Then bumpers around to the man of the day—
The "grip" and the "word," and let fate have its way;
All true men around the proud standard will draw,
Which, in famed fifty-six, bears the name of George Law.
Live-oak George,
Live-oak George,
Like one of his own clippers,
Into port he'll surge.

Then here's to the man who has made himself all
That wealthy, respected, and honored we call;
Too long, under soldiers and lawyers, we saw
Our country degraded—we'll now try George Law.
Live-oak George,
Live-oak George,
'Tis he will make the Galphin crew
Their gains disgorge.

SONG OF THE NATIONAL DEMOCRACY.[45]

To the Albany chiefs the War Democrats spoke,
Ere you play the old game, there are slates to be broke;
Your words are all right if they only were true,
But beneath the war flag you've a Copperhead crew.

So fill up the cup, be it brandy or bier,
Resurrect the war-hatchet and sharpen the spear;
In November we'll have an almighty big row,
And to Copperhead doctrines be—well, if we bow.

Dean Richmond his stomach may pat, and may pinch
His jolly red nose till it lengthens an inch;
But he can't make us think his professions are true
While he sails his war ship with a Copperhead crew.
So fill up the cup, whisky, claret, or bier,
Resurrect the war-hatchet and sharpen the spear;
There are braves on the war-path prepared for a row,
And to Breckinridge doctrines be—well, if we bow.

The bold Pete de Cagger, with mystery big,
May adjust each stray hair in his amber-hued wig,
But his arts, though potential, are well understood--
If his platform be honest, why runs he with Wood?
So fill up the cup—things look certainly queer—
Resurrect the war-hatchet and sharpen the spear;
With the lords of the "Central" we're in for a row,
And to Richmond and Cagger be—well, if we bow.

To the tenets of Douglas we tenderly cling,
Warm hearts to the cause of our country we bring;
To the flag we are pledged—all its foes we abhor—
And we ain't for the "nigger," but are for the war.
So fill up the cup—pleasant tipple is bier—
Resurrect the war-hatchet and sharpen the spear;
With the Albany chiefs we are in for a row,
And their sceptre we'll break, or their heads they shall bow.

It may suit the subservient old War Horse to say
He is "willing to follow where Pete leads the way;"
That, with gayety, he as blank paper will yield
Himself to the power which the Regency wield.
Oh, so great doth your gayety, Purdy, appear,
That we drink your good health in a bumper of bier;
And after November's slate-smashing grand row,
We'll, with gayety, make you our very best bow.

Such things do for some folks, but don't do for us,
Who for Pruyn, Cagger, Cassidy, don't care a cuss;
To the flag we are pledged—all its foes we abhor—
And first, last, all the time, we are in for the war.
So fill up the cup—healthy drinking is bier—
Resurrect the war-axe and sharpen the spear;
In the Wigwam, next April, all factions we'll hush,
And for new men to lead we'll go in with a rush.

The platform of Logan, Grant, Gillmore, and Dix
Is better than any that managers fix:
"Our flag in its glory! our Union restored,
And, till treason cries quarter, no sheath to the sword!"
So fill up the cup with much better than bier,
The big spring is bubbling, its waters are clear—
Democracy's fountain—and thus at its brink,
"To the memory of Douglas" with bowed heads we drink.

A DEMOCRATIC RALLY.

Bring forth the ancient standards, the old time faith renew,
March all and march together, brothers tried and ever true;
Fall in and take your places, call the roll, and let us hear
Who are for us, who against us, in the strife that draws anear.
Now Treason stands with bloody hands,
Her long-worn mask discarded,
And we are they by whom to-day
The Union must be guarded.

Forget all past dissensions in the greatness of the hour;
For Union let the Empire State send forth a voice of power;
When villains league to do a wrong, let the true combine for right,
And we'll soon choke out the mutiny which traitors would incite.
Revealed, opposed, their plot disclosed,
Treason shall sink confounded;
No servile strife, with torch and knife,
Shall through our land be hounded.

Oh, brothers, rally to the flag, for ours the glorious mission,
True to the bond that Jackson sealed to banish all division;
A common fame, a common name, a common good to cherish,
These are the rights which freemen claim content for these to perish.
No frantic hordes with reeking swords
Our sister states shall plunder;
And they whose thought first hatched the plot,
Its wreck let them lie under.

Come all who love our fatherland, and reverence each name
Shouted from Freedom's hill-tops in the morning of our fame;
On Treason let the Empire State be first to place a brand,
And foremost of all cities let the Empire City stand.
Let all combine who will not join
In treason's foul communion,
And let our shout ring boldly out
For nationhood and Union.

The good and great of every state will hail our restoration,
New York once more shall take her place as vanguard of the nation;
East, West, and South—a thrill, a cheer, our victor war-cry pealing,
Shall rouse again in all true men the old time's holy feeling.
Our ship of state will ride elate,
In Union's harbor anchored,
And future days shall live to praise
The peace New York hath conquered.

SENATOR TOM ON CLAMS.[49]

From the cool bosom of the sand,
Washed by the flood and ebbing tide,
These savory bivalves come to hand,
And form the theme of Develin's pride.
More sweet than venison's roasted haunch,
Or birds of paradise stewed with yams,
Are these rare bivalves of Long Branch—
This precious breed of Develin's clams.

These female clams, from sand and foam,
Rise up exemplars to our life;
For they are always found at home,
As should be each domestic wife.
No bills for dry goods do they launch,
Nor diamonds—whether true or shams—
These prudent bivalves of Long Branch—
These rarely prudent Develin clams.

Seldom, if ever, do they talk;
Their mouths with maiden pride they close;
Nor ever in the moonlight walk
Too long and late with clammy beaus.
Their love is pure, their hearts are stanch,
They are just as innocent as lambs—
These coy, young bivalves of Long Branch—
This precious breed of Develin's clams.

No crinoline enshrouds their limbs,
Nor penciled lash, nor paint's endeavor,
But each in the pure water swims,
"A thing of beauty and joy forever."
They never quit their native ranche,
Hotels of cost in summer wooing—
These patient bivalves of Long Branch,
They live in bliss, and die in stewing.

No "rats" or "mice" are in their beard,
  They never like promiscuous gadding,
And in their plumpness, who has heard
  Of any "artificial padding?"
Their simple souls no fear can blanch,
  They envy not their prettier neighbors—
These simple bivalves of Long Branch,
  Whose bake now claims our Develin's labors.

To Weed, whose pen with bolder lines
  Our lady-clams can paint more truly,
My feebler pen the task resigns
  Of picturing all their virtues fully.
To him—yet vigorous, fresh, and stanch,
  Sound in the chest, and head, and hams,
I leave these bivalves of Long Branch—
  This dear sweet brood of Develin's clams.

SENATOR GWIN TO BUCHANAN.

Air: "When first I knew thee, warm and young."

When first I knew thee, gray and old,
  Such treachery gleamed about thee—
So heartless wert thou, and so cold,
  That instinct bade me doubt thee.
I knew thee false in every trait,
  A vain and cruel master,
But hoped that bonds of common hate
  To me would tie thee faster.
      But go, deceiver, go,
        No tears my grave may water
      Like those which ever flow
        O'er Broderick's bed of slaughter.

When every tongue to freedom born
  Denounced thy party treason,
I found in this prevailing scorn
  For faith in thee fresh reason—
"He must be true, for all are foes
  Except the slaves of custom;
The leper with the leprous goes,
  And therefore we may trust him."
      But go, deceiver, go,
        Bright and Fitch will leave thee later,
      And Bigler, with despairing throe,
        Confess he served a traitor.

And yet, J. B., the time is near
  When even Slidell shall leave thee;
And Davis, seized with ghastly fear,
  To death and ruin heave thee;
Missouri Greene shall kick thee down,
  Bayard thy bones will batter,
And puffs from Constitution Browne
  Will lose their power to flatter.
    But go, 'tis vain to curse,
      And weakness to upbraid thee,
    Hate can not wish thee worse
      Than Black Lecompton made thee.

Even now, though still some months are left
  For public pay and booty,
Thy minions, of all pride bereft,
  Yet scorn their abject duty.
Augustus Schell, that veriest slave
  Of all the slaves beneath you,
Will throw no flower upon your grave—
  With naught but curses wreathe you.
    But go; the task was thine
      Our land to rend asunder;
    And many a vote of mine
      You bought for so much plunder.

Even Breckinridge, who on bent knee
  Thy favor now importunes,
Shall curse the day he linked with thee
  His erstwhile lucky fortunes.
And on our country's record-page
  Thy name, in scarlet letters,
Shall glisten to the latest age,
  With Arnold's linked in fetters.
    But go, thou poor old man;
      'Tis Heaven from ruin kept her;
    And now, beneath thy country's ban,
      Resign her sullied sceptre.

THE SEVENTH TO JOHN COCHRANE.

Accept, oh prince of phrases round,
This token of esteem profound
    From those you made your care—
From those to whom, with generous hand,
In words that made each heart expand,
    You tendered "princely fare."

High was the summons, great the need,
And splendid the reward decreed
    To all—so said your pen—
Who'd share the task of rendering praise
To Washington, and those "stern days
    Which tried the souls of men."

Those dreary days of gloom and want,
Discomfort plenty, rations scant,
    Long marches, and hard fighting—
Your splendid art recalled the whole,
And verily you tried each soul
    With hunger sharp and biting.

Knee-deep in mud, no welcome given,
Drenched with the frozen sleet of heaven,
    No roof—no tent provided;
No drop to drink—no food to eat—
Shivering and starving in the street,
    Cold, hungry, and derided.

As thus we slept upon our arms,
Thinking of home's deserted charms—
    The comforts vanished from us—
There rose before each grateful mind,
With sweetest memories entwined,
    Your highly "princely promise."

And then we vowed, in whispers low,
Some fitting presents to bestow
    (You're cute, but we'll be cuter)—
These slop-bowls, tea and coffee kettles—
This set of plate our debt half settles,
Cast in the most appropriate metals
    Of nickel, brass, and pewter.

So take them, Cochrane, and you'll find
In this tall coffee-pot enshrined
    Promotion coming faster:
A testimonial which repeats
That the great Lodge of Healthy Beats—
The Clean, the Dead, Past Grands, and Sweets—
Admiring your astounding feats,
Without once rising from their seats—
On the first ballot—the first choice—
Without even one dissenting voice—
    Have voted you Grand Master.

GRAND ROUT OF THE NABOBS.

CONTINUATION OF THE ILIAD BY ANOTHER HAND. SERMONS AND SODA-WATER NEEDED.

Time—*Early morning.* Scene—*Parlor in the Fifth Avenue Hotel. Cigar-stumps, empty Champagne bottles, and Vigilant-Salamander-Safe-Committee-men lying loose around. Enter the chaplain of the movement with a tray of cocktails. He surveys the room and sings:*

Oh, the nabobs came down like the wolf on the fold,
And their noses were purple, their shirt-studs were gold
In political life every man strove to shine,
And the liquor they quaffed it was Verzenay wine.

Like young sprouts of asparagus, sappy and green,
At the Everett, a month since, these nabobs were seen;
But, like frostbitten pumpkins, all wilted and blue,
They now turn up their toes in the Fifth Ave-noo.

For St. Tammany's trumpet aroused a great host,
And the spirit of manhood rebelled at their boast;
Mere toadstools of lucre, the growth of a night,
These nabobs have wilted beneath the dawn's light.

Here lie Sam and Cisco—with nostrils all wide—
No more with the nabobs allowed to abide;
And, wearied from laughing at all that has been,
Lo! here sleeps the red-bearded Indian serene.

And Baldwin, the polywog pale-face, lies there;
And Forrest, all withered in wintry despair;
And Coleman—these three, stiff as icicles lie,
With a very big Verzenay drop in each eye.

And the spirits of Wolfe weak and sluggishly flow,
While that resolute gentleman, Sammy Barlow
(A jolly good fellow—the harder his lot),
Keeps eternally asking of Sherman "Watts what?"

Now gone all the golden delights of their dream,
And vainly may bubble the Verzenay stream;
For with headache and nausea, awakening in haste,
Each but finds in his mouth a green coppery taste.

And in vain to rekindle their hopes and their lives
Are political cocktails commingled by Ives;
Though the Herald has bitters and Wolfe offers gin,
Yet the feast was too deep for their cure to begin.

Oh, bitter the wails in all boudoirs select
For the mighty fine hopes in their enterprise wrecked;
And at Washington many the shrugs and ahems
At the brittle success of our "national gems."

For "national men" in the true sense were they,
No local affinities hampered their sway;
And "gems" were they also—sharp, brilliant, and nice,
Though, as Phelps will declare, "not at all beyond price."

Now the prospects of Dix they have all gone to grass,
And Ike Townsend insists he be written an ass;
Scoffers leer when they talk of the mammonite squad,
And the Verzenay movement is stiff as a clod.

For control of the movement its starters may whistle,
The Verzenay nabobs have fizzed their last fizzle;
Extinguish the lights, fold their hands, close their eyes—
Unregarded it lived, and uncared for it dies.

WHO KILLED THE NABOBS?

Oh, who killed the nabobs?
"'Twas I," said the Leader;
"You may count me the pleader
Whose words killed the nabobs—"
And this, gentle reader,
This sheet is the Leader.

Who first raised the nabobs?
'Twas Sam, Wolfe, and Cisco,
All jolly and brisk, oh!—
'Twas they raised the nabobs,
Who now lie as solemn
And flat as this column.

To whom gave they trouble?
"Oh, to me," says the Herald;
"My lungs I imperiled
Inflating their bubble;
'Twas a stiff operation
Each morning's inflation."

For whom did they do this?
"Oh, for Sam, Wolfe, and Cisco,
All jolly and brisk, oh!
Who yet have to rue this,
And a fourth man, quiescent,
Who by proxies was present."

What shroud will best suit them?
  "Oh pshaw!" cry the masses,
  "They are but dead asses;
Just bundle and boot them;
  Collapsed, and in flat case,
  They'll fit in a hat case."

And their grave? "None is needed;
  Lock them up with a sermon
  In the safe of Watts Sherman,
And leave them unheeded;
  We are sick of the trouble
  And fuss of this bubble."

Now who'll toll the bell?
  "I'll do it," said Baldwin,
  "If properly called on,
I'll toll it out well—
  My last act of devotion
  To dead hopes of promotion."

And who for the nabobs
  A headstone can carve us?
  "I'll do it," said Jarvis,
"Hic jacet the nabobs;
  The stereotyped model
  Requiescat in—twaddle."

Who'll bury the fellows?
  "Oh I," answered Ives—
  "I, the friend of their lives—
Their inflater—their bellows;
  Let me, late their teacher,
  In death be their preacher."

Who'll give the responses?
  "I'll do it," cries Leary,
  Brisk, jovial, and cheery,
"I'll give the responses;
  I am knee-deep in clover
  Since their fizzle is over."

Who'll turn undertaker?
  "I'll do it," said Coleman,
  A dismal but droll man,
"I'll play mute and waker;
  But, to keep the wake frisky,
  Give me snuff, pipes, and whisky."

EPITAPH.

"'They lived—a world's wonder
Of folly and weakness;
But, whipped into meekness,
They caved and went under.
Their Verzenay bubbled,
Their poor brains grew muddled;
Their pamphlet a fizzle,
Their rallies a mizzle;
Their funds a delusion,
Their plans all confusion;
No friends to abet them,
No friends to regret them;
Neglected and scouted,
Pasquinaded and flouted;
With golden pretensions
Of shrunken dimensions,
And headache and sickness—
Oh, blame not the quickness
With which—just as fast as Jack Robinson whistled—
The Verzenay-Vigilant Fizzlers have fizzled."

THE RING-STAMP FATAL.

Just stay where you are—you had betther far,
Than attimpt to breast the tornado
Which the Ring chiefs know is to lay them low,
Despite all their false bravado.
The storm's on the wing, an' aich craft o' the Ring
Will find it a roarer an' wrecker;
While to victhory sails, undher favorin' gales,
The popilar ship—John Hecker.
Just so sure as you're born, "a receipt for the corn"
Next election the Ring will be findin',
And wid Hecker's strong will in conthrol of our mill—
Faix! we'll do some almighty grindin'.

THE NIGHT RIDE OF ANCIENT ABE.

Not a drum was heard, not a party cry—
We were all most terribly flurried,
As, with kindling horror in heart and eye,
Old Abe to the rail-cars we hurried.

We hurried him quickly, at dead of night,
  A disguise o'er his long limbs throwing,
By the struggling moonbeam's misty light,
  And a bull's-eye dimly glowing.

No useless pageant or pomp we had,
  But with Sumner's cloak around him,
And canny Sim Cameron's cap of plaid,
  To put through in the dark we bound him.

Few and short were the words he said,
  As we looked in his face of sorrow,
But sadly we thought of the row to be made
  In the Herald and Times of the morrow.

We thought, as we jostled him into the car
  Without either cheer or ovation,
What a laugh there would be when the news spread afar
  Of the Rail-splitter's ass-ass-ination.

We started the train, and the hero was off,
  Evading each Plug-Ugly sentry;
But, Lord! how the heathen will guffaw and scoff
  At this new kind of "national entry."

Gayly the Post of the plot may make light,
  And talk of the "Tooley Street tailors,"
But, snugly installed in the mansion of white,
  The Rail-splitter laughs at all railers.

THE ANCIENT ABE.

Air: "The Shan Van Vocht."

"Let us up and do or die,"
  Says the ancient Abe;
"Let us up and do or die,"
  Says old Abe;
"We will rear our banner high
As the stars are in the sky,
And our enemies shall fly,"
  Says the ancient Abe.

Then to Washington he flew,
  Did the ancient Abe—
Then to Washington he flew,
  Did old Abe;

And he swore by black and blue
All seceders to "put through,"
And the forts to man anew,
Did the ancient Abe.

Has he kept his solemn vow,
Has the ancient Abe?
Has he kept his solemn vow,
Has old Abe?
By the Lord! we see him bow
At the shadow of a row—
'Tis an ugly case of "cow"
With the ancient Abe.

For without a cannon fired
By the ancient Abe—
Not a gun or cracker fired
By old Abe—
He has peacefully retired,
Granting all the South desired,
Sinking down as it aspired,
Has the ancient Abe.

"Major Anderson's to blame,"
Cries the ancient Abe;
"It is he that is to blame,"
Says old Abe;
And thus to hide the shame
Of a heart that is not "game,"
He befouls that honored name,
Does the ancient Abe.

Oh, friends, we've had enough
Of this ancient Abe—
Much more than was enough
Of old Abe;
He is made of such weak stuff,
The South beats his game of bluff,
And I fear they'll ride him rough—
Ride the ancient Abe.

Let us watch, and wait, and pray
For the ancient Abe—
For our country let us pray,
And for Abe;
Let us help him if we may,
When he falters on the way,
Guide him back when gone astray—
Poor bewildered Abe.

For though all the saddest fates
Link with ancient Abe—
All the most despairing fates
Link with Abe—
He is captain in the gates
Of these grand United States,
And must be till time abates—
Hapless ancient Abe.

Let us therefore, though we squirm
Under ancient Abe—
Though we writhe, and groan, and squirm
Under Abe—
Let us all stand true and firm,
Of his courage nurse the germ,
And in patience bear the term
Of the ancient Abe.

PHILADELPHIA.

Air: "The Hunters of Kentucky."

In politics a fear intense
Has seized on friend and foe, sir;
The favorite seat is on the fence,
The favorite word, "Lie low, sir;
Our pea beneath the thimbles keep,
Not telling where it lurks,"
And the cry is, "See before you leap
How Philadelphia works!"
For it's all a problem,
Prob-prob-problem,
'Tis all a problem
How Philadelphia works.

The Johnson men pretend to feel
The game is theirs alone, sir,
While the "Rads" proclaim the winning deal
Is safely made their own, sir.
Lord Greeley's face is full of glee,
While Raymond squirms and shirks,
And the prudent ones cry, "Wait and see
How Philadelphia works."
For here is the problem,
Prob-prob-problem—
A mixed and curious problem
How Philadelphia works.

The Blairs, who pull the wires and threads,
  Have plunged into the business
With a zeal which gives to cooler heads
  A sort of swimming dizziness.
They have seized the boat from stem to stern,
  And are fighting it like Turks,
While the older hands stand back to learn
  How Philadelphia works.
          For a ticklish problem,
            Prob-prob-problem,
            'Twould be for any one to guess
          How Philadelphia works.

Has Johnson nerve to make the fight
  A fight to the bitter end, sir?
Has he the pluck his foes to smite,
  And foster every friend, sir?
If he have, his star may yet arise
  O'er the Radical glooms and murks,
And a child may tell with a glance of the eyes
  How Philadelphia works.
          For this is the true problem,
            Prob-prob-problem—
            The kernel of the problem
          How Philadelphia works.

But if he let the Copperheads guide,
  And keep Seward as chief in office,
And hold in their seats of power and pride
  The fanatic knaves who scoff us,
Then riddled will be his official cloak
  With Radical knives and dirks,
And none need ask—save by way of a joke—
  How Philadelphia works.
          For this is the problem,
            Prob-prob-problem—
            The body and boots of the problem.
          How Philadelphia works.

THE NEW "SPIKE" FOR POLITICAL GUNS.[50]

Air: "Villikins and his Dinah."

When a gun opens sharp on the Tammany crew,
And they don't know, to save them, what next they shall do,
Straight for Taylor (Fort Gansevoort, James B.) they will strike,
And they use his big body in place of a "spike,"
          Singing tooral-li-ooral, etc.

Oh Taylor, dear Taylor, thou henchman of Weed,
Assist us, thy partners, in this hour of need;
To Raymond repair, and to Greeley make moan,
And command them to let your co-workers alone,
Singing tooral-li-ooral, etc.

Make Greeley forget how you poisoned his cup
When Evarts and he for the Senate were up—
When Owen, Sim Draper, and all of your breed,
Cut his throat on the sly at the bidding of Weed,
Singing tooral-li-ooral, etc.

There's a "Cork-in" the Herald—a cork that won't budge
For Anse of the Atlas or Nelson the judge;
With silver 'tis fastened as tight as you please,
And when drawn, out flows pure "Aqua Peter de Griese,"
Singing tooral-li-ooral, etc.

To say we're against you you know is all fudge,
For Owen is brother to Matthew the judge;
A Democrat this—a Republican that—
And 'tis hard if, between them, they can't catch the fat,
Singing tooral-li-ooral, etc.

There are more city bonds, and the time is not far,
When such friends as are useful can have them at par;
You will be our "dear Doty," and may make a strike,
If the guns that now vex us you only can spike,
Singing tooral-li-ooral, etc.

"West Washington Market" to our aid you owe,
And Fort Gansevoort—a job not yet finished, you know;
Still, Matthew must pass on that very big claim,
And to let Matthew now be annoyed were a shame,
Singing tooral-li-ooral, etc.

So Taylor, dear Taylor, to Greeley repair,
And caution him sharp of his course to take care;
As for Raymond—we know you have stock in the Times,
You must therefore spike that, or forfeit the dimes,
Singing tooral-li-ooral, etc.

MYSTERIOUS VERSES FROM A PINK-EYED BARD.

The Dead-Beat Club in silence had spent the afternoon,
For election day was coming—for some, alas! too soon.
All things appeared unsettled, such numbers in the field,
And they feared, without harmony, they would be forced to yield.

Then up spake Richard Connolly—"I'll take him by the hand;
We'll make some nice arrangement, and save this fated land.
'Tis the most distressed district that ever yet was seen,
And the only way to save it is by wearing of the green."

Then Charley Baker said "Agreed; this thing we have to do;
And to fix the matter, Sweeny, we'll leave it all to you.
Let's have a joint committee—get Moloney to back down—"
"The very thing," said Richard; "we Beats can do him brown;
For I'll step up to Moloney, and I'll take him by the hand,
And treat him with such favors as no mortal can withstand;
I'll show him, if we both must run, defeat is plainly seen,
And I'll do Moloney easy by a wearing of the green."

They met—that hopeful party—at the hotel kept by Hank,
And while Dick and P. G. treated, their mutual rounders drank;
The committee were in session—Charley Baker, from a hat,
Drew forth a little paper near where Fernando sat.
Then a smile came o'er Wood's features—he took Sweeny by the hand,
Saying, "Dick's the Union candidate—now, Peter, will you stand?
But, although it's the worst district that ever yet was seen,
I believe that Dick can win it by a wearing of the green."

The Dead-Beat Club are jolly now each week-day afternoon,
For election day is over, and Dick is high-per-coon;
At Mataran's they gather—Charley Baker in the chair—
And they drink to Patrick Henry, who acted on the square.
There Dick Connolly meets Moloney, and takes Hughy by the hand,
Saying "How does Bricks John Murphy, and how does Bradley stand?
Mine is the gayest district that ever yet was seen,
And the only way I won it was—a wearing of the green."

FANDANGO'S APOTHEOSIS.

A DAM FROM THE DUTCH (*i. e.* HECKER) DIKES.

When we use the word "dam" in the following song,
We mean such a "dam" as the Croton Dam,
Or such dams as the beaver builds along
The quiet shores of the Aquietam;
And it is in this sense—this pious sense—
We desire to be clearly understood—
When we cry, with a fervor most intense,
"Everlastingly dam Fandango Wood."

His mustache is white, and his wig is brown,
  His heart is the hue of a buried nigger,
And, walking abroad, he delights the town
  With the grace of his lank pretentious figure;
And so this time, boys, in the Croton sense—
  Not the beaver, be it understood—
We cry with a zeal that is most intense,
  "Everlastingly dam Fandango Wood."

His mechanical manners have all the grace
  Of a patent gallows or steam garroter;
His dollars and crimes run a high old race,
  Though each crime is by odds the swiftest trotter.
And so this time, boys, in the beaver sense—
  Not the Croton, be it understood—
We cry, with a fervor most intense,
  "Everlastingly dam Fandango Wood."

"There lived a man"—so a story said—
  "Who was, in his own bad olden time,
From head to heel, and from heel to head,
  And in marrow and vitals, one living crime."
But away with the sickening picture hence!
  He is nothing like this, be it understood,
Whom we mean when we cry, with a zeal intense,
  "Everlastingly dam Fandango Wood."

SONG TO THE SONS OF ST. TAMMANY.

Ho! treaders of the war-path,
  Who round these council-fires
Now gather on the battle eve
  As gathered oft your sires—
Ho! all whose hands have lifted
  The banner-spears of states,
And heard the war-dance circling, while
  The foe was at the gates—

All ye who stand with covered heads
  Before the highest chief,
And ne'er have stooped except to help
  A hapless brother's grief—
All ye on whose high foreheads
  (More than diadem's renown)
The crimson cap of Liberty
  Hath rested as a crown—

All ye who unto Freedom
  Bear consecrated lives,
Up! and against this golden lie
  Unsheathe your vengeful knives.
Up! and against this wretched fraud
  Of proud and boastful wealth,
Show that the good old Jackson blood
  Still flows in ruddy health.

Down with the spawn of venal trade—
  These squatters, make them start—
Who hold in breast a money-bag
  Where true men hold a heart.
Send on your shouts to Washington,
  Where the Great Father dwells,
And let him hear from fearless lips
  This tale which manhood tells.

We tell these men who brag of gold.
  That, though their gains were piled
Higher than highest pyramid
  On which the sun hath smiled,
There is not one of us would shake
  Their leprous hands to win
The aggregate stock-plunder
  Of their boast and of their sin.

HORACE GREELEY AS HEROD.

Seward has bit the bloody dust,
  To cold oblivion fated;
Ben Wade now sleeps as sleep the just,
  And Bates has been abated.
Above the early grave of Banks
  The old Bay State is sighing,
And Hate through philanthropic ranks
  In fiery car is flying.

The Keystone over Cameron's grave
  Sends up a wailing clangor;
Kentucky Clay, the wild and brave,
  Is dumb and white with anger;
Ohio Chase is cold and stiff
  As pig on hook of grocer;
And dead as any hippogriff,
  John C., of Mariposa.

They lie all round—the killed and cold
  In friendly weeping watered;
The badly hurt, the dead, the sold,
  The massacred and slaughtered;
But still they all, with latest breath—
  The last light of life's taper—
Charge Horace Greeley with their death,
  And curse his fatal paper.

Meantime in coat of ancient white,
  And boots of dubious pattern,
And breeches very short and slight,
  And necktie of the slattern,
That mild but philosophic man
  Bears all his honors meekly,
While thunders in the party-van
  His myriad-utteranced weekly.

He talks of Abe—of honest Abe—
  That chief of Western Vandals—
And, just as mother might her babe,
  His candidate he dandles.
That sucking statesman must be fed
  On pap that he has tasted,
And not a thought in Abe's old head
  On other men be wasted.

But still New York for Seward weeps,
  And never seems to weary,
And one loud cry of anger sweeps
  From Montauk Point to Erie.
"A bolt! a bolt! no Western craft
  Shall steal our Seward's thunder;
Better to build another craft,
  And let the ship go under."

In fact, our philanthropic friends
  Are in a peck of trouble,
And, ere recrimination ends,
  Clean burst will be their bubble.
Split into factions, soon will blaze
  The flames that now are lambent—
Young Sam again his head will raise,
  And Gerrit Smith grow rampant.

But Horace smiles a placid smile—
  Serene, sublime, victorious;
No shouts of wrath can stir his bile—
  Revenge—revenge is glorious.

The man whose friendship Seward banned,
  Long service ill requiting,
Has got at length the upper hand
  By steady, ceaseless fighting.

Long life to all our gallant sons
  Who fight to hold their own,
And fame to him who, slighted once,
  His power at length hath shown—
Who stays at watch through weary years,
  Giving no cry or frown,
Then sudden on the stage appears,
  And strikes his wronger down.

May Horace Greeley's fame expand—
  The way his wrongs were righted—
And may the moral sweep our land,
  In every home recited,
Until the old white hat and coat
  Become in song and story
Themes ringing in the minstrel's throat—
  Parts of a hero's glory.

THE BALLAD OF LORD LOVELL.

A NEW EDITION, AS SUNG BY THE CLERKS IN THE STREET DEPARTMENT.

Manse Lovell jumped into an avenue car,
  With his seven-shooting pistol jumped he—
"Now I'm off," he exclaimed, "to take part in the war,
  And I'll fight on the side of Dix-ee,
                    Ee-ee,
  And I'll fight on the side of Dix-ee."

"Oh, where are you gwine," John A. Kennedy said,
  "Oh, where are you gwine," said he;
"For you know you late swore by your honor and head
  To have nothing to do with Dix-ee,
                    Ee-ee,
  But to live in New York peaceablee."

"My parole I don't vally," Manse Lovell replied,
  "Not a cuss—not a rush," said he;
"But as soon as I'm down on the Southering side,
  You shall see, sir, what then you shall see,
                    See-see,
  You shall hear, sir, and often, from me.

"My salary's drawn to the very last day—
I've spoiled the Egyptians," sez he;
"And now I make off with my plunder and pay
To enlist on the side of Jeff D.,
Dee-dee,
And before me 'Abe's minions' shall flee."

From the bold Street Department there rises a wail—
All the clerks there are sad as can be;
And they ask, "Do you think Captain Smith too will fail
To return from his home in Dix-ee,
Ee-ee,
To return from his home in Dix-ee."

Gus Purdy, and Ryer, and O'Brien have "the blues,"
Johnny Richardson's sad as can be;
But old Jonathan Trotter says, "Bully good news;
God prosper the cause of Dix-ee,
Ee-ee,
And send to the South victoree."

Fernando looks on with a muscular grin,
And the aldermen smile full of glee;
For they see a good chance to get Shepherd Knapp in,
If Gus Smith stays away in Dix-ee,
Ee-ee,
If Gus Smith don't return from Dix-ee.

MY SAMBO OF THE KOM-HERAUS.[51]

Give me your hand, my Sambo,
Come to my heart, my Sambo,
Friend of my soul, my Sambo,
Great chief of the Nix-kom-heraus.
Long are your heels, my Sambo,
Crisp is your wool, my Sambo,
Fragrant and rich is your odor,
Oh chief of the Nix-kom-heraus.

Trust not Fred Douglass, my Sambo,
Trust not to Greeley, my Sambo,
Trust not Ward Beecher or Tilton,
Great chief of the Nix-kom-heraus;
But trust your own Raymond, my Sambo,
Who'll never desert you, my Sambo,
While you're good for a vote or a dollar,
Oh chief of the Nix-kom-heraus.

You shall marry us white folk, my Sambo,
We'll marry you black folk, my Sambo,
You shall eat with us, vote with us, sleep with us,
Great chief of the Nix-kom-heraus;
And the whites of the South, my Sambo,
Shall have nary a right, my Sambo,
Which a Nig shall be bound to respect, if
Not pleasing the Nix-kom-heraus.

SAMBO A BAD EGG.

You're a bad investment, my Sambo,
You're nice, but don't pay, my Sambo,
And so you may go to the—hot place
Befitting each Nix-kom-heraus.
Your skin is nigrific, my Sambo,
And your heels they are long, my Sambo,
And your wool has a horrible odor,
And your shin-bones are Nix-kom-heraus.

Get back to your kennel, my Sambo,
There grovel and rot, my Sambo,
Take off your blue coat and equipments,
For the war was all Nix-kom-heraus.
You had nothing to fight for, my Sambo,
And you gallantly won it, my Sambo,
With your blood and your labors you won it—
Enjoy now your Nix-kom-heraus.

You may work for us white folk, my Sambo,
Black boots and shake carpets, my Sambo,
Steal chickens and do some whitewashing·
When our kitchens are Nix-kom-heraus;
But you can not vote with us, my Sambo,
You had nothing to fight for, my Sambo,
In the war, and you gallantly won it—
Hip! hip! for the Nix-kom-heraus.

THE BOARD OF CONTROL PROGRAMME.[52]

Abolish the mayor, and abolish the Boards
Of Aldermen, Councilmen, Supervisors;
For our city and county have tempting hoards,
And Albany's teeth are sharp incisors.

Abolish all powers that are not of our Church;
  There are no honest men that are not in our party;
And both Weed and the Wigwam we'll leave in the lurch,
  "Played out" just as clean as a hand at ecarté.

This, now, is the programme devised by the saints
  Who fight under Waldo's immaculate banner;
And if true be the picture that great artist paints,
  The millennium will come in this very brief manner.

For the Board of Control will have plenary power
  To make good honest men of all rogues in our borders,
And all vices and crimes will expire the same hour
  That our city is placed under Albany orders.

For of all pious towns—not excepting Sing Sing—
  We all know that Albany's far the most pious,
And that "lobby corruption" or "schemes of the Ring"
  Must vamose right away when Saint Fenton is by us.

So hip, hip, and hurra for the Board of Control!
  The earth is the Lord's and its fruits for his people;
We shall purify Gotham with Albany's soul,
  And whoever objects—let him swing from the steeple.

To Saint Waldo we bend—to King Greeley we bow,
  Who to absolute rule in this bill will have risen;
For their Board of Control is—I solemnly swow—
  The biggest darned thing ever seen out of prison.

That we need great reforms in our corporate life,
  These columns of ours have been faithful recorders;
But this wholesale hack-slashing with Albany's knife
  Is just killing the patient to cure his disorders.

LYRICS OF ALBANY.[53]

LEPROSY SOMEWHERE—WHERE IS IT?

Unhappiest of all mortal men,
  We pity Glenn, we pity Glenn,
For fast he lies in the lion's den,
With a hundred and thirty injured men
  All crying aloud for the blood of Glenn.

The courage of a thousand men
  Shone bright in Glenn, shone bright in Glenn,
When, bearding the animals in their den,
He first with tongue, and then with pen,
  Gave out his indictment, and signed it Glenn.

But, alas! a derision to gods and men
  Hath grown poor Glenn—our piteous Glenn!
He is shunned as are Eastern lepers when
Their leprosy is thick; and then
  How they worry and madden the soul of Glenn!

But this point is strange, and a thing for men
  To ponder about in regard to Glenn;
For he swears "'tis seven score of leprous men
Who are driving out one untainted, when
  Our Albany fathers shall banish Glenn."

Now who are the lepers? the beasts in their den,
  Or only poor Glenn—or only Glenn?
Have we found seven score of leprous men?
Or is there but one, to whose tainted ken
  All others appear as diseased as Glenn?

Delavan House, Albany, April 9, 1868.

CORPORATION COUNSEL CHARGERS (THEY CHARGE HIGH) ON THEIR METTLE.

"Next heat!" the circus-master cried;
  The Mayoralty-men rode out;
While trooping from the other side
  Dashed in a second rout.
"The Corporation Counselship,
  What knight the prize can win?"
And eagerly, with trip and slip,
  The candidates rode in.

Came "Glorious Dick" most glorious,
  Exalted, true, and wise;
And Tom C. Fields uproarious
  To win and wear the prize.
Elijah Ward on tiptoe stood,
  And seemed his way to grope,
While George G. Barnard's marriage mood
  Was full of joy and hope.

Came Bainbridge Smith, who means to hatch
  This egg beneath his wing;
Came Sam J. Tilden, sure to catch
  Whate'er the fates may fling.

Came Malcolm Campbell, hot in view
  Of all the chances round;
And ex-Recorder Frank Tillou,
  On "high" achievements bound.

Came Tomlinson of lofty claims,
  A bright and shining ember;
And So-and-so Morange—whose names
  We really can't remember.
Came Greene C. Bronson, he whose son
  Augustus Schell hath spared;
And John E. Develin, on a roan,
  Which kicked, and pranced, and reared.

Their riding was not of the best,
  Their horses were not Arabs,
And all, with lances couched in rest,
  Looked fierce and wild as Caribs.
They seemed a grim and ghastly crew,
  Each pledged to be victorious,
While all kept steadily in view
  The dripping scalp of "Glorious."

So with clatter, dust, and jingle,
  O'er the sawdust and the tan,
Mounted double, riding single,
  Went this legal caravan,
In cotton tights and spangles,
  Much like scarecrows on the wing,
And with bells around their ankles
  Which Tom Carroll strove to ring.

MAYORALTY NAGS AND RIDERS.

With a jingle, jingle, jingle,
  O'er the sawdust and the tan,
Mounted double, riding single,
  Comes the Wigwam caravan—
In cotton tights and spangles,
  Their buskins duly chalked,
And with bells around their ankles,
  In they cantered, rode, and walked.

"Prize one," which Pantaloon brought forth,
  Was labeled "City Mayor"—
A gaudy thing of little worth—
  A gilded pewter chair;

The cushion stuffed with nettles,
  The back all rough with spikes—
"Now, horsemen, to your mettles!"
  Out cantered the three Ikes.

Ike Fowler, brown and burly,
  On a stallion trotted out;
Isaac Townsend, grim and surly,
  In a sudden fit of gout;
Ike Bell, who best of all succeeds
  In coloring meerschaum clay—
All these dashed out on bitted steeds,
  Impatient for the fray.

Came Father Kennedy along,
  His scalping-knife was keen;
Came John R. Briggs, serene and strong,
  With brave and courtly mien.
Came John Kerr, with a bottle
  Of good ale beneath his arm;
And Whitlock (Ben), whose throttle
  From good ale ne'er suffered harm.

Came Wilson Hunt, reformer fine;
  Came Tiemann—room for Dan;
And Father David Valentine
  Kept pricking to the van.
Came true and tried Judge Ingraham,
  Our bench's pride and boast;
Came Gunther, happy as a clam—
  By Teutons talked of most.

Came Royal Phelps, with royal "cheek;"
  James Lee, true, frank, and plain;
Came Charley Secor, who may seek
  Dan Tiemann's place in vain;
Came Havemeyer, who has mire enough
  For any city pickle;
And, last of all, broad, red, and bluff,
  Our old friend, Andie Mickle.

And with jingle, jingle, jingle,
  O'er the sawdust and the tan,
Mounted double, riding single,
  Passed the Mayoralty caravan,
In cotton tights and spangles,
  Their buskins duly chalked,
And with bells around their ankles,
  Which kept tinkling as they walked.

And after James Mahoney
  Gallops William A. Turnure
On a stout New-England pony—
  Not so fast, but very sure.
Patrick Henry follows after,
  With a name to win applause;
While Tom B. Tappan's laughter
  Argues gayly for his cause.

Ed Donnelly, since he failed to moor
  His fortune at Sing Sing,
Thinks governing our city poor
  Would be the next best thing.
Dan Norris grows defiant
  In the safeness of his schemes;
While Martin Luther Bryant
  Is called "Governor" in his dreams.

But of all the straw and real men,
  Including Simeon Meyer,
Who fiercely to be one of Ten
  Doth labor and aspire—
Overlooking all preceding names,
  Commend us at a pinch
To our own beloved, immortal James—
  The namesake of Judge Lynch.

So with Democratic jingle,
  O'er the plowed and beaten tan,
Mounted double, riding single,
  Sweeps the Almshouse caravan;
Through hoops of colored paper
  Each one jumps on riding out,
And at each more lofty caper
  The applauding audience shout.

A SQUADRON OF MOUNTED SAILORS—THE MARINE COURT.

"Now clear the ring for other bouts"—
  The ostlers change the scenes;
And, heralded with laughing shouts,
  Ride in the horse marines.
"Marine Court Judgeship"—come and see
  The Inguns who pursue
Poor Albert Thompson ("with a *p*"),
  And seek to put him through.

Here's Wally Cone, with Frenchy phiz
  And long Zouave mustache;
The Sunday Times his charger is—
  He makes it feel the lash.
Comes Winthrop Chanler dashing through,
  A good and gallant claimant,
And Mr. R. C. Downing, who
  Believes in "prompt cash payment."

Comes Bob E. Livingston, half dead
  With keeping up a canter;
Comes Charley Shea, whose pleasant head
  Is full of joke and banter.
John Anderson—no cousin he
  To "Solace John, my joe;"
And old Dan Clarke, whose policy
  Is still to rail and blow.

Comes Richard Winne, who would win
  If worth were most regarded,
And poor Tom Pearson, who appears
  Among the long discarded.
On comes M'Gregor—Johnny D.—
  Astride a brace of ponies,
And Art Delaney mounted on
  Two asses—his dear cronies.

Cardoza dozes on his mule,
  Dick Clark grows thin and paler,
While nine parts of a decent hope
  Are left for Dan B. Taylor.
'Tis a sight to make outsiders
  Split their sides with fun and spleen,
For ne'er were seen such riders
  As this troop of horse marines.

So round the column passes
  O'er the sawdust and the tan,
On their piebalds and their asses,
  Each one striving for the van;
On their mules, giraffes, and geldings,
  Trot and prance these riders bold,
And their spangles, tights, and beltings
  Are most "gorgeous to behold."

MAGNIFICENT SUPREME COURT EVOLUTIONS.

A louder bell hath tinkled,
  These horsemen stand aloof,
While the ring is raked and sprinkled
  To record anew each hoof.
"Supreme Court Judgeship" is the cry,
  And, cantering from the stable,
On four black chargers, stepping high,
  Come athletes proud and able.

Judge Roosevelt leads the squadron—
  From the fight he does not flinch;
He never made a bad run,
  And is "game" in every inch.
John E. Burrill rides behind him,
  With his tomahawk on edge,
But Leonard's lance will find him—
  William H. hath made the pledge.

Ambrose Pinney is the fourth man
  Of this more than common group;
But Roosevelt, riding in the van,
  May distance yet the troop.
He has bottom and good breeding,
  But if fall and fade he must,
The blow that lays him bleeding
  Will be Leonard's knightly thrust.

Tinkle, tinkle, jingle, jingle,
  O'er the sawdust and the tan,
With no common herd to mingle
  Deign this su-preme caravan.
They somersault and straddle,
  Pirouette, and leap, and fling,
Then, with one foot on the saddle,
  Each man bows and quits the ring.

BILL OF ANOTHER WEEK'S EXHIBITION.

Thus the entertainment closes
  For at least the present week;
Let the candidates count noses,
  And survey extents of cheek.

Immediately or sooner,
  When convenience prompts the same,
Our lyrical harpooner
  Will go round for other game.

For senators, assembly-men,
  And other such small deer,
For all the tribe who now and then
  Turn up to tempt his spear—
For the big fish and the little fish,
  The minnows and the whales—
The fish with very scaly sides,
  And the fish with golden tails;

For horny beasts, which much abound,
  For birds of changing wing,
Each tenant of our hunting-ground,
  Each quaffer of the spring;
For squatter game (to make it pack
  Immediately or sooner)
We mean to send upon the track
  Our lyrical harpooner.

CATTLE OF THE BOARD OF SUPERVISORS—GRAND FANCY DANCE AND MASQUE.

Clear the ring for Supervisors!
  The candidates are few,
And hoard their hopes as misers
  Hoard their gains from common view.
They are masked and thickly painted,
  Quaintly dressed in odd attire,
But with some we are acquainted,
  And the rest—we may inquire.

Him with cloak of purple border,
  James B. Nicholson, we guess;
Douglas Taylor, next in order,
  Wears the sachem's Indian dress;
Bob H. Ellis is no slattern
  In the tights which fit him well;
And that dress of Chinese pattern
  Must hide Charley G. Cornell.

By the Lord! there goes Tom Adams
  On his milk-white steed; he's some;
Pay attention, girls and madams,
  Boys and men, pay heed to Tom.

Not a bolder rider prances
  In the Democratic ring;
Not a truer man advances
  For the bouquets which ye fling.

MUSTERING OF THE CLANS.

I.

Call out the city regiments, every chieftain and his clan;
Place the sinewy First Warders, with Pat Curry in the van;
Let Miner lead the Sappers of the Second's bold brigade,
While M'Carthy's ensign o'er the Third Artillery is displayed;
The Fourth will come with fife and drum, the veteran Purser leading,
All feuds forgot, and but one thought—the duty of succeeding.

II.

The Fifth Zouaves, with Savage, come with eager spring and bound,
Swart veterans of many fights, and ever faithful found;
The Sixth has archers grim and stanch, and numerous as the sea—
Democracy's knight-errants, never known to halt or flee;
The Seventh is bold, and well may hold its place among the best,
When the gallant Rynders couches his deadly lance in rest.

III.

Comes on the Eighth, an Indian tribe, with Delavan commanding;
Biggest of all big Indians, his martial breast expanding;
And marches steadily the Ninth, a battery masked and mortal,
With Kennedy to open fire on every hostile portal.
With stirring tunes the Tenth Dragoons, led by the War Horse, enter;
The Eleventh appears—its grenadiers, with Kelly, form the centre.

IV.

And next to these, with bugle-blow and cymbals pealing glorious,
Led on by Vance, the Twelfth advance, resistless and victorious;
The Thirteenth Voltigeurs file in with Mitchell, prompt for action,
Resolved to conquer open foes, and quell each private faction.
A roar of drums—the Fourteenth comes, a sea of plumes and sabres:
Fill high and toast this noble host; with them John Kelly labors.

V.

With flashing helmets, golden belts, and swords of glittering lustre,
The Chasseurs of the gay Fifteenth around Ike Fowler cluster.
Hart leads the Sixteenth Riflemen, most dangerous under cover;
In all bush-fighting skirmishes these braves are bound to suffer.
With ringing spurs, and shout which stirs our blood, the Seventeenth rallies;
Now Chanler leads, now Smith succeeds as champion of its sallies.

VI.

Room for the Eighteenth chivalry! Ed Cooper rides along,
While fierce and fast as winter waves his men behind him throng.
Room for the Nineteenth Legion, with Herrick at its head,
Four lieutenant colonels fighting to be colonels in his stead.
The Twentieth Ward in sweet accord lifts up its oriflamme,
With Nelson J., the lion-lord, and Peter B., the lamb.

VII.

The Twenty-first is never cursed with envy's base appeal;
There Froment leads his infantry—a wall of fire and steel.
The Twenty-second, a border Ward, to border feuds a prey,
Hath draped its flags in mourning for the young man passed away;
Round William Henry's early tomb each weeping chieftain stands—
The judge, Ward, Nick, and Pete, and Helk across his grave strike hands.

VIII.

Then, brothers, rally round the flag, the old-time faith renew;
March all, and march together, soldiers tried and ever true;
Fall in and take your places, call the roll and let us hear
Who are for us, who against us, in the strife that draws anear.
Our ship of state will ride elate, in Union's harbor anchored,
And future days will live to praise the peace New York hath conquered.

HOFFMAN, DEAR.

Musha, Hoffman, dear, the thing looks queer—
The machine doesn't run to ordher;
An', despite the Ring's views, we're not willin' to lose
Your sarvices as Recordher.
'Tis a bully ould place, which we think you grace,
Arrayed in the judge's armine;
An' 'twould make us despair if we saw you med mayor
As the tool of the Lobby-Ring varmin.
An' so, John T., we'll let you be,
Till your terrum expires, the Recordher;
An' when played is that game, we'll examine your claim
To another "posish" in its ordher.

BIG THING HOFF. HAS HAD.

Thirty thousand a year you've been makin' clear
For more years than we care to reckon;
An' to warn you back from the mayoralty thrack,
All the fingers o' friendship beckon.

"Don't go into it, Hoff, or your head goes off—
 Don't be fooled by the Ring to do it,"
Is the cry o' your friends, wid no selfish ends,
 "Or but once, an' for life you'll rue it.
An' should you, Hoff, at this warnin' scoff,
 Never blame the thrue men who have killed you,
For you'll soon be found to a powdher ground,
 Just as fine as if Hecker had milled you."

CAN ANY ONE FIND US A SPEAKER?

BY OUR CITY POICK.

Say, have we a Bourbon among us?
 Who struck Billy Patterson—say?
These queries, which formerly stung us,
 Are passing like moonshine away.
'Tis now—and our hope becomes weaker
 From hearing it evening and morn—
Can any one find us a Speaker?
 And where was "the tailor's son" born?

God knows that of talk they have plenty,
 But never a Speaker is there;
At Washington, candidates twenty
 Tuck up their coat-tails for "the chair."
There is Banks, full of beans and benignity,
 But another is Fuller, we feel;
While Richardson stands on his dignity,
 And Wheeler keeps watching the wheel.

At Albany things are no better—
 "Young Sam" holds his own at the game,
Though Prince John has indited a letter
 To prove Hard and Soft are—the same.
A dozen, like Barkis, "are willin'"
 To take the responsible toil,
While Seward and his "little villain"
 With sharp sticks are after the spoil.

By just such another queer caper
 The Almshouse directors are floored—
There is Oliver, Smith, and Sim Draper,
 Who wish to "preside" at the Board.
Let us deputize Branch as a seeker,
 Let him mount on his crocodile steed,
And search through the world for a Speaker
 To help us along in our need.

Yes, Branch is the hope that we stand on,
'Tis he that has proved of "our chief"
That the brand on his cradle was Brandon,
Despite his good "mother's belief."
If Branch will not act as our seeker—
If he will not answer our prayer—
We may give up all hope of a Speaker,
And—write a complaint to the mayor.

The mayor—who, of course, feels his hosses
(They kill about thirty a day,
Which accounts for the cheapness of sausage)—
Complains of the stones of Broadway.
But all questions grow fainter and weakei,
And the public ignore them with scorn,
While they ask, Can you find us a Speaker?
And where was the tailor's son born?

Is there no spirit-rapper can tell us
Where "speakers" are now to be found?
A curse on the chance that misfell us,
For "speakers" used once to abound.
Let us pick out a sensible "talker,"
For business is pressing us hard,
And the Central American Walker
Has played Parker French his trump card.

Of England—whose envoys have tramped on
Our rights as a neutral—we ask
That her crimp-sergeants Mathew and Crampton
Be quickly recalled from their task.
And Denmark—we'll soon make her meeker—
Her claim for "Sound Dues" is unsound:
If you only will find us a Speaker,
By the Lord! we can whip them all round.

Branch swears on his family Bible
That "the chief" is a Cockney and bore;
Poor Briggs is arrested for libel,
And horses are killed by the score;
Nicaragua Walker (related
To "Hookey") calls on us in vain,
And, though England is loudly berated,
Her criminal envoys remain.

Oh give us, we beg you, a Speaker,
Our bliss then would reach the sublime;
We will bumper him round in a beaker,
And wish him a jolly good time.

"A Speaker at Washington needed"—
  Advertise, for that is the mode;
Oh say, shall our prayer be unheeded—
  Old hoss, "will saltpetre explode?"

PSALMS OF IMPEACHMENT.

CANTICLE II.—ACCORDING TO THE PROPHET MILES,

Air: "Jeannette and Jeannot."

"Put it through at railroad speed,"
  Bottled Butler fiercely cries;
"For unless we haste, I fear indeed
  Our farce of trial dies.
Bring the ropes and tie him tight,
  Bind his feet and gag his mouth,
Or we else may lose our sovereign right
  To rob and rule the South—
    May lose our job
    To rule and rob,
  Chain, whip, and starve the South.

"Seize the country by the throat,
  Force the black dose through its lips,
For, unless we cast the negro vote,
  Away our sceptre slips.
Every bridge behind is gone,
  No retreat for us remains;
We must either perish one by one,
  Or bind the land in chains;
    A desperate band,
    Forlorn we stand,
  And no retreat remains.

"As to Johnson, who hath been
  An "obstruction" in our path,
Let him taste the rapid guillotine
  Of Radicals in wrath.
Fling aside restraints of law,
  At each oath and duty scoff,
And if Chase to aid we can not draw,
  Then drag his ermine off—
    Ay, quick indeed,
    'At railroad speed,'
  We'll drag his ermine off.

"Since the South is fairly floored,
Men like us may show their teeth;
Let the negro wield a flaming sword,
And cast away the sheath.
Revolution is our end;
Throw disguise off—give it mouth;
And our bayonet-rule shall soon extend
O'er North as well as South—
Black swords and votes
At white men's throats
In North as well as South.

"Is it true that through the war,
Of all rebels—meanest, worst—
Were the black men we were fighting for,
To break their chains accursed?
In no rebel state they rose
To assist us in the fray,
While they labored hard to feed our foes,
And give them arms and pay;
But now, alack!
We need the black
To prop our tottering sway.

"So let black ex-rebels reign
O'er their white ex-rebel lords,
For without them all our plots are vain—
Without their votes and swords;
But with Johnson stricken down,
The Supreme Court bound in chains,
Oh, we Jacobins shall wear the crown
While breath of life remains—
Ay, rule the land
With Marat's hand
While breath of life remains.

"So on with railroad speed,"
The savage Butler cries;
"For, unless we haste, I fear indeed
Our farce of trial dies.
Bring the ropes and quench the light,
Bind his hands and gag his mouth,
For if Johnson wins, we lose the right
To rob and rule the South—
Yea, lose our job
To rule and rob
Both North as well as South."

CANTICLE III.

BOTTLED BUTLER'S SCREECHING IMPEACHING SPEECH.

With a voice in which mingles a hiss as of asps,
With the squeal of a pig, and the grating of rasps,
And the drone of a bagpipe, the bottled one gasps,
  And splutters, and raves of impeachment.
He charges all crimes, from the highest e'er known,
To the lowest and meanest—as mean as his own
(And on crimes Bottled Ben as an expert is known)—
  Against Johnson when urging impeachment.

But of all "bogus babies," unboned and ungristled,
And of all merry tunes by "the dying cow whistled,"
And of all the vile fizzles that ever were fizzled,
  Commend us to Butler's impeachment.
Such a weed-crop of Radical nightshade and wrath,
Of political stinkweed and partisan froth,
No mower hath mowed in a single wide swath
  As Ben Butler when urging impeachment.

MILES RUNS FOR REGISTER.

Say, here! How is it, misther—
  Are you for the Boy or no?
For he's bound to be Re-gisther,
  Let the wind blow high or low.
All the Germans an' the Irish here
  For him have dhrawn the skean,
For Von Halpine trinks zwei lager bier,
  And Miles he "wears the green."
        All the Germans, etc.

He's "too young?" Your granny's sisther!
  I tell you 'tisn't so;
An' he's bound to be Re-gisther,
  Let the wind blow high or low.
All the Celtic and the Teuton vote
  Are friends of his, I ween,
For Von Halpine schpeist mit pretzel brodt,
  And Miles on mild poteen.
        All the Celtic, etc.

Oh, the Wigwam wants a glysther
  For to purge away her ills,
So we'll make him our Re-gisther,
  An' he'll bate even Radway's pills.

All the girls are for him; this is how
  That wondher came to pass—
Von Halpine liebt ein blond-e frau,
  And Miles an Irish lass.
                All the girls, etc.

May my tongue be all a blisther
  If I tell a lie to you,
For he's bound to be Re-gisther,
  And we all must put him through.
Oh, he suits the men of every race,
  This gossoon undefiled—
Von Halpine schpeist mit Schweitzer kaase,
  An' the Boy on p'raties biled.
                Oh, he suits, etc.

So here's to Hans von Halpine,
  And to Miles who wears the green;
Fill your can and dhrink it all, man,
  Or in Rhine wein or poteen;
For Miles he fit mit Sigel,
  And mit Asboth trinks poteen;
And you can't find Halpine's equal
  For "a-wearing of the green."
                For Miles, etc.

A FRAGMENT.[54]

Oh, more than tongue hath power to speak,
  Or my hand the skill to pen it,
I long, I burn, I strive, I seek
  Promotion to the Senate.
For this Lord Thurlow hath my praise,
  For this I let him run my paper,
For this I work through weary days,
  And waste the midnight taper.

MORTON MUST GO.

The mayor at last has found a way
  To get out Morton; this his plan:
With a new Directory, they say,
He will commence at the letter A,
Proceed in regular course to Z,
Skipping one M. by the rule of three;

And, should the new Directory fail,
An army-list he will next assail;
Then get a navy-book, and try
Each "salt" that is laid up high and dry,
Until at last the opposing board,
From weariness no longer able
To lay the new names on the table,
Owns itself bored and fairly floored,
And "lets him spin his man."

TO JUDGE M'CUNN.[55]

[Ye poet complimenteth his hero on belligerent parentage.]

M'Cunn, M'Cunn, you son of a gun,
You'll be the death of us ere you've done;
At honest old Abe you first poked fun,
And now with M'Clellan you've just begun,
While high up promotion's high ladder you run,
My sweet-scented beauty,
M'Cunn, M'Cunn.

[He entreateth him, for reasons assigned, to be less facetious.]

M'Cunn, M'Cunn, will you ever have done,
Or is it but now that you've just begun?
Here we laugh till the tears down our noses run,
While at soldier and sage you keep poking your fun,
You charming young creature—you wonderful one,
My bright, gushing hero,
M'Cunn, M'Cunn.

[Ye poet payeth due homage to ye splendor of his hero's appearance.]

M'Cunn, M'Cunn, you're enough to stun—
You're a sight for all nervous old ladies to shun,
While, flashing and dancing beneath the sun,
Clear down to your elbows your epaulettes run,
Each spire of the bullion alive with the fun
Of its wonderful wearer,
M'Cunn, M'Cunn.

M'Cunn, M'Cunn, you'd better have done,
Or an end will be put to your rollicking fun;
The romances you tell are enough to stun,
As round from hotel to hotel you run;
Nor does every one see that you're only in fun,
My young caucus hero,
M'Cunn, M'Cunn.

GENERAL HALLECK.

"Who raised the price of pork and mutton-pies?
Who filled our butcher-shops with large blue flies?"
Quick our Committee on the War replies,
"'Twas Halleck."

"Who should be blamed for Gotham's filthy streets?
And for our markets filled with poisonous meats?"
Quick answers these Congressional Dead Beats,
"Blame Halleck."

GASTRONOMIC.

Dear Philadelphia! when I view
Thy streets, and think of what thou art—
Thy terrapin, in soup or stew—
And learn that from thee I must part,
I do protest against the deed
With streaming eye and watering mouth,
And swear it is no "knightly meed"
That sends Meade wandering to the South.

TO MARY.

Thou bounding river,
I fly thy tranquil shore;
Farewell! Oh, never
Shall I behold thee more.
Ye rocks, ye woods that quiver
To echo's plaintive cry,
Farewell forever—
We part, and part for aye.

Thou shady grotto,
In raptures deep and true,
When near to Mary,
How quick the moments flew.
Thy dark retreat, all lonely,
Where mystery ever dwells,
Was to me only
Full of delicious spells.

Days when we were glad,
Ye fleet away like dreams—
Days when we were sad,
Oh, how long each seems;
Far from my own loved Mary,
Forever severed wide—
Dark, dark and dreary,
Time rolls its sudden tide.

Oh valley, fairest,
Dear valley of my youth—
Oh Mary, dearest,
Thee have I loved in truth.
Ye rocks, ye woods that quiver
To echo's plaintive cry,
Farewell forever—
We part, and part for aye.

HOLLAND GIN.

The brandy hath a beaming hue,
But no one knows what it is made of;
Though red itself, it makes us "blue"—
A thing the doctors are afraid of.
Sweeter far the Holland gin,
Which looks as clear as bubbling water,
But yet turns out, when taken in,
Intoxication's subtlest daughter.
Oh, my darling Holland gin—
My deadly-drunken, resinous Holland—
Brandy's hue
Is bright to view,
But strength is thine, my beaded Holland.

The pure French brandy would not hurt,
But here with such foul trash they mix it—
One half is vitriol, t'other dirt,
And that's the toper's "ipse dixit."
Oh, the Holland gin for me,
So purely bright and so transparent,
That even a drunken eye could see
A dead fly or the slightest hair in't.
Yes, my sparkling Holland gin—
My innocently-colored Holland—
Clear to view
As mountain dew
Art thou, my most destructive Holland.

Yet still in one point both combine
 To poison, sicken, and distract us,
So that it proves the same, in fine,
 If either or if both attacked us.
Beggary, horror, falsehood, woe,
 To still more grievous crimes expanded,
Are now retailed with every "go"
 Across the groggery counter handed.
  Oh, my brandy, devil's blood;
   And sin, pale sister unto brandy;
    Brain and heart
    Alike depart
   From him who worships gin or brandy.

NOTES.

Note 1, page 25.

A VESPER HYMN.

This composition was found among the posthumous papers of the deceased. The circumstances under which it was prepared were not known to his friends, and it had no title; but its sentiments seemed peculiarly appropriate to the occasion of its first publication, which took place immediately after the author's sudden demise, and the title of Vesper Hymn was then attached to it. Indorsed on it, however, was the following sentence, in the handwriting of General Halpine, "Dedicated to the lady at whose request these hasty lines were written, with the warmest and most grateful wishes of the author for her health and happiness. C. G. H."

Note 2, page 26.

ON RAISING A MONUMENT TO THE IRISH LEGION.

This was the last poetical production of the pen of the author. Its title explains the occasion of its composition—the preparation of a suitable monument to Irish valor displayed during the war for the Union.

Note 3, page 29.

AFTER THE BATH.

The composition of this poem exemplified in a remarkable manner the wonderful poetical fluency of the writer. He had written the first two verses when in the country, and with the exhilaration of beholding the beautiful vision which he was depicting fresh upon him; he wrote the last verse at the Citizen office, late one afternoon subsequently, and read it to the editor of this volume, saying it was either very good or very bad. The gentleman addressed ridiculed the closing sentences as absurdly and abruptly extravagant, and made fun of the closing paragraph, until he feared his associate's feelings were a little hurt, although the latter usually took such affairs very good-humoredly. General Halpine handed the poem, which consisted of the first, second, and last verses only, to the compositors, and left the office to walk home. By the time he had reached Canal Street, however, he had become inspired, and, returning to the office, sat down, and in a few minutes wrote the four additional verses, making it one of the most beautiful of his love sonnets.

Note 4, page 30.

THE MAN OF THREESCORE.

A translation from the French.

Note 5, page 36.

MY TOAST.

This was written as a tribute to the grace and beauty of a charming and fascinating niece of the editor of this work, at whose home General Halpine had met her on two occasions, when he was much struck with her peculiar and unusual style of beauty. The name, Lucie Ellice, was sufficiently altered to conceal the individuality of the person addressed, without greatly changing the sound. The publication of the piece in the Citizen led to the contribution of several others, some by the writer of this, and others by different persons, winding up unexpectedly with one from a new and unknown Lucie Ellice of the South. The series caused a good deal of amusement and excitement in literary circles at the time of its publication.

Note 6, page 40.

TO RAYMOND ON HIS TRAVELS.

A dinner was given at Delmonico's to Henry J. Raymond, the well-known editor of the New York Times, on the eve of his departure for Europe. Many of the prominent editors and authors of the day were present, and countless good things were said. Charles A. Dana presided in the happiest manner, and so many capital speeches were made that it was felt desirable to have some report made of the meeting. This labor was placed upon Halpine's shoulders of course, and he passed the residue of the night in writing out the account. Next morning he came into the room of the editor of this work and commenced reading the song, which he had put in the shape of a serenade into the mouth of his hearer. He had covered fifty pages of foolscap, besides composing half a dozen verses of poetry, between two o'clock at night and six in the morning. The report of the dinner can be found in the number of the Citizen of July 13, 1867.

Note 7, page 46.

DELMONICO'S DREAM.

At a dinner given to General Sheridan by General Halpine, at Delmonico's, the caterer had served trout at a time when, by the laws of nature and man, they were utterly out of season. The fish were sent away from the table untouched, the breach of law and good taste was strongly condemned by the public press, the matter was taken up by the Sportsmen's Club, and Mr. Delmonico was compelled to explain that they had been served without his knowledge, and during his absence from the city, and that such an occurrence should not happen again. It was in the course of the controversy that this poem was written.

Note 8, page 50.

AN ACROSTIC BIRTHDAY OFFERING.

Addressed to Mrs. James Gordon Bennett, a lady for whose beauty, talents, and uncommon intellectual cultivation General Halpine had the deepest respect and admiration.

Note 9, page 51.

JAMES GORDON BENNETT, JR.

In commemoration of the ocean yacht race, that plucky contest in which Mr. Bennett carried off the prize.

Note 10, page 51.

THE KNIGHT'S ADDRESS.

Written on the occasion of crowning a lady Queen of Beauty and Love at a tournament at which he was not present, the words of the ode to the contrary notwithstanding.

Note 11, page 57.

PHILADELPHIA.

Written at the time of the attempt in Philadelphia by the conservative leaders of the Republican party to form a new party by a coalition of loyal Southern War Democrats and moderate Republicans. A lamentably unsuccessful effort.

Note 12, page 69.

STAMPING OUT.

There appeared in the London Times, at the commencement of the Fenian insurrection, a vindictive and bloody suggestion to put down the Fenian rising as the cattle plague had been arrested, that is, by stamping it out, or destroying every animal attacked with the disease—a bloody and brutal proposition, unparalleled on the page of history. The article read as follows, and the poem was a reply to it: "We must stamp out the fires of this Fenian insurrection, and quench its embers in the blood of the wretches who are its promoters."

Note 13, page 77.

WASHINGTON'S BIRTHDAY.

These lines were written by General Halpine as the poet of the day on the first annual celebration of the inauguration of the Military Order of the Legion, held in the Academy of Music, Philadelphia, on the 22d day of February, 1866. The meeting was presided over by Major General Cadwallader, and many of the most prominent officers of the army were present.

Note 14, page 83.

MILES ON THE WHITE FAWN.

A spectacular drama, exhibiting much of female charms unadorned, produced at Niblo's Garden, in New York City.

Note 15, page 91.

LOAFING AS A FINE ART.

Addressed to the editor hereof, and eliciting a reply which was published in a subsequent number of the Citizen.

Note 16, page 109.

SPECIAL ORDERS, A., NO. I.

This was written when the author was adjutant general to Major General Hunter, and was published for distribution among the staff officers. The young lady referred to was a great favorite with them, and expressed no displeasure over the harmless pleasantry at the time; but when it was afterward inserted in the columns of the Citizen, her family took offense, and General Halpine expressed to the editor of this volume his intention of changing the name, and thus depriving the damsel of her only chance for immortality. As he forgot to carry out this fell design, however, the piece is left as it was originally written.

Note 17, page 111.

PERSONAL.

It is almost superfluous to say that this poem refers to the editor of this volume. The persons spoken of are Matthew T. Brennan, who was city comptroller; Orison Blunt, who voted himself a testimonial out of the people's money in consideration for his public services; Nathaniel Sands, agent of the Citizen's Association, of which the writer was one of the founders; A. J. Hackley, who had a questionable contract with the municipal government for street cleaning; and F. I. A. Boole, who was city inspector, and spent a million in not cleaning the streets. Most of these gentlemen were supposed to have cause to bear the "Boy Bob" in lasting, but not friendly remembrance for his attempts, by the aid of the Citizen's Association, to reform the municipal government.

Note 18, page 116.

TO THE CHIEF JUSTICE.

Addressed to Chief Justice Salmon P. Chase, when presiding in the Senate over the impeachment trial of President Andrew Johnson, at a time when every effort was being made by the Republican press to force a conviction as a party measure, and when it was feared that the accused would not have an impartial hearing.

Note 19, page 117.

TO FENTON.

The New York City tax levy had been passed by the Legislature, and was awaiting the signature of Governor Fenton, when this jocose effusion was written. There was a rumor that the governor would veto the measure, and leave the city without any government for the ensuing year, and with all the outstanding claims against it unpaid. The members of the Union League Club had recommended the governor to pursue this unusual and dangerous course, but he was finally convinced by the humorous arguments of Miles O'Reilly, and signed the bill.

Note 20, page 129.

INDIFFERENCE.

On the manuscript of this piece was found, in the handwriting of General Halpine, the expressive and appropriate word "Twaddle."

Note 21, page 130.

ONE DEAD SURE THING.

John B. Haskin is a New York politician, and the song refers to a resolution complimentary to President Johnson, which he introduced into a Democratic Convention.

Note 22, page 130.

MOTTO OF THE MASS.

There was indorsed on the revised manuscript of this poem, in the handwriting of the deceased author, the words "Social and reflective."

Note 23, page 131.

TIME.

Indorsed by the author "Reflective."

Note 24, page 132.

FIERY ELOQUENCE.

Indorsed by the author "Reflective: boyish—a revised copy."

Note 25, page 133.

FAUGH AU BEALLACH.

The author characterizes this as "Extremely boyish."

Note 26, page 134.

MATRIMONIAL COMPLACENCY.

Indorsed "Feminine: boyish."

Note 27, page 136.

IRISH ASTRONOMY.

Manuscript indorsed "Boyish."

Note 28, page 137.

TO A FRIEND.

Indorsed "Pathetic and philosophical."

Note 29, page 159.

BARON RENFREW'S BALL.

Descriptive of a public ball given to the Prince of Wales, on his visit to this country, at the Academy of Music, in the city of New York. The ladies referred to are Mrs. Senator Morgan and other leading belles of New York society. The reference to the breaking away of the floor applies to an actual occurrence—an accident that fortunately resulted in no injury to any one, and not even in any considerable interruption to the festivities. On the occasion referred to the benevolent Mr. Peter Cooper took special charge of the prince.

Note 30, page 184.

O'MAHONY OF THE COMERAGHS.

O'Mahony, an intimate friend of the author, was the first Head Centre of the Fenian organization; but factions subsequently broke out, accusations of neglect and malfeasance were brought against Mr. O'Mahony by his enemies, and a new wing of the party was formed under Mr. Roberts. General Halpine had full confidence in O'Mahony, in his good intentions and his entire sincerity, and wrote this effusion at the time when the difficulties referred to were rife, and as an expression of his opinion.

Note 31, page 207.

ADVERTISEMENT EXTRAORDINARY.

Mr. Thurlow Weed, while returning from Washington to New York, had his pocket picked in the cars. The various allusions are to the events of the day in which he and others were, or were supposed to be, mixed up. Mr. Andrews was then surveyor of the port under Mr. Weed's recommendation; Mr. Greeley, it was supposed, would like a place in the Cabinet; Henry J. Raymond preferred a foreign mission, as did also Mr. James Gordon Bennett, or, at least, such were the suspicions of the public. The Cummings referred to was Mr. Alexander Cummings, then proprietor of the World, which at that time was a pious Republican newspaper.

Note 32, page 216.

BREVET RANK.

This refers to Lafayette C. Baker, Stanton's wretched tool and spy, at the time it was proposed to brevet him brigadier general for his infamous, albeit, where honestly performed, necessary services—

services which civilized nations scarcely class with bravery in the field of battle, and usually pay for in so much hard money. Fortunately the effort to convert a spy, who was not popularly regarded as peculiarly scrupulous, into a hero, failed.

Note 33, page 232.

THE DIFFERENCE.

There was an unfounded report circulated through the press, at about the time these lines were written, to the effect that General James Lane, of Kansas, had committed suicide. The beauty of this piece consists in its truth.

Note 34, page 232.

LECOMPTON'S BLACK BRIGADE.

This was written while the author was closely allied to Stephen A. Douglas politically, and refers to the Democratic Convention which met at Charleston, and which was adjourned to Baltimore in consequence of the violence of the Southern leaders, who were then initiating their movements toward secession—movements which resulted later in rebellion. The references are to men prominent at the time in politics, many of whom were distinguished subsequently in the struggle to destroy the Union.

Note 35, page 234.

THE LYRIC OF TWEDDLE HALL.

The Democratic organization in the city of New York, founded by General Halpine, John Y. Savage, and Nelson J. Waterbury, in opposition to Tammany Hall, had applied for and been refused recognition by the State Convention, and, in consequence of this indignity, had resolved on political vengeance. Cagger and Cassidy were heads of the Albany Regency, Samuel J. Tilden was chairman of the State Committee, and the "Central" referred to was the Central Railroad, which up to that time had been used to help the Democracy.

Note 36, page 236.

GIVE ME GUANO OR GIVE ME DEATH.

Jeremiah Black, attorney general of the United States, declined to defend the President of the United States when on trial of impeachment unless he could obtain the aid of the government in enforcing claims held by certain of his clients to an island of guano—a curious phase of the impeachment trial of Andrew Johnson, which will live in history with an odor worthy of the subject, and not of sanctity.

Note 37, page 236.

TO UNCLE SAM.

England having abused this country for suspending the *Habeas Corpus* Act during the terrible struggle for the Union, herself suspended that "great palladium of freedom" in consequence of a few Fenian riots, and imprisoned Irishmen, naturalized American citizens, whom she suspected of complicity in Fenian plots, on their revisiting the land of their birth.

Note 38, page 237.

THE PRESIDENT TO CONGRESS.

This was written at the time when the impeachment of Andrew Johnson was threatened. The quotations are mainly from speeches made by him in his famous tour through the country. Uncle Thad is Thaddeus Stevens; Ashley is the representative in Congress who first proposed impeachment; Phillips is Wendell Phillips; Mrs. Cobb, a lady popularly accused of being a successful place and pardon broker. The "Cleveland scrape" was the movement for a new party, to which the assent of Henry Ward Beecher was obtained—an assent that he hastily recalled.

Note 39, page 240.

MANHOOD AGAINST THE MACHINES.

A political screed referring to local New York combinations. The "Lunch Club" consists of the Tammany leaders who dine daily at the City Hall, but, it is simple justice to add, at their own expense. The references are to Michael Connolly, the "big judge;" John Hardy and Billy Walsh, ex-aldermen; Nelson J. Waterbury, the "long judge," formerly district attorney; Smith Ely, supervisor—leaders of the Democratic Union, the organization opposed to the dictation of Tammany Hall in city politics; and to Peter B. Sweeny, chamberlain; John T. Hoffman, mayor; William M. Tweed, supervisor, deputy street commissioner, and state senator; A. Oakey Hall, district attorney—the head men of Tammany, and constituting its sacred "Ring."

Note 40, page 243.

JOHN MORRISSEY MY JO, JOHN.

Mr. Morrissey was elected as fitting representative of New York City in Congress, and these lines were written in his honor. He was a pugilist and gambler, but it was reported that he would not cheat, and always "fought fair."

Note 41, page 245.

FERNANDO'S CARD.

The virtuous Fernando Wood announced in a card his desire for re-election to Congress solely as a public refutation of the calumnies heaped upon him by his enemies.

Note 42, page 245.

FOURTH CONGRESSIONAL DISTRICT.

S. S. Cox and John Fox, New York politicians, were both aspirants for a seat in Congress from this district.

Note 43, page 249.

CHURCH, CAGGER, AND PIPER.

The references are to Sanford E. Church, Peter Cagger, S. B. Piper, Dean Richmond, president of the New York Central Railroad, and Erastus Corning, who were members of the New York State Democratic General Committee, and some of whom belonged to what was known in politics as the Albany Regency.

Note 44, page 251.

LINES TO A CONGRESSMAN.

Refers to Henry J. Raymond, editor in chief of the New York Times.

Note 45, page 255.

TWEEDLEDUM AND TWEEDLEDEE.

Refers to the newspaper controversies between Horace Greeley and Thurlow Weed. "Sid. Gay" is Sidney Howard Gay, then managing editor of the Tribune.

Note 46, page 256.

THE HEALTH BILL.

This was a measure of reform carried by the Citizen's Association, with the help of the Republicans, to take the control of sanitary matters in the city of New York from a body of political inspectors, several of whom testified before a legislative committee that they considered "hygiene" to be a "bad smell" or a "collection of dirty water," and give it to a medical board. Reference is made to Thomas C. Acton, president of the Metropolitan Board of Police, and Lyman Tremaine, attorney general.

Note 47, page 258.

RING RHYMES.

This collection of fugitive poetical screeds refers to political matters in the city of New York, and to the great contest which the author waged as Head Centre of the Democratic Union Organization against the Tammany Hall clique, popularly described as the "Ring." These references can only be understood by persons well versed in that greatest of mysteries, New York politics, and to such it would be a work of supererogation to explain them. The following short and condensed statement may be worth the type it requires. On the side of the Democratic Union were Michael Connolly, nicknamed the "Big Judge;" William Walsh, a Fourth Ward ex-alderman; Daniel M. O'Brien, candidate for the state Senate, and Smith Ely, supervisor. And opposed to them were Matthew T. Brennan, then city comptroller, subsequently deprived of power, and shelved on the Board of Police Commissioners; Charles G. Cornell, street commissioner; Terence Farley, alderman, and city contractor on very profitable jobs; Peter B. Sweeny, brains of Tammany Hall, subsequently made city chamberlain; William M. Tweed, supervisor, and later a very fat pluralist, great executive officer of the combination; Francis I. A. Boole, a low scamp from Canada, city inspector, and later a lunatic; Fernando Wood, absolute owner of an organization called Mozart, which he ran as a tender or an opponent to Tammany, according as either paid him best; Thomas C. Fields, state Senator, mouthpiece of the "Ring." To explain all the allusions in this and other political effusions, the space of a volume would be required.

Note 48, page 289.

SONG OF THE NATIONAL DEMOCRACY.

Written when it was proposed to nominate General Dix for governor of the State of New York. Richmond, Pruyn, Cagger, and Cassidy were members of the controlling political Democratic clique called the Albany Regency. Elijah F. Purdy, city supervisor, was nicknamed the "War Horse."

Note 49, page 292.

SENATOR TOM ON CLAMS.

John E. Develin, corporation counsel, was celebrated for giving delightful clam-bakes. On a certain occasion Senator Thomas Murphy was invited to one of these famous entertainments, and this song is supposed to have been written to express his appreciation of the particular dainties that were put before him.

Note 50, page 303.

THE NEW "SPIKE" FOR POLITICAL GUNS.

James B. Taylor was connected with the two greatest swindles ever perpetrated against the city of New York—that of West Washington Market and of Fort Gansevoort—and it was said he had bought an interest in the New York Times, to prevent that paper exposing him. The references are to Owen W. Brennan, Republican Commissioner of Charities and Corrections, brother of Matthew T. Brennan, Democratic comptroller, who had to pass on the Fort Gansevoort matter; Anse was Anson Herrick, editor of the Atlas; Peter Griese was the name of a "dummy" on a railroad bill before the Legislature, and supposed to stand for Peter B. Sweeny; Nelson was Nelson J. Waterbury, head of the opposition to Tammany Hall, and Doty was the fictitious name of a subscriber to city bonds, which were given to him at par when they were selling in market above par, and was supposed to stand for an eminent Democratic judge.

Note 51, page 310.

MY SAMBO OF THE KOM-HERAUS.

This and the next song were first published in the Citizen under the pretense that they were written by Henry J. Raymond, and as a specimen of his style, in retaliation for the publication in the Times of a fictitious letter purporting to come from Miles O'Reilly.

Note 52, page 311.

THE BOARD OF CONTROL PROGRAMME.

A bill was introduced into the Republican Legislature at Albany to cure the evils of New York City politics by putting the municipal government into the hands of a Board of Control. This scheme was mainly promoted by Waldo Hutchings, a Republican wire-puller.

Note 53, page 312.

LYRICS OF ALBANY.

Mr. Glenn, a member of Assembly, denounced his associates for receiving bribes, but failed to prove his case, and was forced to resign.

Note 54, page 327.

A FRAGMENT,

attributed by Miles to Henry J. Raymond—a performance of which the latter has never yet been able to see the joke.

Note 55, page 328.

TO JUDGE M'CUNN,

refers to the famous adventures of the eminent Judge M'Cunn, of the New York Superior Court, when he donned his spurs and sallied out to the war, where he won high renown in an extremely limited period.

INDEX.

THE END.

www.ingramcontent.com/pod-product-compliance
Lightning Source LLC
LaVergne TN
LVHW010159110826
845151LV00002B/557

* 9 7 8 1 4 2 5 5 3 6 5 8 9 *